THE PRESUMPTION OF INNOCENCE IN IRISH CRIMINAL LAW

JUSTICE IN CONTROVERSY SERIES

Editors: Mike Milotte and Donncha O'Connell

This series of monographs addresses a range of controversial legal topics in a format that will appeal to audiences beyond the purely professional and academic legal worlds. It is written by a combination of established and emerging authors with legal, academic, journalistic and other backgrounds. By virtue of their subject matter on the interaction between law and society, the books will inform academic debate; but, given the profound and enduring effect of the law on the lives of all citizens, it is also envisaged that the books will have a much wider appeal and impact. The series aims to provide a distinctive contribution to public discourse by providing a publishing platform for authors who wish to transcend the rather exclusive borders that separate public and academic debate.

Already published in the Justice in Controversy series:

An Ambition for Equality, by Niall Crowley

The Blame Game: Rethinking Ireland's Sustainable Development and Environmental Performance, by Brendan Flynn

Youth Justice in Ireland: Tough Lives, Rough Justice, by Ursula Kilkelly

Forthcoming in the Justice in Controversy series:

Roadmaps to Reunification, by Richard Humphreys

Exploitation or Employment? Prostitution and the Law, by Ivana Bacik

The Future of Irish Nationality and Immigration Law, by Bernard Ryan

The Presumption of Innocence in Irish Criminal Law

'Whittling the Golden Thread'

Claire Hamilton
Dublin Institute of Technology

Foreword by
The Hon Mr Justice
Adrian Hardiman

IRISH ACADEMIC PRESS
DUBLIN • PORTLAND, OR

First published in 2007 by
IRISH ACADEMIC PRESS
44, Northumberland Road, Dublin 4, Ireland

and in the United States of America by
IRISH ACADEMIC PRESS
c/o ISBS, Suite 300, 920 NE 58th Avenue
Portland, Oregon 97213-3644

***Website*: www.iap.ie**

British Library Cataloguing in Publication Data
An entry can be found on request

ISBN 0 7165 3407 X (cloth)
ISBN 978 0 7165 3407 5 (cloth)
ISBN 0 7165 3408 8 (paper)
ISBN 978 0 7165 3408 2 (paper)

Library of Congress Cataloging-in-Publication Data
An entry can be found on request

Typeset in 11/13pt Sabon by FiSH Books, Enfield, Middx.
Printed by MPG Books Ltd, Bodmin, Cornwall

Throughout the web of the English criminal law one golden thread is always to be seen, that it is the duty of the prosecution to prove the prisoner's guilt subject to . . . the defence of insanity and subject also to any statutory exception . . . No matter what the charge or where the trial, the principle that the prosecution must prove the guilt of the prisoner is part of the common law of England and no attempt to whittle it down can be entertained.

Viscount Sankey LC, *Woolmington v. DPP*

Contents

Foreword

This is an important and timely book on a very significant subject. The phrase 'Presumption of Innocence' has an almost totemic status in our system of justice and indeed in many international legal instruments as well: see the judgment of Costello J. in *O'Leary v. Attorney General.*[1] It is the foundation of the rule that guilt must be established beyond reasonable doubt, and that the onus of proof normally rests on the prosecution. It is not a mere shibboleth: in the ringing words of Ó Dálaigh C.J. in *A.G. v. O'Callaghan,*[2] the Courts owe more than verbal respect 'to the principle that punishment begins after conviction and that every man is deemed to be innocent until tried and duly found guilty'. In the same case Walsh J. importantly asserted: 'The presumption of innocence is a very real thing and not simply a procedural rule taking effect only at the trial.'

The foregoing is not seriously controversial. There has not, to my knowledge been any express attack upon the presumption in itself in this jurisdiction. But its scope has been narrowed, as in certain decisions in the historic child sex abuse cases, and statutory provisions have eroded it to some degree in a number of ways, carefully outlined by Ms Hamilton. It is not necessary to be in agreement with all of the opinions she expresses to see that her book is a valuable service to the Irish legal community.

First, she offers a full analysis of the history and jurisprudence underlying both the presumption and the exceptions to it. This exercise is of particular importance in dealing with a concept which has become so verbally familiar that its true significance is sometimes only vaguely grasped. Secondly, she analyses the consequences of the presumption and the related rights to which it gives rise. Thirdly, she carefully and critically analyses a large number of recent and proposed changes in the law in terms of their effect upon the presumption, and thus on the basic principles of our system of criminal law.

Ms Hamilton's book is, in the best sense of the term, an opinionated one. She sees the criminal justice system as 'struggling to reconcile due process with a more managerial notion of crime control', and she unashamedly favours due process. She is critical both of the substance of recent statutory changes and of the thinking and rhetoric behind them. She provocatively examines the genesis of some modern statutes in terms of what she sees as panic and populism. She does not accept the 'myth of the benign State', a term coined by Helena Kennedy, and trenchantly rejects the view, so often proclaimed and so little examined, that the balance has swung too far towards the accused. She counters this, in part, with a chapter on the huge role played by pleas of guilty in the Irish criminal justice system with thoughtful observations on the significance of this. Only about 5 per cent of prosecutions on indictment end in acquittal: scarcely a doomsday scenario.

Would even the most ardent advocates of 'law and order' favour a higher conviction rate? Would ninety-nine point something per cent as in China, be more satisfactory, or is it possible that there are drawbacks in a system that so weakly scrutinises State allegations against individuals? Ms Hamilton discusses points such as these and disparages the concept of 'meaningless acquittals and meaningful convictions', the view that only a conviction is a valid or appropriate end to a criminal trial. Some who speak publicly on criminal justice themes seem dangerously close to this view.

It is natural that Ms Hamilton should call in aid of her argument famous cases of doubtful convictions or proven miscarriages of justice. To these must now be added the recent Irish cases of *Wall and McCabe* and of *Shortt*. It is good that our law now provides for the recognition of actual miscarriages when they occur. It is unfortunate that none of these cases has, as far as I know, prompted any serious examination of how miscarriages occur and, where maliciously caused, how they are concealed.

Many of Ms Hamilton's themes are controversial: too controversial at least for any extra judicial comment by a judge. But I have no hesitation in saying that this book substitutes analysis for platitude and invites the reader to think, rather than to declaim or emote, about important aspects of our criminal justice system. Those who differ from her are thereby challenged to rigorous, rather than merely rhetorical, rejoinder. Whether her critique of recent statutory measures commends itself to the reader or not, it is a principled and closely argued one. Legal changes in the area of fundamental rights should be closely watched for their general tendencies as well as their individual content, lest we one day find with surprise that our law has altered in an undesired way while our attention was elsewhere.

The price of liberty is eternal vigilance. Ms Hamilton with this book takes her place as one of the most vigilant watchers on our wall of fundamental rights.

Adrian Hardiman

Notes

1 [1993] 1 IR 102.
2 [1966] IR 501.

Acknowledgements

I have accumulated many debts since I began work on this book. I would like to thank my former colleague and good friend, Fiona Murphy BL, whose sound knowledge of both the theory and practice of criminal law was of tremendous assistance. Thanks should also go to John Brosnan, Irish Prison Service, for his willingness to share his dissertation on pre-trial custody in Ireland with me and his patience in answering questions in relation to same. I am also grateful to Jim Mitchell, Irish Prison Service and to the library staff in Dublin Institute of Technology, Mountjoy Square. The author also wishes to extend her thanks to Ian O'Donnell, University College Dublin, for his comments on the conclusions of this book and to her editors for their insightful comments and attention to detail. All errors are of course the author's own. Last but by no means least, I would like to thank Brendan and my family for their unswerving support in what can often prove to be a lonely enterprise.

Introduction

Honouring the presumption of innocence is often difficult; sometimes we must pay substantial social costs as a result of our commitment to the values we espouse. But at the end of the day the presumption of innocence protects the innocent; the short cuts we take with those whom we believe to be guilty only injure those who are wrongfully accused and ultimately ourselves.

Marshall J. in *US v. Salerno*

In 1931, the prominent jurist, Sir Carleton Allen,[1] claimed that 'if the average Englishman were asked what he considered to be the outstanding characteristic of English criminal law, or indeed of the whole legal system, he would probably answer without a moment's hesitation: "A man is presumed innocent until he is proved guilty"'. A generation later, it is likely that if a similar enquiry were made of the ordinary Irish man or woman this same reply would be given.[2] It is indeed trite law in this country that every individual charged with a criminal offence enjoys the right to be presumed innocent. Indeed, it is no exaggeration to state that it is perhaps the best known of the fundamental principles underlying the common law legal systems.

The law is replete with encomia to the presumption of innocence. Legal scholars have employed different arithmetic to give expression to the bias which is inherent in the principle.[3] Blackstone's[4] maxim is the best known: 'better that ten guilty persons escape than that one innocent suffer'. Fortescue[5] thought it better that 'twenty guilty persons should escape the punishment of death than that one innocent person should be condemned', and Hale[6] determined the ratio to be as low as five. In the US, the presumption has been called 'a general principle of our political morality',[7] 'as irresistible as the heavens till overcome',[8] 'a cornerstone of Anglo-Saxon justice'[9] and a 'bedrock, axiomatic and elementary principle' whose 'enforcement lies at the foundation of the administration of our criminal law'.[10] Every law student will also be familiar with the poetic flourish of Lord Sankey in *Woolmington v. DPP*[11] on the burden of proof: 'Throughout the web of the English law one golden thread is always to be seen, that it is the duty of the prosecution to prove the prisoner's guilt.' Our own superior courts have also acknowledged the principle as a 'fundamental postulate' of the criminal law which is constitutionally protected as part of the right to fair trial.[12] Indeed, the Supreme Court famously held in *People (AG) v. O'Callaghan*[13] that the courts owe more than verbal respect to the principle. The Court went on to note that the presumption is 'a very real thing and not simply a procedural rule taking effect only at the trial'.

Yet, in a legal system which now accommodates preventative detention, the use of silence as evidence against an accused and significantly increased police powers among other developments, the 'reality' of the presumption is increasingly placed in question. There is a danger that, as Lacey *et al*[14] have argued:

> We take [the presumption of innocence] so much for granted that even the widespread institutional and social practices which sit unhappily with it (the treatment of suspects at police stations; use of custody for "suspects" refused bail; pressure on people to plead guilty; prejudicial media reporting, to name but a few) do not threaten to displace it, and rarely even call forth critical comment.

It is important to distinguish here between the practice of the law and the law itself. It is not so hard to believe that there is a considerable gap between the rhetoric of the law and its operation in practice. In real life, the values espoused within the Gardaí may not correspond with laws designed to promote due process; barristers negotiate deals on the basis of pleas of guilty and judges, intentionally or not, do not place enough weight on the presumption of innocence in considering applications for bail. This is not the whole picture, however. The difficulty is not just with the gap between rhetoric and practice but also with the dissonance between the rhetoric and the law itself. Such departures from the rhetoric of innocence have been lamented throughout history. As Laufer[15] notes, since the emergence of the presumption, 'jurists and lay observers alike have noted that the criminal process, from beginning to end, defeats presumptions of innocence and invites presumptions of guilt'.[16] More recently, McBarnet[17] has argued as a result of her study in the Scottish courts: 'Police and court officials need not abuse the law to subvert principles of justice; they need only use it. Deviation from the rhetoric of legality and justice is institutionalised in the law itself.'

While McBarnet's study was primarily concerned with the way in which the law had been developed by the courts, one of the main concerns of this book will be to explore whether the presumption of innocence has been subverted through recent legislative developments. There is little doubt that the criminal justice landscape has been dramatically altered in the last few decades. As Walsh[18] has recently noted, there have been twenty-seven major criminal justice enactments since the *Criminal Justice Act 1984* enhancing the powers of the police and the prosecution. Most worrying among these changes has been a drift away from the criminal law itself towards civil mechanisms to regulate criminal activities, a trend given increasing affirmation by the introduction of anti-social behaviour orders in this jurisdiction. The implications for our society are considerable and, as Walsh has argued, the likelihood is that further inroads will continue to be made into due process rights:

> I view this Bill [*Criminal Justice Bill 2004*] as yet another dangerous concession to those who have argued persistently, and who will no doubt continue to argue, that the criminal justice system is weighted in favour of the suspect. If that argument was ever true it has surely been neutralized at some point in the past 20 years under the flood of pro police and prosecution measures.[19]

In light of this depressing diagnosis, the aim of this book is to attempt to take stock of the law impacting upon the presumption of innocence, arguably one of the most important principles of our criminal law. Those readers with a certain familiarity or interest in civil libertarian issues may be aware of the many legislative inroads that were made into due process rights in the period following the murders of Jerry McCabe and Veronica Guerin in the summer of 1996. It is my contention that the current backlash against these rights has had a longer gestation and that a dilution of the tangible effects flowing from the presumption had already been in train prior to these murders. It would be false to present this period as a one-off aberration, an argument which is borne out by the controversial provisions contained within the most recent Criminal Justice Act. The exercise has necessitated an examination of an eclectic range of topics and the book touches upon areas as diverse as the laws of evidence, criminal law, criminal procedure, sentencing law and prison law. Breaches of the presumption of innocence can be found in the highly controversial human rights abuses in Guantanamo Bay as well as in the more prosaic reverse onus clauses in statutes and it is the very breadth of the rule which may allow it to act as a litmus test for our criminal justice system. The limitations of the undertaking should also be noted, however, as it is not purported to examine the causes underlying the attenuation of the presumption or provide a theoretical framework within which this development can be examined. Readers interested in such analyses may find much to consider elsewhere.[20]

In Chapter One the definition to be accorded the presumption itself is considered, together with its history and *raison d'etre*. Chapter Two discusses the main judicially-created exceptions to the presumption of innocence and the ancillary evidential requirement that the prosecution prove its case beyond all reasonable doubt. This chapter reconsiders the arguments advanced for these exceptions such as the reverse onus burden of proof imposed on the defendant who pleads insanity and questions their validity. Also included in this chapter is a discussion of the Irish jurisprudence on delay in cases of alleged child sexual abuse, a controversial subject which has forced the courts into an uneasy compromise with the right of the accused to be presumed innocent. The next Chapter looks at rights which are normally affiliated with the presumption such as the right to proof beyond all reasonable doubt and the right to silence. The relationship between these rights is complex and their interdependence is much contested in the academic literature.

Chapters Four to Six have as their focus legislative innovations which have arguably curtailed the presumption, from the *Criminal Justice Act 1984*, which first introduced detention for the purpose of interrogation in Ireland, to the *Criminal Justice Act 2006*. A central focus of this section is the murders of Garda Jerry McCabe and journalist Veronica Guerin in the summer of 1996 which spawned a legislative response with particularly significant policy consequences. The period has been viewed by some commentators as a 'textbook case of moral panic' and a 'catalyst for a hardening in political attitudes.'[21] Chapter Five examines the implications of the legislative changes for the presumption of innocence. Chapters Seven and Eight scrutinise established practices which sit uncomfortably with the presumption, namely the sentencing discount for a plea of guilty in the criminal courts and the treatment afforded remand prisoners in Ireland, a growing cohort within the prison estate. The book is primarily concerned with domestic law but Chapter Nine examines current relevant developments in two countries to which Ireland often looks in policy matters: Britain and the United States. It examines the provisions of the Labour Government's flagship piece of legislation, the English *Criminal Justice Act 2003*, as well as serious abrogations of the presumption of innocence which have occurred as part of the 'war on terror'.

Overall, the book poses a challenge to both those who would wish to rest on our laurels as a nation committed to due process and those who would argue that the balance of the criminal justice system has swung too far in favour of the accused. It is a much vaunted proposition that we are a country that is generous to our accused persons. The Minister for Justice, Michael McDowell, stated in April 2003 that Ireland is 'the only member state of the EU in which individual citizens are guaranteed the constitutional right to due process, to the exclusion of illegally obtained evidence, to trial by jury in all non-minor cases, to fair bail, to the presumption of innocence, to *habeas corpus*,[22] and the right to have any law invalidated in the courts which conflicts with his or her rights-and the right not to have any of these rights altered except by referendum'.[23]

There is also a consensus among the media that the rights of the accused have been purchased at the expense of victims' rights and should be curtailed. Writing in the wake of the Brian Murphy manslaughter case, Carol Coulter,[24] legal affairs correspondent of the Irish Times, asserted that 'victims' feelings are not at the centre of the criminal justice system'. Interestingly, Ms Coulter pinned the blame for this unsatisfactory state of affairs on the presumption of innocence and argued for change along the lines of the inquisitorial system that pertains in most European jurisdictions where the accused does not benefit from the presumption. The argument confuses the fact that the prosecution does not bear the burden of proof in these countries with a presumption of guilt. The presumption of innocence, which is fundamental to any civilized system of law, is in fact respected in such jurisdictions and is enshrined in the European Convention on Human Rights. It is proposed in the chapters which follow to move the debate in a different direction: does our claim to a presumption of innocence in this country form an empty boast? Can we really lay claim to a presumption that is more than merely theoretical or illusory?

Notes

1 C. K. Allen 'The Presumption of Innocence' in *Legal Duties and Other Essays in Jurisprudence* (Oxford, Clarendon Press, 1931) p.253.
2 Perhaps this is overly optimistic. A recent public survey conducted by the American Bar Association (1999) found that over one-third of Americans were unaware that a defendant is innocent until proven guilty.
3 For a full exploration of the ratio of innocence, see A. Volokh 'N Guilty Men' (1997) 146 *University of Pennsylvania Law Review* 173 available at http://www.law.ucla.edu/volokh/guilty.htm#56.
4 W. Blackstone *Commentaries on the Laws of England* Vol. IV (1765–1769) p.358.
5 J. Fortescue *De Laudibus Legum Angliae* (1775), Chapter 27, p.63.
6 M. Hale *Historia placitorum coronæ* (1778) p.289.
7 W. Twining *Rethinking Evidence: Exploratory Essays* (Oxford: Basil Blackwell, 1990) p.208.

8 D.J.B. Thayer *A Preliminary Treatise on Evidence at the Common Law* (1898) at p.553 (quoting Bradner *Evidence* p.460.

9 H.J. Abraham *The Judicial Process* (Oxford: Oxford University Press, 1993) p.96.

10 *Coffin v. US* 156 US 432 p.453.

11 [1935] AC 462 at 481.

12 *O'Leary v. Attorney General* [1993] 1 IR 102.

13 [1966] IR 501.

14 N. Lacey, C. Wells and D. Meure *Reconstructing Criminal Law* (Weidenfield and Nicolson, 1990) p.155.

15 W.S. Laufer 'The Rhetoric of Innocence' (1995) 70 *Washington Law Review* 329 p.350.

16 Laufer *ibid.* cites by way of example William Darling *Ten Years as a Police Judge* (1884) (quoted in Wigmore *Evidence in Trials at Common Law* (1981) p.531) who noted in strong terms: 'It is greatly to be feared that the so-called presumption of innocence in favor of the prisoner at the bar is a pretence, a delusion, an empty sound. It ought not to be, but – it is.' He continues: 'The secrecy of complaint-making at the magistrate's office, the mysterious inquisition of the grand-jury room, the publicity of the arrest, the commitment to the lock-up, the demand of bail, the delay of trial, the enforced silence of defence till prosecution had done its worst, are all so many steps and strokes to blacken the accused before he is to open his mouth with a syllable of evidence to break the force of the damaging array of circumstances. To suppose that the presumption of innocence, with its unbiased nature prompts, is not before this time choked and strangled to death is an absurdity too gross to dispute.'

17 D. McBarnet *Conviction: Law, the State and the Construction of Justice* (London, MacMillan Press, 1981) p.156.

18 D. Walsh 'The Criminal Justice Bill: Completing a Crime Control Model of Criminal Justice?' paper delivered at Conference on the Criminal Justice Bill 2004: Implications for Human Rights and Legal Practice, Trinity College Dublin, 20 April 2005.

19 *Ibid.* p.5.

20 See, for example, S. Kilcommins, I. O'Donnell, E O'Sullivan and B. Vaughan *Crime, Punishment and the Search for Order in Ireland* (IPA, 2004) for a consideration of whether Garland's 'culture of control' has application to Irish criminal justice policy. Garland suggests that society is in transition – a reconfiguration is taking place in which priorities have been realigned to focus on features such as offences committed, the rationality of offenders and the utility of punishment goals such as just desserts, incapacitation and retribution. Applying this theory to Irish criminal justice policy, Kilcommins *et al* have argued that it may be applicable not only to state-offender relations (post conviction) but also to state-accused relations (pre-conviction). They note at p.173 that 'in the same manner by which judicial discretion is curbed to create a more efficient system of punishment, so too, in the broader trial process are

the fairness of procedure rights of accuseds limited so as to allow for more result-orientated outcomes. Both of these increasingly streamlined processes are part of the same over-arching continuum.'

21 I. O'Donnell 'Crime and Justice in the Republic of Ireland' (2005) 2(1) *European Journal of Criminology* 99 p.106.

22 The issuing of a writ by a judge ordering that a prisoner be produced before it for the purpose of determining the legality of his/her detention.

23 *The Irish Times* 24 April 2003, cited in S. Kilcommins *et. al. op. cit.* p.173.

24 *The Irish Times* 10 March 2004.

Chapter One

The Presumption of Innocence

(I) What is the Presumption?

(a) Procedural Ambit

A preliminary, but crucial, point relates to definition. It is difficult to define the presumption as it is often used to denote different things. As Schwikkard[1] puts it: 'Despite the laudatory rhetoric associated with the presumption of innocence, there is little consensus regarding, its contents and scope leading to considerable variation in respect of its normative value.' Ashworth[2] has also observed: 'This apparently simple right has a number of ramifications . . . The presumption of innocence, as it is usually termed, points in an at least two different directions.'

In its narrowest sense, the presumption can be viewed as merely giving expression to the more prosaic evidential rules that the prosecution bears the burden of proof and that guilt must be proved beyond a reasonable doubt.[3] This view has been espoused by many commentators on the law of evidence. Cross and Tapper,[4] for example, state that 'when it is said that an accused person is presumed to be innocent, all that is meant is that the prosecution are obliged to prove the case against him beyond reasonable doubt'. Morton and Hutchinson,[5] who have written a book on the presumption in Canadian law, adopt a similar view.

> In relation to the first requirement that the prosecution at all times bears the legal burden of proving the facts in

> issue, it follows that the defendant is not compelled to participate in the trial process and does not have to give evidence in his or her own defence. He or she may simply elect to put the prosecution to proof and test their evidence by way of cross examination. It is here that the presumption of innocence and the right to silence interact in that it affords the accused the right to say 'prove it.'

It should be noted that the principle that the onus rests with the prosecution also extends to any defence raised by the accused. Once the accused can point to some evidence on which to base his or her defence, (satisfies the 'evidential burden' in the case), then the prosecution bears the burden of disproving it beyond a reasonable doubt.[6] Thus, in a trial for murder, the prosecution at all times bears the legal burden of proving the accused caused death with an intention to kill or seriously harm. If self-defence is raised as an issue by the accused, defence counsel must point to some evidence on which this claim can be substantiated. In most cases, this will appear on the evidence led by the prosecution although the accused always retains the option of giving evidence himself or herself as to an attack. Once the evidential burden is satisfied, or the issue can be said to have 'passed the judge', then the prosecution bears the additional burden of disproving the possibility of self-defence beyond all reasonable doubt. The requirement that the accused meet an evidential burden in relation to defences is a pragmatic measure to avoid the prosecution having to negative every defence to a criminal charge, however unrelated to the evidence.

It is useful at this juncture to devote some space to an explanation of the terms 'evidential' and 'legal' burden as these are terms which will appear with some frequency throughout the book. The legal or persuasive burden is the onus which is placed on the prosecution at the start of a case to establish the case against the accused beyond all reasonable doubt. This attaches to all elements of the offence, including any defences to the charge, and ensures that the prosecution shoulders the burden of proving all the facts pertinent to guilt (the exception is the defence of insanity which is discussed further in Chapter Two). The evidential burden, on the other hand, does not require proof of facts, but does require that sufficient evidence is adduced to raise a reasonable doubt or, put more simply, to raise an issue as to a fact (such as self defence in the example above). The prosecution must discharge an evidential burden in order to successfully bring a prosecution (after hearing the prosecution evidence the judge may decide that there is 'no case to answer' and dismiss the case) and it also carries the legal burden in a case.

Generally, the only occasion on which the defence bears a burden is when it will be required to satisfy an evidential burden in relation to a defence it wishes to raise or in the case of insanity where it bears a legal burden. However, this basic situation may be altered by statutory devices which seek to place the evidential or the legal burden on the defence (these are termed 'reverse onus provisions'). The important point to remember is that the difference between the two burdens is the degree of evidence required to satisfy the burden – the evidential burden requires evidence sufficient to raise a reasonable doubt while the legal burden requires sufficient evidence to be adduced to establish that a fact does or does not exist.

To return to the question of the ambit of the presumption, the definition of the presumption can also be extended to include the requirement of neutrality for fact finders. Wigmore[7] has identified the presumption as incorporating a requirement that the adjudicator ignore all pre-trial indicators of guilt and determine guilt or innocence solely on the evidence presented in court. This facet of the presumption would appear to be a well-recognised principle of Irish criminal law. Irish juries are told as a matter of course by prosecution counsel at the start of a case that the fact that the Director of Public Prosecutions (DPP) has seen fit to bring an indictment against the accused is a matter of no moment in relation to the accused's guilt and that they must base their decision solely on the evidence adduced before them in court. It is an aspect of the presumption which may assume an increasing relevance in this jurisdiction, however, as our society becomes increasingly racially and ethnically diverse. It is noteworthy that in the US, a country with severe racial divisions, Laufer[8] has argued for a reconceptualisation of the presumption as a factual assumption of innocence to counter juror predispositions which are inconsistent with it. He argues that in order to give real meaning to the presumption juries should be instructed at the start of the proceedings that they must assume the accused did not commit the crime charged.

Finally, in its broadest sense, the presumption may also be seen as a means of demanding treatment of a person charged with an offence which is consistent with innocence. This view reinforces a more general principle of liberty within the criminal justice system which extends beyond the trial event itself to the whole criminal justice system and into the realm of police investigation.[9] The influential writer, Packer,[10] has adopted this view of the presumption of innocence. Packer famously wrote of the criminal justice system as struggling to reconcile due process with the more managerial notion of crime control. Within this system, he spoke of a presumption of guilt as well as of innocence. In his view, the presumption of guilt is a factual presumption which arises once there is sufficient evidence on which to arrest and detain the accused. From that point on all further dealings with the accused by the authorities are based on the view that he is probably guilty. The presumption of innocence, however, is not the opposite of the presumption of guilt. The presumption of guilt, he argues, is merely a prediction of the outcome, whereas the presumption of innocence is a normative judgment: '[It] means that until an adjudication of guilt by an authority legally competent to make such an adjudication, the suspect is to be treated, for reasons that have nothing whatever to do with the probable outcome of the case, as if his guilt is an open question.'[11] The authorities are therefore mandated to ignore the presumption of guilt in their treatment of the suspect. Packer saw the functional reason for the presumption of innocence as being bound up with the concept of legal guilt:

> A man who, after police investigation, is charged with having committed a crime can hardly be said to be presumptively innocent, if what we mean is factual innocence. But if what we mean is that it has yet to be determined if any of the myriad legal doctrines that serve in one way or another the end of limiting official power through the observance of certain substantive and procedural irregularities may be appropriately invoked to exculpate the accused man, it is apparent that as a matter

> of prediction it cannot be said with confidence that more probably than not he will be found guilty.[12]

In other words, it is necessary to assume innocence as the concept is defined in a legal sense rather than a factual one at the trial. It is therefore logically prior to a fair trial in accordance with law as it ensures that the state fulfils its burden to prove legal guilt: 'By forcing the state to prove its case against the accused in an adjudicative context, the presumption of innocence serves to force into play all the qualifying and disabling doctrines that limit the use of the criminal sanction against the individual.'[13] Thus, in Packer's definition, the presumption shrouds the accused with protection from the moment of charge or just before (when the presumption of guilt arises) to the conclusion of the trial. The eminent writer on criminal law, Glanville Williams,[14] has taken a similarly expansive view of the presumption through his argument that the poor conditions in which pre-trial prisoners are held repudiates the presumption of innocence.

This view of the presumption is perhaps best expressed by Professor Tribe:[15] '[The presumption] represents far more than a rule of evidence. It represents a commitment to the proposition that a man who stands accused of crime is no less entitled than his accuser to freedom and respect as an innocent member of the community.' It is worth quoting his definition at length, not least for the interesting distinction he draws between the tangible and intangible benefits which accrue to accused persons: 'In terms of tangible consequences for the accused, this commitment is significant because it can protect him from a variety of onerous restraints not needed to effectuate the interest in completing his trial; because the suspension of adverse judgment that it mandates can encourage the trier to make an independent and more accurate assessment of his guilt; and because it may help to preserve an atmosphere in which his acquittal, should that be the outcome, will be taken seriously by the community.' The intangible or symbolic effects of the presumption comprise 'a refusal to acknowledge prosecutorial omniscience' and 'an affirmation of respect for the accused' through the law's refusal to convict prior to a hearing. This idea of the presumption giving rise to tangible, as well as symbolic effects, is one which will be revisited throughout this book.

From the above it can be seen that a major point of contention with the formulation of the presumption as a normative value is whether its protection extends to the pre-trial period. Ní Raifeartaigh[16] has examined this question in her article on the presumption and bail law. She identifies three incarnations of the presumption within the common law world which she terms the narrow, broad and intermediate approaches:

- The Narrowest View: the presumption of innocence has no application at the pre-trial stage;
- The Broadest View: the presumption of innocence applies at the pre-trial stage and prohibits all restrictions on the accused's liberty which are based on a view that he or she is guilty of criminal conduct; and
- An Intermediate View: the presumption of innocence applies at the pre-trial stage but merely prohibits punishment of the accused for alleged criminal conduct.

The first view confines the presumption to the trial event itself. In thereby reducing its scope, it essentially becomes an expression of the two evidential rules that the prosecution bears the burden of proof and guilt must be proved to a standard beyond a reasonable doubt. On this view of the presumption, it follows that wide restrictions on pre-trial liberty and other rights are permissible. Rather surprisingly, given the express protection of the presumption of innocence in the Charter of Rights and Freedoms,[17] the Canadian courts have settled on this view of the presumption in its application to bail law.[18] Indeed, the adoption of this approach is all the more surprising given the decision of the Supreme Court in *R v. Oakes*[19] where it was held that, at a minimum, the presumption of innocence required not only that the state prove guilt beyond a reasonable doubt but that criminal prosecutions must be carried out in accordance with lawful procedures and fairness.

The third, intermediate view, which allows interferences with the presumption for regulatory purposes, has been the preferred approach of the US Supreme Court. In considering the constitutionality of provisions which authorized preventive detention in *US v Salerno*,[20] Rehnquist C.J. found that the provisions did not violate due process under the Fifth Amendment as the restriction in question was regulatory rather than punitive. The regulatory/punitive dichotomy was criticized by Marshall J. in a strong dissent as a mechanism whereby one can 'merely redefine any measure which is claimed to be punishment as "regulation" and magically, the Constitution no longer prohibits its imposition'.[21] Further, as Ní Raifeartaigh points out, the line between 'regulatory' and 'punitive' is a difficult one to draw. The distinction appears particularly tenuous in the bail context when one considers that the practical effect on the offender is similar whether pre- or post-conviction.[22]

The second, broadest view of the presumption has traditionally found favour in this jurisdiction. This approach received the wholehearted endorsement of the Supreme Court in the seminal decision on bail law in *People (AG) v. O'Callaghan*[23] where Walsh J. stated that 'the presumption of innocence until trial is a very real thing and not simply a procedural rule taking effect only at the trial'. Recent Irish decisions lend support to this view. In *People (DPP) v. O'Toole*[24] Hardiman J., delivering the judgment of the Court of Criminal Appeal, was critical of a trial judge's charge to the jury which did not adequately address the issue of the presumption of innocence. The decision in *O'Toole* is a particularly significant decision on the scope of the presumption in Ireland in that it treats the issue of the relationship between the presumption of innocence and the evidential principle that the burden of proof rests with the prosecution.

In *O'Toole*, the defendant was convicted of a number of sexual offences, including a count of rape. The trial judge was requisitioned[25] by counsel after the jury had retired on the basis that he had omitted to mention the presumption of innocence. In his recharge he stated that the presumption was a very serious one and that the onus to rebut that presumption was on the prosecution. He went on to state that there was an onus on the prosecution at all stages with respect to every question 'where there was a difference'. Hardiman J. held that the charge was unsatisfactory in a number of respects. First, the presumption of innocence should have been explained separately from the burden of proof and not presented as 'merely an alternative way of stating it'. The failure by the trial judge to direct the jury in this way could lead them to regard the presumption as a 'mere technical rule'. The Court felt it was necessary to explain to the jury the 'cause and effect' relationship between the presumption and the evidential rules. Secondly, the statement that the prosecution bore the burden of proof 'where there was difference' gave the impression that the onus only arose where there was difference of account between the prosecution and defence. Thirdly, the learned judge had not made reference to the standard of proof of beyond a reasonable doubt. In sum, Hardiman J., in quashing the conviction, stated that the 'fundamental importance of the presumption of innocence' which was of 'high constitutional significance' meant that the judge's charge had serious implications for the integrity of the trial.

This decision is clear authority for the principle that the presumption of innocence is a cornerstone principle of Irish criminal law in its own right and not simply a proxy for the evidential rule of proof beyond all reasonable doubt. The Supreme Court found that these two rules are separate and distinct, although conceptually related. Further, it is of note that in a series of historic sexual abuse cases (discussed in greater detail in Chapter Two), the majority of the Supreme Court did not endorse arguments of counsel that the presumption of innocence only applied at trial.[26] The decision can be contrasted with the view taken by the US courts, which have held that the failure to instruct a jury on the presumption is harmless as long as instruction on the reasonable doubt rule has been given.[27] Such a finding reduces the presumption of innocence to a proxy for the reasonable doubt rule.

It is proposed in this brief exploration of the doctrine to take a broad view of the presumption which incorporates both pre-trial protections and evidential rules at trial. While cognizant of the view that a broad definition may weaken the presumption in terms of its enforceability,[28] it has long been acknowledged that the presumption of innocence is a somewhat slippery concept and this is to some degree inevitable given its status as the focal point of due process. When the presumption is understood as a general doctrine which underpins the right to silence, the burden of proof and other rights of an accused prior to and at trial, its enforceability is much less problematic. This approach is one which would appear to resonate with the Irish case law discussed above and, as will be seen below, with the recent jurisprudence of the European Court of Human Rights. This last point is important since Irish courts are now required to interpret Irish law in light of the European Convention on Human Rights ('ECHR').[29] Finally, this interpretation will also afford the presumption the greatest impact on the criminal justice system. Given that the vast majority of defendants will not experience trial, to understand the presumption as little more than a rule of evidence at trial is to confine its benefits to the few. An expansive interpretation is therefore to be preferred.

(b) Substantive content

A distinct question from the ambit of the presumption in a procedural sense is the extent to which the presumption may impact on *substantive* criminal law. While an instinctive reaction might be that the presumption has no implications outside the realms of what might be loosely termed 'procedural justice', the incorporation of the ECHR in England has given rise to a real possibility that Article 6(2), (which enshrines the presumption of innocence under the Convention) may force reconsideration of the content of criminal law provisions. The debate has arisen out of two recent decisions of the House of Lords, namely, *R v. DPP, ex parte Kebilene*[30] and *R v. Lambert*[31] which are discussed in much greater detail in Chapter Two. Suffice it to note here that it has been contended by Roberts and Zuckerman[32] that in both these decisions the House of Lords took a much broader view of the presumption of innocence than is traditionally understood, thereby imbuing it with a degree of substantive content. The authors maintain that:

> The striking feature of both these decisions is that Article 6(2) was extended to the proof of facts that were not elements of the offence that the prosecution had to prove to secure a conviction. In *Kebilene* both the Divisional Court and the House of Lords proceeded as if 'terrorist purpose' were an element of the offence, when, on the face of it, the statutory language provides no warrant for

> requiring any such criterion of criminal liability. *Lambert* is, if anything, an even stronger example. The House of Lords expressly stated that knowledge of the nature of the substance is not an element of the offence of possession of a controlled drug with intent to supply, contrary to section 5(3) of the *Misuse of Drugs Act 1971*, and yet proceeded to find that section 28's reverse onus clauses [requiring the defence to prove lack of knowledge] would breach Article 6(2) unless read down to impose merely evidential burdens.[33]

The difficulty with this approach, according to Roberts and Zuckerman, is that, quite apart from the expansive role that this would give the European Court of Human Rights, English judges, unlike their US counterparts, are not equipped for this level of judicial review. Further, such rigorous scrutiny of legislative reverse onus clauses may have the result that Parliament resorts to creating offences of strict or absolute liability, as has occurred in the US. (Strict liability offences are criminal offences which do not require proof of any type of fault although a defence of reasonableness may be available to a defendant while absolute liability offences are offences which do not require proof of any type of fault but in respect of which no such defence is available.) They argue this potential difficulty may be avoided by means of a planned programme of decriminalization.

In contrast to what may be termed the 'classical' school of thought on the presumption embodied in Roberts and Zuckerman's arguments, Tadros and Tierney[34] claim that a substantive reading of the presumption is necessary in order to adequately protect individuals from wrongful conviction. The authors eschew the technical definition of offence in favour of the concept of the 'gravamen' of the offence, as employed by the Divisional Court in *Kebilene*. While the Divisional Court interpreted gravamen to mean 'the wrong at which the offence is aimed',[35] Tadros and Tierney argue that the word should be read to mean 'purpose' or the 'conduct which the creation of the offence was intended to deter or control'. On this view, it should be for the prosecution to prove all elements of the offence in order to demonstrate the defendant's behaviour is criminal in line with the underlying purpose of the offence; if the prosecution cannot do so, the presumption has been interfered with.

They cogently argue that by adopting such a formula, a state can be prevented from evading the protections afforded by Article 6(2) through the criminalization of a mere evidential requirement of what would be an incompatible offence. By way of illustration, they discuss possible permutations of the offence of possession of drugs with intent to supply. If Parliament were to create an offence where, once the prosecution proved that a payment had been made to a known drug dealer, the burden fell to the accused to prove that no drugs had come into his or her possession, that offence would clearly on the classical theory breach the presumption of innocence. If, however, the state created another offence, under the *Making Payment to a Known Drug Dealer Act 2004*, whereby it was an offence to make a payment to a known drug dealer, this would pass the test under the classical theory even though the practical effect is much the same as the first hypothetical act. They continue:

> This shows quite clearly why the purposive approach to Article 6(2) that we are proposing is preferable to the classical theory. The purposive approach allows the court to consider not just the form in which the offence was drafted but the purpose of the legislation. And where Parliament has attempted to evade the evidential structure guaranteed by the presumption of innocence by failing to reflect the underlying purpose of the legislation in its actual terms, the courts should find that the presumption of innocence has been interfered with.[36]

Whether or not the purposive test will ever find firm favour with the English or Irish courts (and this approach does not remain without its difficulties, such as uncertainty in the law),[37] there can be little doubt that it is dangerous to consider the presumption in isolation from the substantive criminal law, precisely for the reasons identified above. It is, after all, futile to express concern about reverse onus provisions in statutes when Parliament remains free to rewrite offences in terms of strict or absolute liability as both methods permit conviction of an accused despite the presence of a reasonable doubt as to moral culpability. This has led Ashworth and Blake[38] to call for a fleshing out of the presumption so that both its letter and spirit can be honoured: 'The argument that it should be the prosecution's duty to prove a defendant guilty must be given greater substantive content: 'guilt' should be interpreted as requiring "fault".' They suggest that a lead may be taken from the Canadian courts in this regard which have forged a link between procedural requirements and substantive criminal law provisions by interpreting section 7 of the Charter of Rights, (which provides that there should be no deprivation of liberty that is not in accordance with 'the principles of fundamental justice') as invalidating most strict liability offences which attract a penalty of imprisonment.

The burden of the authors' argument is that greater emphasis should be placed on the relationship between the presumption of *mens rea*[39] and the presumption of innocence. At common law there is a presumption that *mens rea* or the 'guilty mind' required to prove the crime is an essential ingredient unless Parliament has indicated a contrary intention either expressly or by necessary implication. The common law presumes that, unless Parliament has indicated otherwise, the appropriate mental element is an unexpressed ingredient of every statutory offence. An expansive reading of the presumption of innocence works in tandem with this presumption in that it requires that the prosecution prove fault as well as the external element of the offence or *actus reus*.[40]

Further, as Tadros and Tierney point out, this may well be the favoured interpretation of the presumption at European level. In *Salabiaku v. France*,[41] the seminal case on Article 6(2), the European Court of Human Rights referred to the need for the court to have 'a genuine power of assessment' so as to avoid the presumption of innocence being deprived of its 'substance'. It is significant that the Strasbourg Court did not draw on the distinction between procedural and substantive criminal law in order to reject out of hand the submission in *Salabiaku* that an offence of strict liability offended the presumption of innocence in Article 6(2). The court appeared to accept such an argument as valid although it was conceded that strict liability offences are permitted 'under certain conditions'.

(II) THE ORIGINS OF THE PRESUMPTION

Given the rhetorical purchase of the presumption of innocence, it may come as a surprise to learn of its modern origins and historical contingency. Allen[42] notes that while statements emphasizing the importance of protecting the innocent, even at the expense of letting the guilty escape, (described by him as the 'platitudes of innocence') were in evidence through the works of eighteenth century legal writers such as Fortescue,[43] Hale[44] and Blackstone,[45] it is not before the beginning of the nineteenth century that an explicit presumption of innocence is formulated. It is important at this juncture to distinguish between the development of evidential requirements such as the reasonable doubt rule and a broader conception of the presumption of innocence as their evolution is related but distinct.

(a) Development of Proof Beyond All Reasonable Doubt

Until the nineteenth century, the laying of an indictment by the prosecution was viewed by many trial judges as indicative of guilt and trials were conducted in accordance with this assumption. A number of developments therefore paved the way for the adoption of the rule that the prosecution must bear the onus of proof beyond all reasonable doubt, most notably the increasing recognition of the role of defence counsel in the trial and the related development of a body of evidential principles. Important social developments such as the formation of a professional police force in 1829 were also significant in reducing societal fear of accused persons. Allen surmises that it did not emerge as a doctrine until *circa* 1865 and cites the case of *R v. White*[46] in support of this, where the 'beyond a reasonable doubt' formula was employed by Martin B in his charge to the jury. However, as McAuley and McCutcheon[47] point out, this disregards subsequent important developments in the laws of evidence:

> Martin B's remarks in *White* must be read in light of the fact that defendants were not given the power to compel witnesses to testify on their behalf until 1867 and could

> not themselves give sworn evidence until 1898. In other words, until the egregious impediments affecting the conduct of the defence were finally removed in the late nineteenth century, the claim that the defendant was presumed to be innocent until the prosecution proved both the mental and material ingredients of its case beyond all reasonable doubt was still something of an empty boast.

The views of the authors as to the presumption's historical contingency are borne out by examination of the case law surrounding the decision of the House of Lords in *Woolmington v. DPP*,[48] which decision has been credited with finally 'settling' one of the criminal law's most famous principles.

Woolmington was a young man who was charged with the murder of his estranged wife. He admitted responsibility for the killing, but claimed that his gun had gone off accidentally. He claimed that at the time of the killing he had been trying to convince his wife to return to live with him by threatening to shoot himself and in the process the gun had gone off accidentally and his wife had been killed. At his trial, the judge directed the jury as follows:

> The Crown has got to satisfy you that this woman died at the prisoner's hands. They must satisfy you of that beyond any reasonable doubt. If they satisfy you of that, then he has to show that there are circumstances to be found in the evidence... which alleviate the crime so that it is only manslaughter, or which excuse the homicide altogether by showing that it was a pure accident.

Woolmington was convicted and his appeal to the Court of Criminal Appeal failed. On appeal to the House of Lords, however, he met with more success. The direction was held to be wrong in law as the onus remained at all times on the prosecution to prove that the killing was not an accident. The appeal was allowed and the conviction quashed. Delivering the unanimous opinion of their Lordships, Viscount Sankey LC famously declared:

> Throughout the web of the English criminal law one golden thread is always to be seen, that it is the duty of the prosecution to prove the prisoner's guilt subject to ... the defence of insanity and subject also to any statutory exception. If, at the end of and on the whole of the case, there is a reasonable doubt, created by the evidence given by either the prosecution or the prisoner, as to whether the prisoner killed the deceased with a malicious intention, the prosecution has not made out the case and the prisoner is entitled to an acquittal. No matter what the charge or where the trial, the principle that the prosecution must prove the guilt of the prisoner is part of the common law of England and no attempt to whittle it down can be entertained.[49]

Yet despite the confidence with which Viscount Sankey asserted the antiquity of the presumption, the trial judge in *Woolmington* and the Court of Criminal Appeal, through their directions that the onus of proving accidental death rested on the defendant, were only applying the settled law for over one hundred and fifty years. In the later case of *Jaysena v. R*[50] Lord Devlin commented upon *Woolmington*: '[I]t is not necessary to read more than the speech of Lord Sankey LC himself to see that by far the greater strength of previous authority supported the view which the House rejected.' The trial judge and appellate court in *Woolmington*, who were overruled in the case, both relied on the following passage found in Foster's *Crown Law* of 1762, subsequently quoted in Stephen, Archbold, Russell and Halsbury's *Laws of England*:

> In every charge of murder, the fact of killing being first proved, all the circumstances of accident, necessity or infirmity are to be satisfactorily proved by the prisoner, unless they arise out of the evidence produced against him, for the law presumeth the fact to have been founded in malice, unless the contrary appeareth.[51]

Foreign as the above passage may sound to the ears of criminal lawyers today, it would seem that until the decision in *Woolmington*, the onus of proving defences generally, not just accidental death, was on the defendant. As noted above, Blackstone expressed a clear view that 'it is better for ten guilty persons to escape their conviction and go unpunished than for one innocent person to be unjustly condemned'[52] and further held that in order to establish that the accused has committed an offence, all reasonable doubt in relation to the issue ought to have been eliminated. However, he was equally clear in his assertion that 'all [the] circumstances of justification, excuse, or alleviation, it is incumbent upon the prisoner to make out, to the satisfaction of the court and jury'.[53]

Indeed, so well established was this principle that litigation surrounding the issue of the burden of proof continued well into the twentieth century. Sir John Smith[54] cites various twentieth-century cases in which the pre-*Woolmington* principles in relation to the various defences were finally laid to rest. Authoritative statements of law that the burden rested with the defence to prove duress,[55] self-defence[56] and automatism[57] were not handed down until the 1950s and 1960s. The same is also true of Irish law, with decisions on the burden of proof in relation to various defences all being reached within the last decade.[58] In light of this history, it is clear that modern criminal law owes no small debt of gratitude to their Lordships in *Woolmington*. The decision represented a clear authority that the prosecution should bear the legal burden of proof not only in respect of the constitutive elements of the office but also in respect of any defences raised. As Fletcher[59] puts it: 'Rejecting this extreme application of Blackstone's analysis, the House of Lords in its *Woolmington* decision took the first step toward a new policy of protecting criminal defendants in cases of doubt on "exculpatory" issues.'

(b) Development of the Presumption of Innocence

In contrast to the well-documented evolution of the evidential rules associated with the presumption of innocence, relatively little has been written on the origins of the presumption of innocence. Early mentions of the presumption in the seventeenth century in America relate it to the idea that every person is honest and innocent until proved to the contrary[60] and, as noted above, seventeenth and eighteenth century legal writers in England had written poetically about the importance of protecting the innocent. It was not until the nineteenth century that the presumption began to be linked with the evidentiary burden of proof. As Fletcher[61] notes: '[Relating] the presumption of innocence to the process of proof and conviction was a relatively new development. The doctrine appears in some early nineteenth century civil disputes, but it was apparently not until the mid-century that some commentators began to use the presumption of innocence as a rationale for the prosecutor's burden of persuasion.'

Allen's[62] examination of the history of the presumption of innocence has led him to conclude that the presumption is synonymous with the rule as to prosecutorial proof. Even if the presumption originally evolved in conjunction with the rules of proof, however, this does not discount the possibility, as Summers[63] notes, that the presumption has gradually forged its own identity. It is difficult to pinpoint the precise moment in time when the presumption assumed a wider application but it is possible that it only really emerged as a distinct concept as late as the twentieth century in tandem with a growing awareness of civil liberties and human rights.

(III) A COMPARATIVE EXCURSUS

As jurisdictions which afford the presumption constitutional protection, an analogy can be drawn between the US and Canada and Ireland. The US Constitution demonstrates its antiquity through its failure to refer expressly to the presumption of innocence, or to the burden of proof in its due process clause. The courts have found constitutional authority for the presumption, however, in the Fourteenth Amendment's Due Process clause. The presumption first became prominent in American common law in 1895 in the case of *Coffin v. US*.[64] In *Coffin*, the court refused to instruct the jury as to the presumption of innocence but interestingly did instruct them fully on the subject of reasonable doubt. Relying on Roman law, Fortescue, Hale and Blackstone, the US Supreme Court declared the 'presumption of innocence in favor of the accused' to be 'the undoubted law, axiomatic and elementary' and a protection that 'lies at the foundation of the administration of our criminal law.' Despite the obvious enthusiasm of the Court for the doctrine, a question mark must hang over the decision in that curiously, it appeared to view the presumption as evidence in favour of the accused. A more reliable authority is therefore the decision of *In re Winship*[65] where Brennan J. stated unequivocally: 'Lest there remain any doubt about the constitutional stature of the reasonable-doubt standard, we explicitly hold that the Due Process Clause protects the accused against conviction except upon proof beyond a reasonable doubt of every fact necessary to constitute the crime with which he is charged.' The legal axiom has received express constitutional protection in Canada, however, where section 11(d) of the 1982 Charter of Rights and Freedoms posits the presumption of innocence as a fundamental right.

The presumption is also enshrined in several international human rights instruments. One of the earliest references to the presumption is to be found in Article 9 of the *Declaration of the Rights of Man and of the Citizen* in 1789, which states: 'Every man is supposed innocent until having been declared guilty.' In 1948 the United Nations incorporated the principle of innocent until proven guilty into the *Universal Declaration of Human Rights* which declares: 'Everyone charged with a penal offence has the right to be presumed innocent until proved guilty according to law in a public trial at which he has had all the guarantees necessary for his defence.'[66] The principle was also incorporated into the *European Convention on Human Rights* in 1953 (Article 6(2)) and the *United Nations International Covenant on Civil and Political Rights* (Article 14(2)).

The protection given to the presumption under the ECHR merits particular scrutiny given its recent incorporation into Irish law.[67] The first point to make in relation to Article 6(2) is that it is a specific protection which should always be read in light of the overall fair trial guarantee in Article 6(1). Article 6(2) provides: 'Everyone charged with a criminal offence shall be presumed innocent until proved guilty according to law.' Although the Article does not expressly state that proof should be beyond all reasonable doubt, the Strasbourg Court has held that 'the burden of proof is on the prosecution and any doubt should benefit the accused'.[68] Further, it is implicit in a number of decisions that proof beyond reasonable doubt is necessary.[69] An examination of the jurisprudence of the European Court concerning the presumption reveals that, on the one hand, the Court has interpreted the presumption as being very broad in scope and extending outwith the criminal trial, while on the other hand, it has allowed significant qualifications to its operation. As such, it has been described by some critics as both 'too narrow and too broad'.[70]

To consider first of all the ambit of the presumption, it is clear that it extends beyond the criminal trial itself and requires that treatment of suspects and defendants at the pre-trial stages is consistent with the presumption. In the leading case of *Salabiaku v. France*[71] the Court rejected the notion that the presumption 'merely laid down a guarantee to be respected by the courts in the conduct of legal proceedings [as] its requirements would in practice overlap with the duty of impartiality imposed in paragraph [6]1'. In the more recent case of *CC v. United Kingdom*,[72] 'due regard' for the presumption was also invoked in defence of the presumption in favour of bail for persons charged with an offence, developed under Article 5(3) of the Convention. Significantly, the Strasbourg court has also held that the Article provides that there ought to be consideration of the effect of negative pre-trial publicity[73] and has appeared willing to give effect to the presumption after an acquittal. In *Minelli v. Switzerland*,[74] for example, the court found a violation of Article 6(2) where an acquitted defendant had been ordered to pay costs on the basis that he would 'very probably' have been convicted had he not been saved by the operation of a limitation period for the offence. Similarly, in *Hammern v. Norway*[75] the Court held that legislation which awarded compensation to acquitted persons on the ground that on the balance of probabilities the person 'did not carry out the act that formed the basis of the charge' breached Article 6(2) as, owing to the presumption, this matter was no longer in issue. Finally, the Court has also recognized the affiliation of the presumption with the privilege against self-incrimination, a connection that is hotly contested by some academic commentators as stretching the presumption too far.[76]

The Court is less robust, however, in its defence of provisions reversing the burden of proof. Despite the unqualified wording of Article 6(2), the Court has held that the Article is not absolute. Article 6(2) does not prohibit rules which transfer the burden of proof to an accused to establish a defence, provided the overall burden of establishing guilt remains with the prosecution. Neither does it prohibit presumptions of fact or law. The seminal case in this area is again *Salabiaku v. France*,[77] where the applicant challenged certain provisions of the French Customs Code which allowed for a presumption of guilt once the prosecution proved possession of the goods in question. The Court held that the Convention does not prohibit presumptions of fact or law *per se*, as long as they remained within 'reasonable limits which take into account the importance of what is at stake and maintain the rights of the defence'. On the facts of the case, the Court found that the applicant retained some form of defence and that some discretion remained with the court whether to convict so that there was no breach of Article 6(2). The case is also authority for the proposition that offences of strict liability do not violate Article 6(2) provided that the prosecution retains the burden of proving the commission of the offence: 'The Contracting States may, under certain conditions, penalize a simple or objective fact as such, irrespective of whether it results from criminal intent or from negligence.'

It is unfortunate that the leading case on Article 6(2) speaks in terms of balancing rights rather than adopting a stricter test of 'absolute necessity' as in most of the Article 6 case law. As Ashworth[78] rightly notes, Article 6 rights are not absolute (e.g. right not to be subjected to torture) or qualified rights (e.g. right to freedom of speech) under the Convention but can be categorized as 'intermediate' in nature so that the protection afforded such rights should logically be greater than that given to qualified rights under Articles 8 to 11. *Salabiaku* is therefore out of kilter with case law on Article 6 generally and cannot be credited with recent developments in English jurisprudence stymieing to some extent the retreat from *Woolmington* and the principle that the prosecution should bear the burden of proof. As Ashworth observes: 'The Strasbourg jurisprudence on Article 6(2) is underdeveloped, not to say flaccid, and it is British judges, taking their cue from Commonwealth constitutional courts, who have sought to give greater sharpness to the right and to any exceptions.'[79] The relevant decisions of the English courts are considered in Chapter Two.

(IV) JUSTIFYING THE PRESUMPTION

(a) Justifying the Presumption of Innocence

The aphorism that familiarity breeds contempt, or at least apathy, certainly holds true for the presumption of innocence. Commentators on the topic often decline to advance justifications for it on the basis that its virtues are too obvious to need restatement.[80] This is a dangerous assumption given the poverty of public debate on such issues and the current readiness to sacrifice important liberties at the altar of political expedience. Reiteration of the justifications for fundamental rights such as the presumption of innocence is particularly important if they are to be viewed not as latter-day white elephants but rather as rights which have an intrinsic claim on our attention. Roberts[81] makes the point well:

> It is all too easy to neglect the practical and political significance of our taken-for-granted fundamental principles, but we undervalue them at our peril; the more so at a time when many of our traditional principles of criminal procedure, especially those which are designed to protect the accused, are widely criticized and progressively eroded.

The right to be presumed innocent is closely affiliated with the constitutional right of the innocent in English and Irish law not to suffer criminal conviction and punishment. The inter-relationship between these rights has been emphasized by Roberts and Zuckerman[82] who point out that if justice is frequently found to miscarry, then not only does the public lose confidence in the system of justice but the state would be failing to take the rights of individuals seriously. It is axiomatic that a wrongful conviction can result in unjustified restrictions on liberty or property as well as social stigma. In addition, the person may experience a powerful sense of anger and frustration at the injustice of their situation. Indeed, the long campaigns waged by prisoners who protest their innocence and even forgo parole in order to maintain their protest, provide a powerful illustration that it is a core part of the human condition to rail against unjust censure.

A significant contribution to the debate has been made by the contemporary rights theorist, Dworkin,[83] who has argued that when an innocent person is convicted this results in not only the misapplication of imprisonment or other suffering but also the infliction of a 'moral wrong'. Dworkin distinguishes between the 'bare harm' inflicted on an individual by punishment such as loss of liberty or frustration of desires, which is common to both the justly and unjustly convicted and 'the further injury that he may be said to suffer whenever his punishment is unjust, just in virtue of that injustice'.[84] This is what Dworkin viewed as 'the injustice factor' in his punishment or the 'moral harm' inflicted on the individual by society when a miscarriage of justice occurs. The notion should not be confused with the mental anguish or outrage of the individual who is wrongly convicted. The wrong occurs whether the person in question is aware of the injustice perpetrated upon him or her or not and can best be described as an objective notion of the inherent evil of a mistaken conviction:

> 'Bare harm is best understood, perhaps, in subjective terms: someone suffers bare harm to the degree that the deprivation causes him pain or frustrates plans that he deems important to his life. But moral harm is . . . an objective matter, and whether someone suffers moral harm in some circumstances . . . [is a] moral rather than [a] psychological fact.'[85]

The concept of 'moral harm' led Dworkin to elaborate two other rights which support the right of the innocent not to be convicted and which should trump other public interest considerations. These are, first, the right to procedures which attach the correct importance to the risk of a moral harm and, secondly, the right to a consistent weighting of the importance of moral harm or, put simply, the right to equal treatment. The second right is less obvious than the first but, as Dworkin notes, is of great practical importance as it guarantees proper protection against wrongful conviction even in hard cases where 'the correct answer to the problem of moral harm is deeply controversial'.[86]

In response to Dworkin's arguments, there are many who would argue that the wrong done to a victim when a guilty person is acquitted is of equal gravity. Certainly, this is Tony Blair's view. Speaking on criminal justice reforms on 18 June 2002, the British Prime Minister turned the traditional legal axiom on its head when he commented: 'It is perhaps the biggest miscarriage of justice in today's system when the guilty walk away unpunished.' The first point which should be made in response to this argument is that the criminal justice system aims to avoid both forms of miscarriage of justice and that these aims are not necessarily irreconcilable. Another argument is that the prosecution is brought by the state against the defendant on behalf of society as a whole as the crime is seen as a slight on the nation's values. It is not brought by the victim who acts as key witness. The effect is that when a person is wrongfully acquitted, this wrong is therefore done to society in general rather than one individual. In the same way that society as a whole is implicated in a miscarriage of justice, the escape of the guilty bears upon every citizen. Ashworth describes this wrong as 'a diffused kind of failure of justice, which does not usually impinge on any individual in the same direct way as a mistaken conviction does'.[87]

It can be seen that the presumption of innocence, together with the placing of the burden of proof on the prosecution and the reasonable doubt standard, acts as a means of protecting the accused against wrongful conviction and its consequent effects. The legal, moral and social consequences of an erroneous judgment in a criminal matter mandate a higher level of protection for the individual than in civil litigation and the compromise is struck in the form of the reasonable doubt standard. This standard takes account of the risks of wrongful conviction while not requiring the elimination of all doubt, which would exhaust resources and result in very few convictions.

It may well be asked whether the system can afford such generosity to the accused in modern times. Such an argument recalls Stephen's justification for the presumption in his *History of the Criminal Law*: 'If it be asked why an accused is presumed to be innocent, I think the true answer is, not that the presumption is probably true, but that society in the present day is so much stronger than the individual, and is capable of inflicting so very much more harm on the individual than the individual as a rule can inflict upon society, *that it can afford to be generous*.'[88] There is a social cost to the presumption and the high standard of proof in terms of the acquittal and release of a number of offenders and the possible danger to public safety. Not only does the acquittal of an offender violate the rule of law and compound the suffering of their victims, but it may also undermine the objectives of punishment such as deterrence. In addition, one need look no further than recent opinion polls in the media to conclude that concern about crime has reached record levels, despite low crime rates, and this is reflected in political discourse. If it is accepted that the criminal justice system traditionally pursues the twin aims of truth-finding and due process, should not the latter cede to the former in such a climate?[89]

A preliminary point is that prioritizing truth at all costs would lead us to assume some uncomfortable positions as a society. Most people would agree that individuals should not be tortured or subjected to inhuman and degrading treatment. Yet, as Ashworth notes: 'If we accept this right – which we should do on principle... – then we must accept that there can be values higher than the truth.'[90] Although this is an extreme example, compelling arguments can also be made for respecting the presumption of innocence.

An effective response to the question must first seek, as does Kennedy,[91] with characteristic aplomb, to explode the myth of the 'benign state'. As she writes: 'We should have learned from history that, in the long-run, abuses by the state are far more dangerous to liberty and democracy than individual criminal conduct, dangerous and disturbing as that is.'[92] The history lesson is not confined to the bloody feuds of the seventeenth and eighteenth centuries. The miscarriages of justice in England involving Irish persons suspected of acts of terrorism – the Birmingham Six and Guildford Four – occurred only fifteen years ago. Further, recent research studies in England and America suggest that miscarriages of justice continue to occur on a regular basis.[93] Nor is the Irish criminal justice system beyond reproach. Indeed, abuses by the Garda Síochána in the Kerry Babies', Sallins Train Robbery and Paul Ward cases and the recent revelations in the Morris tribunal invite the opposite conclusion. The inescapable fact remains that in weakening the presumption of innocence society cannot avoid an increased violation of individual rights and convictions of the innocent. These wrongs are further aggravated in that they are done in the name of each and every citizen.

Secondly, it is important to realize that we are *all* at risk of unjust conviction. This requires the explosion of another important myth which acts as a barrier to full appreciation of the importance of the presumption of innocence – that of the 'other'. It is often assumed that only 'criminals' will suffer, that 'the innocent have nothing to fear', yet these rights belong to all citizens. It is therefore no coincidence that with the depersonalization of rights comes an increased willingness on the part of the public to relinquish them. At the start of his series of lectures on serious crime and human rights, Ashworth[94] asks his audience to consider a hypothetical scenario in which the audience member discovers that his or her brother or son and his friend have been accused of burglary. Rights suddenly assume quite a different complexion if the question becomes: 'How would you wish them to be treated by the police? Should it be for the police to decide how long and under what conditions they should be kept, or should they have rights?' Ashworth's exercise served to bring home the significance of rights in a way in which dusty academic arguments about the presumption of innocence and its implications cannot. To quote Kennedy once more: 'We always think it is "other" people's liberty that is being traded, which somehow makes it all right. We do not realize that liberty is not divisible in this way.'[95] This argument also has relevance to the assumption which is sometimes made, particularly in the context of discussions on anti-social behaviour, that the rights of the accused should be reduced in the interests of the rights of the 'community'. Society in general has a clear interest in freedom being respected and fair procedures adhered to as well as in crime control.

A third point relates to the effectiveness of eroding the presumption. It does not follow that adjusting the system in such a fashion would significantly increase the rate of conviction of the guilty or the accuracy of the criminal justice system. Roberts and Zuckerman[96] make the important point that the small number of defendants who escape conviction must be viewed against the 97 per cent attrition rate at the investigative stages where crime is not detected, reported, or recorded. Further, claims that 'the truth' will out if due process protections were dismantled ignore the fact that 'the truth' itself is an inherently contestable notion. The sceptic might claim that the prosecution case in a criminal trial represents the truth of the matter, yet in reality the prosecution case is constructed from facts assembled from certain lines of investigation pursued by the police. Studies have shown that the police do not pursue all lines of enquiry with equal vigour but are more likely to favour one theory of events at the early stages of the investigation.[97] Later on in the process an interpretation is put on those selected facts by several actors within the system, from police officers, to solicitors in the DPP's office, to counsel for the prosecution. It should also be noted that seemingly infallible evidence adduced by the prosecution may, upon closer inspection, be less reliable. Visual identification evidence provides a clear example of such evidence. Although jurors rely heavily on eyewitness identification, there is overwhelming evidence that eyewitness identification is highly fallible and that eyewitness confidence is a poor guide to accuracy. A recent study by Wells *et al.*[98] examined the first 40 cases where DNA exonerated wrongfully convicted people. In 90 per cent of the cases, mistaken eyewitness identification played a major role. In one case, five separate witnesses identified the defendant. All of the above militates in favour of the conclusion that 'reference to "truth" and "facts" carries an aura of objectivity and incontrovertibility that is often exaggerated'.[99]

(b) Justifying the Burden of Proof

A closely related consideration is the reasons underlying the burden of proof. Roberts[100] is one of the few writers in this area who has given careful consideration to the justification for the logistics of proof. The essence of his objections to reversing the onus of proof is the inequity of imposing a burden on the accused, who is at a clear disadvantage in the criminal process. He locates the presumption in its broader political and practical context and advances three reasons for placing the burden of proof on the prosecution:

i. The burden of proof protects a citizen's liberty. If the accused bore the burden of proof in a criminal trial, a presumption of guilt would replace the presumption of innocence which affords an accused the benefit of any doubt. Accordingly, a judge would be forced to direct a jury that, in the event of a 'tie', (where they were satisfied that it was as likely as not that the accused was guilty of the offence charged), the accused has not made out his or her case and they should convict. A presumption of guilt would seriously undermine respect for the freedom of individuals to go about their business without undue interference from the state. As noted by the US Supreme Court in *Winship*: '[It is] important in our free society that every individual going about his ordinary affairs have confidence that his government cannot adjudge him guilty of a criminal offense without convincing a proper fact-finder of his guilt with utmost certainty.'[101] Roberts highlights the impossible task which citizens would face if suddenly called upon to explain periods of their life:

> A moment's introspection reveals, at least to most of us, that we could not guarantee to be able to account for our past movements and motives in order to answer any charge that might, without warning, be brought against us.[102]

Kitai[103] makes an interesting argument in this regard. He has gone further than Dworkin and argued that the state has a moral commitment towards both the innocent *and the guilty* not to convict a defendant in the face of reasonable doubt. This view is based on social contract theory:

> The duty imposed on the state not to condemn a person for violating the law without proper evidence and to regard her as an autonomous end in and of herself is founded on the social contract theory, namely, on the

> partnership between the state and that individual. This duty gives rise to the individual's absolute and inalienable right, innocent or not, towards the state not to be convicted unless her guilt has been proven beyond all reasonable doubt.[104]

ii. The structure of criminal proceedings is such that a defendant is placed at a considerable disadvantage when attempting to prove his or her innocence. The prosecution dictates the structure of the proceedings through its employment of professional investigators to gather evidence and public prosecutors who select the charges to be brought on the basis of the evidence. At all times the defendant is responding to the agenda put in place by the state, not instigating it. In the Irish criminal justice system, the accused is at a particular disadvantage in the early stages of the investigation due to the fact that there is no right to have a lawyer present during interrogation. Only reasonable access is required.

iii. To insist that the accused should bear the burden in a criminal trial when faced with the immense power and resources of the state would tilt the balance overwhelmingly in favour of the prosecution. As Roberts argues:

> The prosecution has access to investigative resources which are vastly superior to those available to most defendants in criminal cases. From the high-tech world of DNA profiling to labour-intensive house to house inquiries, the prosecution is considerably better placed to amass evidence of guilt than is a defendant trying to establish her innocence.[105]

To the second and third points it may be added that the accused is also at a considerable disadvantage in the ability to ensure witnesses are available to give evidence in his or her favour. The defendant cannot bring to bear the authority of the state in this regard. Overall, the asymmetrical onus of proof on the prosecution is essential to redress the balance in the criminal process which is tipped overwhelmingly in its favour.

(c) Justifying the Presumption of Innocence in Ireland

In an Irish context, it is appropriate to take a holistic approach and consider the broader constitutional framework within which the presumption of innocence is located. While the presumption probably has the strongest association with Article 38.1 of the Constitution, which guarantees that no person shall be tried on a criminal charge except in 'due course of law',[106] it should also be considered in the light of the commitment by the state in the Preamble to promote the common good 'with due observance of Prudence, Justice and Charity so that the dignity and freedom of the individual may be assured'. This approach was clearly endorsed by O'Higgins C.J. in *State (Healy) v. Donoghue,*[107] who invoked the Preamble in support of the courts' view of 'fair procedures': 'In my view the Preamble makes it clear that rights given by the Constitution must be considered in accordance with concepts of prudence, justice and charity.' Considered in this light, particularly the concept of charity, the presumption can be viewed as an embodiment of an essentially positive view of humankind. The connection between this view and the presumption was recognized by the Canadian Supreme Court in *R v. Oakes.*[108] Having outlined traditional explanations of the presumption in terms of the social and personal consequences for the accused, Dickson J. continued:

> In light of the gravity of these consequences, the presumption of innocence is crucial. It ensures that until the state proves an accused's guilt beyond all reasonable doubt, he or she is innocent. *This is essential in a society committed to fairness and social justice. The presumption of innocence confirms our faith in humankind; it reflects our belief that individuals are decent and law-abiding members of the community until proven otherwise.*

Shami Chakrabarti,[109] Director of the human rights organisation, Liberty, has also identified faith in the human condition as the broad value underlying the presumption of innocence in a speech on the topic in 2004. Although 'conscious of the rather gloomy picture' he had painted, (the speech discussed recent legislative incursions on the presumption of innocence in Britain) he ended on a positive note:

> We are mostly decent and not corrupt – in need of inspiration rather than coercion from institutions. We are more altruistic than selfish and so on. This is part of why democracy should flourish and not crumble when we are all the subjects of equal treatment, fairness and respect. So the optimism that fearlessly defends the broad value of the presumption of innocence must also believe that it will survive. For we are ultimately too decent, too altruistic, to live with the alternative.

If such a link does exist between the presumption of innocence and the decency of our society, perhaps it is not too much to say that the presumption may act as a barometer of our society as well as of the criminal justice system.

Conclusion

This chapter has reviewed the various interpretations placed on the presumption and argued, in line with Irish law and the case law of the ECHR, for a broader view which extends beyond the rules of evidence and the criminal trial. On this interpretation the presumption is a key principle underpinning the criminal process which guards against treatment inconsistent with innocence prior to and throughout the trial as well as dilution of the requirement that guilt is proved beyond all reasonable doubt. If, as Tribe argues, the presumption mandates respect for the accused and his or her version of events, then it also acts as conceptual guardian of the reasonable doubt rule. Given that the reasonable doubt rule is offended by strict or absolute liability offences which permit conviction of an accused despite the presence of a reasonable doubt as to moral culpability, it is further submitted that the presumption should not be viewed as operating solely within the confines of procedural law.

Discussion of the presumption's limits is essential in order to examine with accuracy the impact of legislation and case law upon it. Although of relatively recent origin, and historically contingent, the presumption is a principle which has received strong endorsement in various international human rights instruments and is recognised, either expressly or by implication, in the constitutions of most common law systems. Its ubiquity may be explained by the powerful justifications for the rule which can be located primarily in the terrible or 'moral' wrong inflicted on an individual who is wrongly convicted. Such considerations, combined with the right to liberty and the power of the state relative to the individual, require that the accused is entitled to a presumption of innocence and that the state should bear the burden of proving guilt beyond all reasonable doubt.

NOTES

1 P. J. Schwikkard 'The Presumption of Innocence: what is it?' (1998) 11 *South African Journal of Criminal Justice* 396 p.396.
2 A. Ashworth *Human Rights, Serious Crime and Criminal Procedure* (London: Sweet and Maxwell, 2002) p.14.
3 S. Summers 'Presumption of Innocence' (2001) 1 *Juridical Review* 37–57 pp.42–4.
4 C. Tapper (ed.) *Cross and Tapper on Evidence* (10th ed., London: Butterworths, 2003) p.135.
5 J.C. Morton and S.C. Hutchinson *The Presumption of Innocence* (Carswell, 1987).
6 *People (AG) v. Quinn* [1965] IR 366.
7 *Wigmore on Evidence* (3rd ed., 1940) p. 2511.
8 W.S. Laufer 'The Rhetoric of Innocence' (1995) 70 *Washington Law Review* 329.
9 See, for example, R. Byrne *et al. Innocent until Proven Guilty? A report of The Irish Council for Civil Liberties* (Dublin: ICCL,1983).
10 H. Packer *The Limits of the Criminal Sanction* (London: OUP, 1969).
11 *Ibid.* p.161.
12 *Ibid.* p.167.
13 *Ibid.*
14 G. Williams *The Proof of Guilt* (3rd ed., Stevens 1963) pp.183–4.
15 L. Tribe 'Trial by Mathematics: Precision and Ritual in the Legal Process' (1971) 84 *Harvard Law Review* 1329 p.1370.
16 U. Ní Raifeartaigh 'Reconciling Bail Law with the Presumption of Innocence' (1997) 17(1) *Oxford Journal of Legal Studies* 1.
17 (1982), Section 11(d).
18 In *R v. Pearson* (1993) 77 CCC (3rd) 124 and *R v. Morales* (1993) 77 CCC (3rd) 91, the Supreme Court held that s.11(d) of the Charter (which enshrines the presumption of innocence) 'created a procedural and evidentiary rule that the prosecution must prove guilt beyond a reasonable doubt at the trial, this rule had no application at the bail stage, where the guilt or innocence of the accused was not determined nor punishment imposed'. See U. Ní Raifeartaigh *op. cit.* at 11.

19 [1986] 1 SCR 103.
20 481 US 739 (1987).
21 *Ibid.* at 760.
22 U. Ní Raifeartaigh *op. cit.* pp.17–18.
23 [1966] IR 501 at 513.
24 *People (DPP) v. O'Toole* Unreported 10th December 2003, Hardiman, Lavan and de Valera J.J. [2004] 4 ICLMD 18. See K. Ennis 'Cases and Comment' in (2004) 14(1) ICLJ 28.
25 A requisition is the legal name given to the formal objections made by either the prosecution or defence to any aspect of the trial judge's charge after the jury has retired.
26 See *PC v. DPP* [1999] 2 IR 25 and *JO'C v. DPP* [2000] 3 IR 478 and *PO'C v. DPP* [2000] 3 IR 87. Two judges have disagreed with this view, namely Denham J. in *PC v. DPP* [1999] 2 IR 25 at 58 ('These are civil proceedings by way of judicial review. Thus, the presumption of innocence is not a determining factor, that presumption is part of a criminal trial not a civil trial.') and Lynch J. in *PC v. DPP* [1999] 2 IR 25 at 77 ('The imposition of the onus of proof on the applicant does not impinge in any way on the presumption of innocence which applies on the trial of criminal proceedings and which will of course apply in favour of the applicant if this prosecution is permitted to proceed.') See further Chapter Two.
27 *Taylor v. Kentucky* 436 US 478 (1978); *Arizona v. Fulminate* 499 US 279 (1991).
28 See for example, Schwikkard *op. cit.* and also P. Healy in 'Proof and Policy, No Golden Threads' [1987] *Crim LR* 355 at p.365: 'As a reason of policy or principle, it is indeterminate in scope and theoretically could be invoked as a reason for any decision or rule that seeks to control the jeopardy of the accused by minimizing the risks of prejudice, unfairness, error or miscarriage of justice. But so broad a notion would transform the presumption of innocence into a vaporous euphemism for fairness in the administration of criminal justice, and as such it would lose any practical utility or coherence.'
29 Section 2 of the *European Convention on Human Rights Act 2003.*
30 [2000] 2 AC 326.
31 [2002] 2 AC 545.
32 P. Roberts and A. Zuckerman *Criminal Evidence* (Oxford: Oxford University Press, 2004). See also P. Robert's analysis of *Kebilene* in '*Kebilene* Deconstructed' (2002) 118 *LQR* 41.
33 *Ibid.* p.388.
34 V. Tadros and S. Tierney 'The Presumption of Innocence and the Human Rights Act' (2004) 67(3) *MLR* 402.
35 This is Roberts' interpretation in his 'deconstruction' of *Kebilene.* See P. Roberts, *op.cit.* p.53.
36 Tadros and Tierney *op. cit.* p.415.
37 For a comprehensive discussion of the merits and demerits of a substantive approach to the reasonable doubt rule see S. E. Sundby 'The

Reasonable Doubt Rule and the Meaning of Innocence' (1988–9) 40 *Hastings Law Journal* 457.

38 A. Ashworth and M. Blake 'The Presumption of Innocence in English Criminal Law' [1996] *Crim LR* 306 p.317.

39 This is the Latin term used to describe the mental element of the crime or the culpable state of mind which must be proved in order to secure a conviction for a particular offence, e.g. intention to kill or seriously harm in the case of murder.

40 This is the Latin term used to refer to the external elements of the crime. For example, the *actus reus* of murder is the act of killing someone.

41 (1988) 13 EHRR 379.

42 C.K. Allen 'The Presumption of Innocence' in *Legal Duties and other Essays in Jurisprudence* (Oxford, Clarendon Press, 1931) pp.256–9.

43 For Fortescue see *De Laudibus* (1775) at p.63 in which he maintains: 'One would much rather that twenty guilty persons should escape the punishment of death than that one innocent person should be condemned and suffer capitally.'

44 Hale in his *Pleas of the Crown* (1778) at p.289 writes: 'It is better that five guilty persons should escape unpunished than one innocent person die.'

45 W. Blackstone *Commentaries on the Laws of England* Vol. IV (1765–1769), p.358: 'better that ten guilty persons escape than one innocent suffer'.

46 (1865) 4 F&F 383.

47 F. McAuley and P. McCutcheon *Criminal Liability: A Grammar* (Round Hall Sweet and Maxwell, 2000), p.39.

48 [1935] AC 462.

49 *Ibid.* at 481–2.

50 [1970] 1 All ER 219 at 222.

51 Folio Edition, Clarendon Press, Oxford, 1762 p.255.

52 Blackstone *op. cit.* at p.352.

53 *Ibid.* at *201.

54 J.C. Smith 'The Presumption of Innocence' [1987] *NILQ* 223 p.226.

55 *R v. Steane* [1947] KB 997 until reversed by *R v. Lobell* [1957] 1 QB 547.

56 *R v. Smith* (1837) 8 C&P 160 until reversed by *R v. Gill* [1963] 2 All ER 688.

57 *Hill v. Baxter* [1958] 1 QB 277 until reversed by *Bratty v. AG for NI* [1963] AC 386.

58 See for example *People v. Clarke* [1995] ILRM 355 (self defence); *People (DPP) v. Bambric* [1999] 2 ILRM 71 (provocation) and *People (DPP) v. Kavanagh*, Unreported, CCA, 18th May 1999 (duress).

59 G. Fletcher 'Two Kinds of Legal Rules: A Comparative Study of Burden-of-Persuasion Practices in Criminal Cases' (1968) 77 *Yale Law Journal* 880 p.903. For a contrary view that *Woolmington* did not significantly change the law see A. Stein 'From Blackstone to *Woolmington*: On the Development of a Legal Doctrine' (1993) 14 (1) *Legal History* 14.

60 J. Thayer *A Preliminary Treatise on Evidence at the Common Law* (1989) p.552.

61 *Op.cit.* pp.533–4.
62 *Op. cit.*
63 *Op. cit.* p.54.
64 156 US 432 (1895).
65 397 US 358 (1970) at 363.
66 Article 11(1).
67 *European Convention on Human Rights Act 2003.*
68 *Barbera, Messegue and Jabaro v. Spain* (1989) 11 EHRR 360, paragraph 77; *Telfner v. Austria* (2002) 34 EHRR 7, paragraph 15.
69 See for example *Goodwin v. Ireland* (1993) 16 EHRR CD 26 where the Commission referred to the fact that a tribunal did not apply a standard of proof beyond reasonable doubt in concluding that the proceedings in issue were not criminal for the purposes of Article 6.
70 S. Summers *op.cit.* p.55.
71 (1988) 13 EHRR 379.
72 [1999] *Crim LR* 300.
73 *Ensslin, Baader and Raspe v. FRG* (1978) 14 DR 64.
74 (1983) 5 EHRR 554.
75 [2003] ECHR 75 (11 February 2003).
76 See Chapter Three.
77 (1988) 13 EHRR 379.
78 A. Ashworth 'Criminal Proceedings after the Human Rights Act: The First Year' [2001] *Crim LR* 855 p.863–4.
79 *Ibid.* p.864.
80 See, for example, J.C. Smith *op. cit.* p.224: 'I do not propose to spend time today justifying the presumption of innocence. Its virtue seems to me to be self-evident.'
81 P. Roberts [1995] *Crim LR* 783 p.785.
82 P. Roberts and A. Zuckerman *op. cit.* pp.344–5.
83 R. M. Dworkin 'Principle, Policy, Procedure' in *Crime, Proof and Punishment*: *Essays in Honour of Sir Rupert Cross* (London: Butterworths, 1981) p.193.
84 *Ibid.* p.202.
85 *Ibid.* p.208.
86 *Ibid.* p.211.
87 A. Ashworth *Human Rights, Serious Crime and Criminal Procedure op. cit.* p.113. Ashworth recognizes that there are exceptions to this, of course, for example, where an individual was acquitted through the operation of a rule such as the presumption of innocence and this resulted in violence being inflicted on the victim. See Ashworth *op. cit.* p.36 fn 64.
88 *Op.cit.* p.354.
89 A well known advocate of this position is the jurist, Jeremy Bentham, who argued that 'rectitude' should be the primary objective of criminal procedure. See J. Bentham *Rationale of Judicial Evidence* (1827).
90 A. Ashworth 'Crime, Community and Creeping Consequentialism' [1996] *Crim LR* 220 p.221.

91 H. Kennedy *Just Law: The Changing Face of Justice and Why it Matters to Us All* (London, Chatto and Windus, 2004). See in particular Chapter 1 'A Benign State – A Modern Myth' pp.3–30.
92 *Ibid.* p.15.
93 See M. Zander and P. Henderson *Crown Court Study* Research Study No. 19 (HMSO, 1993) and D. Givelber 'Meaningless Acquittals, Meaningful Convictions: Do We Reliably Acquit the Innocent?' (1997) 49 *Rutgers LR* 1317.
94 A. Ashworth *Human Rights Serious Crime and Criminal Procedure op. cit.* pp.5–6.
95 H. Kennedy *op. cit.* p.8.
96 P. Roberts and A. Zuckerman *op. cit.* p.359 citing a Home Office study *Digest 4: Information on the Criminal Justice System in England and Wales* (RDS Directorate, October 1999).
97 Royal Commission on Criminal Justice (*Report of the Royal Commission on Criminal Justice*, London, HMSO, 1993) (Cmnd, 2263)), Chapter 2.
98 G. Wells, M. Small, S. Penrod, R. Malpass, S.D. Fulero and C. Brimacombe 'Eyewitness Identification Procedures: Recommendations for Lineups and Photospreads' (1998) 22 *Law and Human Behavior* 603. See also B. Cutler and S. Penrod *Mistaken Identity* (1995, Cambridge University Press: Cambridge, UK).
99 A. Ashworth (1996) *op. cit.* p.227.
100 Roberts *op cit.*
101 379 US 358 (1970) at 364.
102 *Op cit.* p.786.
103 R. Kitai 'Protecting the Guilty' (2003) 6 *Buffalo Criminal Law Review* 1163.
104 *Ibid.* at p.1187.
105 Roberts *op. cit.* at p.787.
106 See the judgment of Costello J. in *O'Leary v. AG* [1993] 1 IR 102.
107 [1976] IR 325.
108 (1986) 24 CCC (3d) 321 (SCC) at 333–4.
109 S. Chakrabarti, 'The End of Innocence' Director of Liberty, paper delivered to the Centre for Public Law, Cambridge, 15 November 2004. Available at: www.liberty-human-rights.org.uk/resources/articles.

Chapter Two

Judicial Exceptions to the Presumption of Innocence

Despite Lord Sankey's ringing phrases, a careful reading of *Woolmington* reveals that the presumption is far from absolute. Two exceptions were specifically recognised by the court, *viz* the insanity defence at common law and any statutory exception. Although the latter exception is to be expected in a parliamentary democracy, it is disquieting that this derogation now threatens to undermine the principle itself. Glanville Williams[1] has been scathing in his criticism in this regard:

> Unhappily, Parliament regards the [presumption of innocence] with indifference – one might almost say with contempt. The Statute Book contains many offences in which the burden of proving his innocence is cast on the accused ... The sad thing is that there has never been any reason of expediency for these departures from the cherished principle; it has been done through carelessness and lack of subtlety.

More recently, a survey conducted by Ashworth and Blake[2] into legislative exceptions to the *Woolmington* principle on the burden of proof found 219 examples, among 540 offences triable in the Crown Court, of legal burdens or presumptions operating against the defendant. The authors classified all the indictable offences recorded in the 1995 edition of *Archbold* according to whether they explicitly or implicitly shifted the legal burden to the defence. Their finding that no fewer than forty per cent of offences triable in the Crown Court appear to violate the presumption of innocence is all the more shocking given that these are indictable offences (offences in respect of which the defendant is entitled to a jury trial) which attract higher penalties and in respect of which one would expect fewer derogations from principle. The results of the study led them to call for 'a thorough reappraisal of the form and content of criminal legislation'.

While the burden of this book is that the presumption of innocence is being eroded, primarily by the legislature, examination of the case law indicates that, in common with parliamentarians, the judges must accept their share of responsibility. It is the judicial treatment of the presumption and its corollary, the prosecutorial burden of proof, which therefore forms the focus of this chapter. The first section considers the arguments for departing from the rule that the prosecution should bear the burden of proof in relation to the insanity defence. The second section tracks developments in English and Irish jurisprudence impacting upon the presumption such as the recognition by the courts of an implied statutory exception to the rule concerning the onus of proof.

(I) The Insanity Defence as an Exception to Woolmington

The exceptional position of insanity has its origins in the decision of the House of Lords in the *M'Naghten* case,[3] which laid the foundation for the modern criminal law on insanity. The facts of *M'Naghten* are well known in that he suffered from an insane delusion that the Prime Minister, Sir Robert Peel, was persecuting him and believed he had to be killed. In the final result, however, he killed Peel's private secretary, Edward Drummond. In *M'Naghten*, their Lordships referred to the presumption of sanity which applies to all accused persons 'until the contrary be proved to [the jurors'] satisfaction'. In *Woolmington*, Lord Sankey, relying on *M'Naghten*, expressly removed the defence of insanity from the scope of the general principle he had established. He stated:

> M'Naghten's case stands by itself. It is the famous pronouncement on the law bearing on the question of

> insanity in cases of murder. It is quite exceptional and has nothing to do with the present circumstances. In M'Naghten's case the onus is definitely and exceptionally placed upon the accused to establish such a defence ... It is not necessary to refer to M'Naghten's case again in this judgment for it has nothing to do with it.[4]

Whether his Lordship was correct in his assertion that *M'Naghten* and the defence of insanity were *sui generis* in this regard is open to question. In his detailed examination of the area, Jones[5] observes that the decision was made in the mid nineteenth century at a time when the law considered that the burden of proof in relation to all defences rested with the accused. As noted above, *Woolmington* was the catalyst for change in this regard,[6] and in fact went against the preponderance of previous authority in requiring that the prosecution bear the onus on all issues.

Be that as it may, the law appears to be well settled and for the purposes of the present inquiry the main question is whether the reasons behind the exception are valid. It is axiomatic that the current law offends the presumption of innocence as it allows the accused to be convicted despite the presence of a reasonable doubt as to his or her guilt. Indeed, the law requires the defendant to prove the issue of insanity on the balance of probabilities so that even if the issues are finely balanced, and the jury cannot make up their minds either way as to the sanity of the accused, they must convict. Close cases are therefore resolved in favour of the prosecution.

That the law of insanity represents a *prima facie* breach of the presumption of innocence has been recognized by the Canadian Supreme Court in the case of *R v. Chaulk*,[7] although curiously, the European Commission of Human Rights[8] has determined otherwise. Logic would dictate that if the defendant must go further than discharge an evidential burden the presumption has been breached, yet the Commission did not seem to appreciate the distinction between a legal and an evidential burden. It held that 'requiring the defence to *present evidence* [discharge an evidential burden] concerning the accused's mental health at the time of the offence'[9] did not offend the presumption. The Commission also seemed to fudge the issue through its claim that the complaint concerned the presumption of sanity, rather than the presumption of innocence. With respect, this argument is also unconvincing as, when the former presumption displaces the latter, Article 6(2) is correctly invoked.

Of course, even if the current law infringes the presumption, it must be conceded that there can be valid reasons of policy for placing a persuasive onus on an accused pleading insanity. Jones examines three possible justifications for the rule, *viz* prosecutorial difficulties of proof, the peculiar knowledge principle and societal protection and finds them all wanting. In relation to the 'impossibility' of proving the sanity of an accused or disproving insanity beyond all reasonable doubt, he notes that this argument was adopted by the Supreme Court in *Chaulk*, yet the Court did not advance an argument as to why insanity should be distinguished from other criminal defences: 'A prosecutor can be faced with equal difficulties of proof in cases of, for example, sane automatism or voluntary intoxication.'[10] A related difficulty for the Court was the possibility of defendants feigning insanity. In relation to automatism, this problem has been met by way of stringent application of the evidential burden, by requiring the accused to establish a 'proper foundation' for the defence such as medical evidence,[11] and there is no reason why a similar approach could not be taken to pleas of insanity. Further, the consequences of a successful defence based on insanity, namely, indefinite detention in the Central Mental Hospital,[12] render it unlikely that defendants would be tempted to fabricate insanity.

The second argument, which found favour with the Supreme Court in *Chaulk*, is that the accused should have little difficulty in proving insanity on the balance of probabilities given that it is a matter peculiarly within his or her own knowledge. The peculiar knowledge principle as a justification for reverse burdens of proof has a long history in Ireland and is critically discussed below. The significant point, however, is a that there is world of difference between knowing something to be true and actually proving it. This explanation for the singular position of insanity among the criminal defences suffers from a similar defect as the previous argument in that it also fails to explain why defendants who plead insanity are treated differently from defendants who plead, say, provocation or self-defence where the facts are also often within the personal knowledge of the accused.

One of the strongest arguments in relation to the anomalous position of the insanity defence is the need to protect society from dangerously mentally ill offenders who may have committed quite serious offences. As Jones observes: 'The courts are just as concerned with social protection as they are with issues of individual fairness or responsibility...There is a constant tension between these two competing values, which goes some way to explaining (but not justifying) the complexities and paradoxes which pervade this area of law.'[13] If the law was changed, however, so that accused persons pleading insanity would only have to satisfy an evidential burden, it is unlikely the streets would suddenly be filled with crazed violent offenders, for two reasons. First, to a large extent, fears as regards the protection of society must be answered by the special verdict of insanity which does not result in unconditional release but may result in detention for an indefinite period of time in the Central Mental Hospital (CMH). Secondly, a defendant's legal team will still have to satisfy the judge as to an evidential burden, probably by way of medical evidence. In this regard, they will most probably err on the side of caution: 'There is little evidence to support the argument that the evidential burden can too easily be satisfied by an accused. An accused cannot "calculate so finely or divide his evidence so precisely" as to produce just enough evidence to pass the judge but leave the prosecution in ignorance of evidence which is peculiarly inaccessible to it.'[14] In light of these safeguards, it is submitted that the need for any doubt about insanity to be resolved in favour of a finding of guilt (and therefore detention) is both unnecessary and offensive to fundamental principles.

(II) Other Exceptions to the Presumption

In England, controversy has also surrounded the development by the judiciary of a 'third exception' to the *Woolmington* rule, namely, an *implied* statutory reversal of the burden of proof. As will become clear the courts have insisted on tying knots in the golden thread even where the statute was silent as to the burden of proof[15] and these developments have been mirrored in Ireland with the emergence of the 'peculiar knowledge' principle. However, in this jurisdiction the most significant development is arguably in the area of historic sexual abuse cases where the presumption has been reversed.

(a) English Law

The point of departure here must be s.101 of the *Magistrates Court Act 1980*, which governs the trial of summary offences where specified conduct is allowed in permitted circumstances. It reads:

> Where the defendant to any information or complaint relies for his defence on any exception, exemption, proviso, excuse or qualification, whether or not it accompanies the description of the offence or matter of complaint in the enactment creating the offence or on which the complaint is founded, the burden of proving the exception, exemption, proviso, excuse, or qualification shall be on him; and this notwithstanding that the information or complaint contains an allegation negativing the exception, exemption, proviso, excuse or qualification.

The section requires a defendant in such circumstances to prove that he or she falls within an exception to a statutory offence and was intended to facilitate the prosecution of certain regulatory offences such as driving without a licence. This exception to the presumption was considerably extended, however, by the judgment of the Court of Appeal in *R v. Edwards*,[16] which sanctioned shifting the burden to the defendant in a much wider range of circumstances. The Court held that where terms such as 'exception, exemption, proviso, excuse or qualification' appear in a statute they automatically trigger a requirement that the accused prove he or she falls within the exempted class. This did not only apply to summary offences but also those tried on indictment and significantly, where the burden of proof was reversed the accused bore a legal rather than an evidential burden. Thus in *Edwards*, the House of Lords first recognized the existence of an *implied* reverse onus statutory clause in addition to express reverse onus provisions, a development which clearly had the potential to seriously undermine the presumption of innocence.

In *R v. Hunt*[17] the House of Lords confirmed that, in addition to insanity and express statutory exceptions, there exists the possibility of a statute implicitly placing a legal burden on a defendant. While accepting the 'third exception' in principle, the Law Lords moved away from an approach based on the linguistic structure of the statute in question, and sought to reinstate an element of discretion in deciding whether Parliament intended the accused to bear the burden. The decision established that the courts must look not only at the wording of the statute in exempting classes of persons from a general rule but also to several other factors such as the difficulty which the accused may experience in discharging the burden. This is well illustrated by the decision in *Hunt* itself which concerned a charge of possession of morphine contrary to s.5(2) of the *Misuse of Drugs Act 1971*. The concentration of the drug had to be over 0.2 per cent. Their Lordships held that the burden of proving the particular level of concentration remained with the prosecution in this instance and were influenced by the relative ease with which the prosecution could have resolved the issue. Other factors which should be taken into account by the courts included the gravity of the offence and the fact that, *per* Lord Griffith: 'Parliament can never lightly be taken to have intended to impose an onerous duty on a defendant to prove his innocence in a criminal case.'[18]

The decision in *Hunt* has caused much academic ink to be spilt. While most commentators have been critical of the decision,[19] Zuckerman[20] has drawn attention to its positive aspects, such as the extract quoted above which he interprets as a call for restraint from judges and magistrates in too readily imposing a burden on the accused. Zuckerman also places much store by the fact that the House of Lords 'practiced what it preached' in holding that the composition of the drug was an element which the prosecution should prove. This analysis seems overly sanguine given that, first of all, the case itself was one in which the application of all three criteria militated strongly in favour of the accused and secondly, the aforementioned passage along *Woolmington* lines may be viewed as a mere platitude in a judgment which largely ignored the presumption of innocence. While the rejection of the wide-ranging principle in *Edwards* is to be applauded, it is submitted that the decision is open to criticism on two counts. First, the decision opened the door to much uncertainty in that in relation to many offences one cannot be sure of the location of the burden of proof. As Mirfield[21] notes statutes such as the English *Public Order Act 1986* are replete with such instances. While exceptions to the presumption created by Parliament are at least subject to parliamentary debate, an implied exception to *Woolmington* admits of no such scrutiny and allows the presumption to be subverted on an *ad hoc* basis to policy considerations. Secondly, the case represents a missed opportunity to vigorously reassert the *Woolmington* principle. It was surely open to their Lordships, having regard to established policy in *Woolmington*, to hold that in cases of ambiguity, judges should interpret the burden as lying with the prosecution. Instead, the high water mark of the decision may be seen as Lord Griffith's *dictum* whereby he argued against the imposition of 'onerous burdens' on the accused.

In any event, the harsh effects of the decision in *Hunt* have been mitigated somewhat by the implementation of the *Human Rights Act 1998*. The House of Lords considered the impact of the Act, or more precisely Article 6(2), on the allocation of the burden of proof in *R v DPP, ex parte Kebilene*[22] which concerned a charge of possession of articles in circumstances giving rise to a reasonable suspicion that these were being used for a terrorist purpose. The Divisional Court were unequivocal in their finding that the section breached the presumption of innocence. Lord Bingham held: 'Under s.16A a defendant could be convicted even if the jury entertained a reasonable doubt whether he knew the items were in his premises and whether he knew he had the items for a terrorist purpose.'[23] The House of Lords decided the case on a different point but appeared to incline towards this view. The later case of *R v. Lambert*,[24] however, marked the real turning point in the case law in this area. This case involved a challenge under the *Human Rights Act* to s.28 of the *Misuse of Drugs Act 1971*, which requires the defendant to prove that he or she does not know that the substance is a controlled substance. The main issue in the case, and the one on which the appeal was ultimately disposed of in the House of Lords, was whether the 1998 Act could have retrospective effect. The four Law Lords, however, went on to consider *obiter*[25] the compatibility of s.28 with Article 6(2) of the Convention. Reading 'down' the reverse onus clause in issue in the case in the light of Article 6(2) of the ECHR, they considered that both express and implied reverse onus provisions in a statute could be interpreted as imposing an 'evidential' burden only. Lord Steyn observed that in order to determine whether a legal burden or evidential burden falls on the defence, it is necessary to take account of numerous factors including the gravity of the conduct, the seriousness of the offence, the precise justification for placing the burden on the accused, and the degree of difficulty that the accused may have in discharging that burden. Whereas before *Lambert* it was assumed that the *legal* burden was placed on the accused, the issue of whether a statutory clause imposes a legal or evidential burden on the defence now falls to be determined on a case by case basis.

It is difficult to assess with any degree of precision the effects of the *Lambert* decision. While it is clear that the golden thread has been reinforced in a post-*Lambert* legal landscape, it should not be interpreted as a legal 'cure-all'. As Munday[26] cautions: 'One ought not to run away with the idea that *Lambert* has led to wholesale abandonment of the idea that Parliament can legitimately cast a legal burden of proof on a defendant.' A survey of recent cases on the issue lend support to this standpoint. In *L v. DPP*[27] and *R v. Matthews*,[28] two cases concerning a charge of unlawful possession of an offensive weapon, the courts interpreted s.139(4) of the *Criminal Justice Act 1988* as placing a legal burden on the accused to 'prove he had good reason or lawful authority for having [the weapon] with him in a public place'. Although both these cases, in common with *Lambert*, concerned an offence of possession, the courts distinguished *Lambert* on the basis of the knowledge of the accused. As the Court of Appeal stated in *Matthews*: 'The reason for which an accused has a bladed article in a public place is something peculiarly within the knowledge of an accused.'[29] In *Sliney v London Borough of Havering*,[30] the defendant was charged with an offence under the *Trade Marks Act 1994*, s.92(1)(c). Section 92(5) of the Act provides:

> It is a defence for a person charged with an offence under this section to show that he believed on reasonable grounds that the use...was not an infringement of the...trademark

The defendant argued that this section, properly construed, imposed only an evidential burden on him. It was held, however, that the section imposed a legal burden on the defendant justified, in particular, by the difficulty that enforcement authorities would face in proving the absence of a reasonable belief should the burden be on the prosecution. In relation to this offence, the court did not appear to be moved by the fact that the maximum penalty is ten years imprisonment. On the other hand, the courts have found that merely evidential reverse onus burdens apply to the offences of drugs possession (unsurprising in line with *Lambert*)[31] and defrauding a company's creditors in anticipation of the company being wound up.[32]

The most recent ruling of the House of Lords on reverse onus provisions is *Sheldrake v. DPP*.[33] This case concerned the offence of being drunk in charge of a vehicle in a public place contrary to s.5(1)(b) of the *Road Traffic Act 1988*. Section 5(2) afforded the accused a defence if he or she could prove, on the balance of probabilities, that there was no likelihood of driving the car. In finding no breach of the presumption of innocence in Article 6(2), and therefore overturning the decision of the Divisional Court, the House of Lords relied on the gravity of the conduct in question in its potential to cause death, injury or damage on the roads. Lord Bingham was also strongly influenced by the fact that the requisite intention was largely a matter within the accused's own knowledge: '[It was] a matter so closely conditioned by his own knowledge and state of mind at the material time as to make it much more appropriate for him to prove on the balance of probabilities that he would not have been likely to drive than for the prosecution to prove, beyond reasonable doubt, that he would.'[34]

The decision of the House of Lords in *Sheldrake* remedies the anomalous situation whereby a similar offence under the same statutory regime, with similar aims and objectives (the prevention of intoxicated driving), required a different burden of proof than the s.5(2) offence. In *R v. Drummond*,[35] the Court of Appeal had previously held that fully probative reverse onus burdens applied to road traffic offences involving drink or drugs, a decision which is clearly inconsistent with the decision of the Divisional Court. The conflicting decisions serve to illustrate the uncertainty which surrounds this area of law at present. It is of note, however, that three of the cases decided since *Lambert* have singled out the knowledge of the accused as the determinative factor in reversing the onus. As we shall see below, this reasoning finds a resonance in Irish law where reverse onus provisions falling within the 'peculiar knowledge principle' are permitted.

(b) Irish Law

The presumption of innocence has only recently been accorded express constitutional status by the Irish courts, although it was implicitly recognised as being of constitutional pedigree in earlier Supreme Court decisions such as *People (AG) v. O'Callaghan*.[36] The *O'Callaghan* case will be considered in detail in Chapter Five. It concerned the issue of preventative detention and whether an accused could be denied bail on the basis that he or she would commit further offences upon release. While the words of ÓDálaigh C.J. may now ring somewhat hollow in light of the changes introduced in the *Bail Act 1997*, the former Chief Justice based his decision against such a ground of objection to bail on the constitutionally protected right to liberty and the presumption of innocence. In a well-known passage from his judgment, he warned that 'the courts owe more than verbal respect to the presumption of innocence'.[37]

Another early case which bears on the presumption is *King v. AG*.[38] That case concerned a constitutional challenge to section 4 of the *Vagrancy Act 1824* which made it an offence for a 'suspected person' to be found loitering with intent to commit a felony at certain designated places under the Act. The offence required no specified act to demonstrate an 'intent' and a person could be deemed a 'suspected person' if he or she had previous convictions. The High Court and the Supreme Court on appeal declared the section to be unconstitutional. McWilliam J. in the High Court relied on Articles 40.1 (the guarantee of equality before the law) and Article 38.1 in concluding that the presumption of innocence applies to all persons, including those with previous convictions. The Supreme Court emphasized the vagueness of the offence, which vested undue discretion in the prosecutor and the judge. Henchy J. in particular found the section to be 'out of keeping with the basic concept inherent in our legal system that a man may walk abroad in the secure knowledge that he will not be singled out from his fellow citizens and branded and punished as a criminal unless it has been established beyond all reasonable doubt that he has deviated from a clearly proscribed standard of conduct'.[39] Byrne *et al*[40] have described this decision as endorsing 'the fundamental imperative that the accusatorial system of criminal justice in the operation of its guilt eliciting process must reduce to the minimum the possibility of an innocent person being convicted'. As the presumption of innocence is one of the most important ways in which this risk can be minimised, the judgment serves as a powerful endorsement of the doctrine.

The seminal case on the presumption of innocence in this jurisdiction, however, is *O'Leary v. AG.*[41] Costello J. in the High Court noted that the presumption was expressly recognized in all of the major international human rights instruments and had no difficulty in finding that Article 38.1 requires that all criminal trials be conducted in accordance with the presumption of innocence as a 'fundamental postulate' of the criminal law. However, he further held that this constitutional right was not absolute:

> The Constitution should not be construed as absolutely prohibiting the Oireachtas from restricting the exercise of the right to the presumption of innocence. The right is to be implied from Article 38, which provides that trials are to be held in 'accordance with law' and it seems to me that the Oireachtas is permitted in certain circumstances to restrict the exercise of the right because it is not to be regarded as an absolute right whose enjoyment can never be abridged.[42]

The case turned on the interpretation of section 24 of the *Offences Against the State Act 1939* which provides that possession or proof of possession by an accused of certain 'incriminating documents' shall be 'evidence, without more, until the contrary is proved' that the accused was a member of an unlawful organization.[43] This amounts to what is known as a 'presumption' and a brief explanation of these legal concepts will be given prior to a more detailed examination of the judgment.

A presumption can be described as a legal mechanism whereby, on proof of one fact, the courts must find another fact proved, without the necessity of adducing evidence in the normal way. The law recognizes two types of presumption which differ according to whether a legal or an evidential burden is placed on the defendant. Where a presumption requires a defendant to prove or disprove a fact on the balance of probabilities, this is most commonly referred to as a 'legal presumption'. Should he or she fail to satisfy this burden, they will stand convicted of the offence. The second presumption, known as an 'evidential presumption' is not quite as demanding on the defendant. The effect of this type of presumption is to require the defence to raise evidence only of a reasonable doubt as to a fact which can be achieved, for example, by testifying him or herself. If the evidential burden is discharged by the defence, it is then the duty of the prosecution to disprove the fact beyond all reasonable doubt. While both presumptions arguably offend the presumption of innocence as the prosecution is no longer required to prove certain matters, the legal presumption has particularly serious consequences as it allows a defendant to be convicted even where he or she has established a reasonable doubt as to their guilt.

Costello J. concluded that section 24 only imposed an *evidential* burden of proof on the defendant, not a legal burden. Thus, the defendant could elect not to call evidence in the case and would still be entitled to an acquittal if the evidence did not establish his guilt beyond a reasonable doubt. His decision was upheld on appeal to the Supreme Court.[44] O'Flaherty J. held that the effect of the section was to amount to evidence only, the value of which could be shaken by cross examination, or by pointing to the mental capacity of the accused or circumstances by which he or she came to be in possession of the document.

The second decision on the presumption was *Hardy v. Ireland*,[45] which this time related to section 4 of the *Explosive Substances Act 1883*. The section provided that it was an offence for any person who makes or has knowingly in his possession or under his control any explosive substance under such circumstances as to give rise to a reasonable suspicion that he is not making it or does not have it in his possession or under his control for a lawful object, *unless he can show that he made it or had it in his possession or under his control for a lawful object* (emphasis added). While a majority of the Supreme Court recognised that the legal burden was transferred to the accused under the section, they did not hold the section to be unconstitutional. Murphy J. opined: 'I do not see that there is any inconsistency between a trial in due course of law as provided for in Article 38.1 of the Constitution and a statutory provision . . . which affords to an accused a particular defence of which he can avail if, but only if, he proves the material facts on the balance of probabilities.'[46] Hederman J. found, despite the employment of the words 'unless he can *show*', that the section placed an evidential burden on the accused. The final member of the Court, Egan J., appeared to base his decision on the fact that the defence was created by statute and operated in a 'saving or excusatory' context.

The difficulty with the judgments in *O'Leary* and *Hardy* is the complete lack of guidance in an area impacting directly on the parameters of a cornerstone principle of the criminal law. As Ní Raifeartaigh remarks:

> Notably, the presumption of innocence and its ramifications are barely touched on; . . . No indication is given of whether there are limits to statutory restrictions of the presumption of innocence or what these limits might be; indeed, the approach of the majority almost appears to envisage that statute may restrict the presumption at will. If so, it is difficult to see any difference between the Irish position and that in England, where there is no constitutional guarantee of the presumption of innocence.'[47]

The judgments beg the question as to what test is to be applied in determining the constitutionality of future statutory incursions on the presumption. Certainly, *Hardy* is sufficiently broad to permit of a statutory reversal of the burden of proof in respect of criminal defences such as self-defence, provocation, and intoxication. Moreover, a coda may be added to Ní Raifeartaigh's argument. English law has moved on since *Hunt* with the incorporation of the ECHR and the *Lambert* judgment. As will be recalled, the House of Lords held that a statute may place a legal *or* evidential onus on the defence depending on the gravity of the conduct, the seriousness of the offence, the precise justification for placing the burden on the accused, and the degree of difficulty that the accused may have in discharging that burden. In Ireland, *Hardy* is clear authority for the proposition that reversals of the legal burden of proof (and therefore *prima facie* breaches of the presumption of innocence) are constitutionally permissible but little else. Given the existence in English law of criteria which can be said to afford some protection to the accused, at least in relation to more serious criminal offences, it would appear that, paradoxically, the 'golden thread' currently enjoys greater protection in a jurisdiction where it has not been elevated to the level of a constitutional guarantee.

Further, Irish decisions on implied, rather than express, statutory exceptions to the burden of proof do little to inspire confidence in judicial commitment to the presumption of innocence. Unlike English jurisprudence, which has evolved since *Edwards* to consider a variety of factors in deciding whether a defendant should bear a legal or evidential burden, the Irish case law has remained focused on one factor, namely the facility with which the matter in question can be proved by the defendant or the 'peculiar knowledge principle'. This principle was first expounded by the courts in *Ministry for Industry and Commerce v. Steele*,[48] a case which concerned the alleged sale of pork sausages with over 65 per cent pork content thereby breaching a wartime order. The Supreme Court felt that the content of the sausages was a matter which afforded the accused better opportunities for proving the truth and once the prosecution had made out a *prima facie* case that the sausages fell within the prohibition, the onus moved to the defendant to disprove same. In several Irish cases since, however, the rule has not been applied where the prosecution has failed to meet the *prima facie* case requirement.[49] In one of these cases, *AG v. Shorten*,[50] Davitt P. took the opportunity to express his clear dissatisfaction with the peculiar knowledge principle:

> I do not feel happy about the application to criminal cases of . . . the peculiar knowledge principle . . . I find it very hard to regard resorts to the 'peculiar knowledge' principle even in its modified form or to any similar principle as other than attempts to whittle down the presumption of innocence.

Davitt P. was right to be concerned. Although most of the criteria against which implied legislative exceptions are to be measured in England are open to attack on consequentialist grounds (i.e. the end justifies the means), one at least has the consolation that a greater number of hurdles are placed in the path of a shift in the legal burden of proof. In Ireland, it must be a source of some concern that this constitutionally protected principle can be traded in simply on the basis of prosecutorial convenience. As Roberts[51] notes, it would be much easier for the defendant to prove defences such as provocation, duress and self-defence, yet these must traditionally be disproved by the prosecution beyond all reasonable doubt. Indeed, in *R v. Spurge*,[52] the English Court of Criminal Appeal observed:

> The facts however relating to a defence of provocation or self-defence . . . are often peculiarly within the knowledge of the accused . . . Yet . . . the onus of disproving them undoubtedly rests upon the prosecution. There is no rule of law that where facts are peculiarly within the knowledge of the accused the burden of establishing a defence based on these facts shifts to the accused.

Tadros and Tierney[53] make a similar point in relation to most forms of *mens rea* which are almost certainly peculiarly within the knowledge of the accused – should the defence therefore have to prove intention and recklessness? Indeed, as the Divisional Court in *Sheldrake* pointed out, the prosecution will generally be able to test an assertion by an accused as to a fact in issue. In criminal matters, 'the courts are well used to testing the state of mind of defendants'. A final, but crucial point, concerns the false assumption that because a matter is within the accused's knowledge, it is therefore easy for him or her to prove. Witnesses or independent evidence to corroborate an account may be difficult to come by or the charge may by its very nature be extremely difficult to disprove, such as offences relating to terrorism.

(I) Historic Sexual Abuse Cases

Hardiman J.'s robust defence of the presumption in *People (DPP) v. O'Toole*[54] has been noted in Chapter One. The learned judge mounted an equally robust defence of the principle in a number of recent cases on delay in sexual abuse cases, although this time he represented the minority view. In Ireland, an accused person who faces charges relating to a delayed complaint can make a judicial review application for an order of prohibition in a civil court.[55] In these applications in prosecutions for sexual abuse the presumption of innocence is called into question when the review court is required to consider the reasons advanced for the long periods of delay by complainants in revealing and reporting these offences. This delay by the complainant may of course be completely justifiable on the basis that it may often be attributable to the defendant either directly through threats or inducements to keep the abuse a secret or indirectly through the psychological effects of the abuse. The difficulty with this analysis, however, is that it is premised upon an assumption of guilt of the accused which would appear to violate the presumption of innocence enjoyed by the accused in relation to the charge(s).

In *PC v. DPP*[56] and *J O'C v. DPP*[57] the Supreme Court developed a three-pronged test in relation to whether an order of prohibition should be made and a trial halted. The first question concerns whether the delay is so long that the trial should be prohibited on account of the delay alone in the absence of specific prejudice. As cases involving twenty or thirty year delays have been held not to fall into this category, it is likely that few cases will meet this requirement. The second question requires an assessment of the reasons for the delay and at this stage the defendant will be presumed guilty of the offences, allowing an inquiry into whether 'the delay in making [the complaint] was referable to the accused's own actions'. The justification advanced by the Keane CJ for infringing the presumption of innocence in this way was that of necessity:

> Without such an assumption, it would not be possible for the court to conduct any such inquiry and the court would be obliged automatically to halt the trial of a person because of the expiry of a lengthy period of time, even though the failure to make the complaint was due to domination exercised by the adult ... Since that patently cannot be the law, the presumption of innocence which applies in its full rigour to a criminal trial cannot apply to inquiries of this nature.[58]

At the third stage of the test, the normal presumption of innocence reasserts itself in determining whether the delay has prejudiced the defence to such an extent that there is a real and serious risk of an unfair trial.

For the minority in *J O'C*[59] on the other hand the only relevant question was whether there was a real risk of an unfair trial. A truncated version of Keane C.J.'s test omitting the second element was favoured by Hardiman J. in his strong dissenting judgment in *J O'C* on the basis that such a test did not impact on the presumption of innocence:

> I cannot subscribe to the proposition that the presumption of innocence applies only in the actual trial of criminal proceedings or is capable of suspension for any purpose relating to the trial, such as the disposal of injunctive proceedings like the present ones ... [E]ven if the presumption did not apply to civil proceedings, or were capable of suspension in such proceedings for some particular purpose there is in my view no basis whatever for assuming the truth of the allegations against the defendant, prior to conviction, for any purpose or in any proceedings. This assumption, even for a limited purpose, is a much greater step than merely not applying the presumption, great as that is in itself. It involves assuming the contrary.[60]

These comments find a resonance in the dissenting judgment of Murray J. in *P O'C v. DPP*,[61] where he held that an assumption of guilt, however contingent, is 'inconsistent with the fundamental rights of a citizen'.

It is possible, as suggested by Lewis[62] in her article on the topic, that the law in this area may be 'born of frustration' given the often circular arguments which characterize this issue. However, as Hardiman J. observes, the willingness of the courts to not only cede the presumption in part of the test, but to *assume guilt*, must give cause for concern. In her analysis of the Irish authorities, Lewis questions the value of the second stage of the test at all given that, once the defendant's guilt is assumed, the inevitable result is that the court will find the delay to be justifiable. If this is the case, then the second limb would appear to add nothing but an additional layer of complexity to an already difficult area of law as well as making a serious inroad into the presumption of innocence.[63]

The dangers implicit in such a process were recognized by the High Court in *PC* where McGuinness J. held: '[T]his Court cannot accept that a situation of domination exists automatically in all cases where a person is accused of sexual offences. The presumption of innocence has to play a part in the Court's considerations and the Court must base its decision on the actual evidence before it.'[64] She went on to make the powerful argument that we should not be so quick to replace past assumptions as to the mendacity of women making allegations of rape or sexual assault with assumptions as to the veracity of complainants in sexual cases: '[I]t would be unfortunate if the discredited orthodoxy of the past were to be replaced with an equally rigid orthodox view that in all cases of delay in making complaints of sexual abuse the delay can automatically be negatived by dominion.'[65] Another source of concern is the ability of the Court to apply the respective presumptions of guilt and innocence in so neat a fashion – the possibility of the former presumption influencing the third stage of the test cannot be ruled out.

In the course of his judgment in *J O'C*, Keane C.J. attempts to mitigate the effects of this incursion into the presumption of innocence: 'The court must proceed on the assumption that the allegations are well founded and, *to that extent only and solely in the context of these specific proceedings*, the presumption of innocence does not apply.'[66] References were also made by the Court in the later case of *P O'C* to the 'special nature of the offences' in question. In *J O'C*, Hardiman J. sought to reinforce the point that the decisions should not be taken as restricting the general scope of the presumption. Responding to arguments advanced by counsel that the presumption is an evidential rule applicable only at trial, he contends: 'Only the judgment of Lynch J. [in *PC*] appears at page 77, expressly to limit the presumption of innocence to the trial of the criminal proceedings.'[67] Yet, the fact that efforts have been made to limit the reversal of the presumption of innocence to a discrete area of law does not provide an answer to the argument that due process protections are being denied the very defendants who need them most. Sexual offenders generally and particularly child sex abusers are, as Fennell[68] notes, society's current 'folk devils'. Society is understandably uncomfortable with such persons but it is precisely at this juncture that the rules of evidence and due process guarantees are 'necessary to counter-balance our prejudices as fact-finders.'[69] Further, it is questionable whether this area of the law can be so conveniently vacuum packed. Fennell evokes the following colourful simile for such judicial tinkering:

> [Such judicial modifications are like] individual body parts waiting to be transplanted. Independently each appears normal, but when combined they create a horrible Frankensteinian creature. The resulting body of law does not at all resemble anything remotely similar to traditional notions of fairness.[70]

Recent decisions of the Supreme Court, however, indicate a willingness to apply the 'fair trial' part of the test in its full rigour. In *P O'C* the applicant was charged with five counts of indecently assaulting the complainant on dates unknown in 1982. The offences were alleged to have been committed during private music lessons which were given by the applicant to the complainant. It was alleged that he had been assaulted in a room and that on each occasion the accused locked the door before committing the offences. The applicant sought an order of prohibition on the grounds that because of the delay involved there was great difficulty in interviewing witnesses or collating evidence which might be of help in defending the allegation made against him. In particular, the applicant's solicitor was unable to discover when keys had been made available to the various rooms in the school. It was argued that if it were possible to demonstrate that the complainant's account in respect of locking the doors was untrue then the credibility of the complainant's entire account of the incident could well be seriously undermined. The High Court found that the complainant's delay was, as a matter of probability, excusable. However, there was a specific prejudice, namely evidence relating to the door locks, which the applicant might suffer as a result of a trial being held at this stage which would result in a real and serious risk of an unfair trial and this decision was upheld in the Supreme Court. In *JL v. DPP*[71] a trial was also halted owing to the specific prejudice which had accrued to the applicant as a result of the twenty-five year delay.

As Lewis notes, however, both cases can be distinguished, particularly *JL* as it was an isolated incident of sexual abuse, and 'it remains to be seen... whether these cases truly mark a move towards a third stage of the test, or are simply aberrations'.[72] In the absence of a Supreme Court decision since these two decisions, it would appear that the preponderance of High Court cases involving delay and sexual abuse have found against the applicant on the fair trial point.[73] This raises the question whether the gravamen of the test remains the second limb with its concomitant assumption of guilt. *Dicta* in previous cases would appear to confirm this suspicion. Denham J. in *P O'C*, while finding that the applicant had established a real risk of an unfair trial as a result of delay, significantly described the case as 'an exception to the general rule'. Similarly in *PC*, Denham J., in rejecting the applicant's case, nearly went so far as to suggest a presumptive rule in favour of allowing prosecutions to proceed: '[The applicant has not] distinguished his case from the growing body of case law which has permitted delayed prosecutions for child sexual abuse to proceed. No factor takes this case out of the norm of this common law...'.[74] The exceptional nature of cases where the defendant's rights are vindicated, taken together with the language employed by the

Supreme Court identifying the interests of the community with those of the victim, lend strong support to Fennell's argument that 'the overarching theme is accommodation of prosecution and pursuit of victim's interests . . . with presumptions of dominion prevailing over innocence rights'.[75]

Conclusion

It is disquieting to note that in both England and Ireland judicial exceptions to the presumption have been readily implied in a manner which suggests the courts do not place sufficient weight on the presumption of innocence. These judicially created exceptions to the presumption, such as implied reverse onus provisions on the basis of peculiar knowledge of the defendant, often do not stand up to scrutiny, the example *par excellence* being the (now well-established) reversal of the burden of proof where the defence of insanity is raised. The arguments for singling out insanity from other defences such as intoxication or automatism, are far from convincing. Further, judicial departures from the presumption are increasingly evident in Ireland where the Supreme Court has embarked on a line of jurisprudence in relation to delayed sexual abuse cases which serves to turn the presumption on its head. It is distinctly possible, as Fennell suggests, that in developing this line of authority the judiciary have been influenced by popular sentiment surrounding the issue of child sexual abuse.

Notes

1 G. Williams *The Proof of Guilt* (3rd ed., Stevens, 1963) pp.184–5.
2 A. Ashworth and M. Blake 'The Presumption of Innocence in English Criminal Law' [1996] *Crim LR* 306.
3 (1843) 10 Cl. & F 200.
4 [1935] AC 462 at 475–6.
5 T. H. Jones 'Insanity, Automatism and the Burden of Proof on the Accused' (1995) 111 *LQR* 475.
6 Jones notes that in practice, judges were already relaxing the legal rules in relation to defences in criminal trials. *Ibid.* p.478.

7 [1990] 3 SCR 1303.
8 Application No. 15923/89 against the UK, 4 April 1990.
9 *Ibid.* p.3.
10 Jones *op. cit.* p.492.
11 See, for example, *Bratty v. Attorney General for Northern Ireland* [1963] AC 386 where the House of Lords referred to a 'proper foundation' being laid before the defence of automatism can be put to the jury. In *Queen v. Falconer* (1990) 171 CLR 30 p.83, Gaudron J. stated: 'In practical terms a claim of involuntariness which is not based on mental illness is almost certain to be treated as frivolous unless supported by medical evidence that identifies a mental state in which acts can occur independently of the will, assigns a causative explanation for the state and postulates that the accused did or may have experienced that state.'
12 Under the *Criminal Law (Insanity) Act 2006* when a person is found guilty but insane, he or she will be sent to a 'designated centre' for detention and treatment which can be either a psychiatric hospital or prison.
13 *Op. cit.* p.513.
14 *Ibid.* p.509.
15 P. Roberts and A. Zuckerman *Criminal Evidence* (Oxford University Press, 2004) p.374.
16 [1974] 1 QB 27.
17 [1987] AC 352.
18 *Ibid.* at 374.
19 See, for example, J. C. Smith 'The Presumption of Evidence' [1987] *NILQ* 223; P. Healy 'Proof and Policy: No Golden Threads' [1987] *Crim LR* 355 and P. Mirfield 'The Legacy of Hunt' [1988] *Crim LR* 19.
20 A. Zuckerman 'No Third Exception to the Woolmington Rule' (1987) 104 *LQR* 170.
21 *Op. cit.*
22 [2000] 2 AC 326.
23 *Ibid.* at 345.
24 [2002] 2 AC 545.
25 Obiter is an abbreviated form of *obiter dictum* meaning 'observation by the way'. It is an observation by a judge on a matter not specifically before the court or not necessary in determining the issue before the court; a side opinion which does not form part of the judgment.
26 R. Munday *Evidence* (4th edition, Butterworths, 2000).
27 [2003] QB 137.
28 [2004] QB 690.
29 *Ibid.* at 695.
30 [2002] EWCA Crim 2558.
31 *R v. Lang and Deadman* [2002] EWCA Crim 298.
32 *R v. Carass* [2002] 1 WLR 1714.
33 [2004] UKHL 43. See further C. Wells 'Reversing the Burden' (2005) *NLJ* 183.

34 *Ibid.* at para. 41.
35 [2002] EWCA 527: the defence of post-accident drinking.
36 [1966] IR 501.
37 *Ibid.* at 508.
38 [1981] IR 233.
39 *Ibid.* at 257.
40 R. Byrne, *Innocent Until Proven Guilty? A Report of the Irish Council of Civil Liberties* (Dublin: ICCL, 1983) at p.13.
41 [1993] 1 IR 102 (HC); [1995] 1 IR 254 (SC).
42 *Ibid.* (HC) at 110.
43 The case as brought in the High Court also sought to challenge s.3(2) of the *Offences Against the State (Amendment) Act 1972*. This line of argument was not pursued in the Supreme Court and it is not proposed to consider it here.
44 Ní Raifeartaigh has questioned the correctness of this decision on the basis that it is 'marred by an apparent confusion between presumptions of fact and evidential burdens of proof'. See U. Ní Raifeartaigh 'Reversing the Burden of Proof in a Criminal Trial: Canadian and Irish Perspectives on the Presumption of Innocence' 5 (1995) *ICLJ* 135 pp.150–2.
45 [1994] 2 IR 550.
46 *Ibid.* at 568.
47 Ní Raifeartaigh *op.cit.* p.153.
48 [1952] IR 304.
49 See *McGowan v. Carville* [1960] IR 330 (prosecution could not prove accused was without a driving licence) and *AG v. Shorten* [1961] IR 304 (prosecution could not prove car driven without consent).
50 [1961] IR 304 at 309–10.
51 P. Roberts '*Kebilene* Deconstructed' (2002) 118 *LQR* 41 p.65–6.
52 [1961] 2 QB 205 at 212.
53 V. Tadros and S. Tierney 'The Presumption of Innocence and the Human Rights Act (2004) 67(3) *MLR* 402 pp.426–7.
54 Unreported, Court of Criminal Appeal, Hardiman J., 10 December 2003.
55 *State (O'Connell) v. Fawsitt* [1986] IR 362.
56 [1999] 2 IR 25.
57 [2000] 3 IR 478.
58 *PO'C v DPP* [2000] 3 IR 87 at 94.
59 Barron J. agreed with Hardiman J.
60 [2000] 3 IR 478 at 517.
61 [2000] 3 IR 87 at 104.
62 P. Lewis 'The Presumption of Innocence in Delayed Criminal Prosecutions for Childhood Sexual Abuse: Lessons from Ireland' [2001] *Crim LR* 636. For a critical examination of the English law in this area see further P. Lewis and A. Mullis 'Delayed Prosecutions for Childhood Sexual Abuse' (1999) 115 *LQR* 265.
63 *Ibid.* p.642.

64 [1999] 2 IR 25 at 40.
65 *Ibid.* at 43.
66 [2000] 3 IR 478 at 486.
67 *Ibid.* at 517.
68 C. Fennell 'The Culture of Decision Making: A Case for Judicial Defiance through Evidence and Fact-Finding' [2001] *Judicial Studies Institute Journal* 25 p.55.
69 *Ibid.* p.65.
70 *Ibid.* p.35 quoting W. Patton 'Evolution in Child Abuse Litigation: the Theoretical Void Where Evidentiary and Procedural Worlds Collide' (1992) 25(3) *Loyola of Los Angeles Law Review* 1009 at p.1019.
71 [2000] 3 IR 122.
72 *Op. cit.* at p.643.
73 See, for example, *S.K. v. The Director of Public Prosecutions* 26 February 2004. High Court; *D.W. v The Director of Public Prosecutions* 21 March 2002 High Court; *B.J. v The Director of Public Prosecutions* 12 February 2002 High Court; *C.K. v The Director of Public Prosecutions* 27 May 2004 High Court; *J.S. v The Director of Public Prosecutions* 2 April 2004 High Court ; *K.M. v The Director of Public Prosecutions, Judge Mary Martin* 14 January 2003 High Court.
74 [1999] 2 IR 25 at 65.
75 C. Fennell *op. cit.* p.41.

Chapter Three

Related Rights

This chapter does not discuss the presumption itself, but rights with which it is often said to be inextricably bound. While the presumption reinforces many other rights such as the right to liberty and the right to fair procedures, it has a particularly close association with rights relating to the discharge of the prosecution's burden of proof. The chapter which follows therefore discusses the evidential requirements of proof beyond all reasonable doubt and the right to silence.

(I) Proof of Guilt

As already noted in Chapter One, twin corollaries of the presumption are that the burden of proof in a criminal proceeding is borne by the prosecution and each element of the crime must be proved by them beyond a reasonable doubt. Having already examined the case law surrounding the prosecutorial onus of proof in Chapter Two, this section concerns the meaning and application of the reasonable doubt rule. The high standard of proof required, short of beyond *all* doubt but greater than the civil standard of proof of the balance of probabilities, reflects the law's concern to minimize the risk of miscarriages of justice. Whereas a claimant in a civil trial may succeed upon proof that it is *more likely than not* that his or her version of the facts is correct, the prosecution in a criminal trial must dispel any reasonable doubt harboured by the jury in order to secure a conviction. While the standard cannot be reduced to an exact mathematical formula, if the balance of probabilities represents a degree of certainty of at least 51 per cent, then beyond a reasonable doubt is much closer to 100 per cent. Lord Denning was one of the first to attempt an elaboration of the phrase in the following oft-quoted passage from *Miller v. Minister of Pensions*:[1]

> It need not reach certainty, but it must carry a high degree of probability. Proof beyond a reasonable doubt does not mean proof beyond a shadow of a doubt. The law would fail to protect the community if it admitted fanciful possibilities to deflect the course of justice. If the evidence is so strong against a man as to leave only a remote possibility in his favour which can be dismissed with the sentence 'of course it is possible, but not in the least probable', the case is proved beyond reasonable doubt, but nothing short of that will suffice.

The issue of the quantum of proof in a criminal trial has had a somewhat unhappy history in the English appellate courts.[2] Williams[3] notes that the 'beyond a reasonable doubt' test established in *Woolmington* was abandoned in *R v. Summers*[4] in favour of an instruction to the jury that they should 'feel satisfied' of guilt or 'feel satisfied so that they can feel sure of it'. This was in turn discredited as affording insufficient protection to accused persons and, more recently in England, a direction that the jury must 'feel sure' has found favour with the Court of Appeal.[5] The 'sure' formula has now been promulgated by the Judicial Studies Board as a model direction and has hopefully brought some degree of finality to the issue. It reads:

> How does the prosecution succeed in proving the defendant's guilt? The answer is – by making you sure of it. Nothing less than that will do. If after considering all the evidence you are sure that the defendant is guilty, you must return a verdict of 'Guilty'. If you are not sure, your verdict must be 'Not Guilty'.[6]

In Ireland, judges are under no obligation to expound the meaning of the 'reasonable doubt' mantra to juries, but in practice they do attempt some explanation of the phrase, commonly instructing juries that a reasonable doubt is the kind of doubt which may affect the mind of a person in the conduct of important affairs such as marriage and moving house. While this formula has been criticized in England due to its subjective slant and reliance on jurors' individual life experiences, it is likely that similar criticism may be levelled at any formulation of the standard. Indeed, studies which have been carried out in England and the US with mock jurors, members of the public and professionals involved in the criminal justice process reveal considerable disparity of approach when asked to quantify the standard in percentage terms, regardless of the formula employed. The results of the US study, using the 'beyond all reasonable doubt' test, ranged from sixty-one per cent to ninety per cent[7] and in the UK, questions posed to a study group on the interpretation of the JSB 'sure' direction produced a similar range with respondents stating that the standard indicated levels of certainty of seventy to a hundred per cent.[8] It may well be that an 'objective' meaning of the term (beyond a comparison with the much lower balance of probabilities standard) is largely illusory and that levels of confidence with which juries may convict will vary with their own life experience, the seriousness of the charge before them, and their enthusiasm for risk-taking.

(II) Origins of the right to silence

The terms 'the right to silence' and 'the privilege against self-incrimination' are often used interchangeably although they have different meanings. The right to silence can be defined as the right not to suffer prejudice by reason of a failure to answer questions, most notably through the drawing of adverse inferences whereas the broader privilege against self incrimination embodies the right not to be compelled to answer questions or supply information. The right and the privilege are closely connected in theory and practice with the main distinction being that the former principle prohibits indirect coercion through the legal mechanism of drawing adverse inferences, while the latter prohibits direct compulsion to supply information on pain of conviction or punishment.[9] Like the presumption of innocence, both principles can be described as fundamental rights. Both have been implied into the fair trial provisions of both the Irish Constitution and the European Convention on Human Rights. The privilege is expressly guaranteed in the Fifth Amendment to the US Constitution and in international human rights instruments such as the International Covenant on Civil and Political Rights. Given their close association and common underlying rationale, it is proposed to treat them in the passage which follows as synonymous.

The precise origins of the right to silence are difficult to locate but it is generally accepted that the privilege against self incrimination developed in England as a response to the notorious practices of the Star Chamber and of the ecclesiastic court of the High Commission which were charged by the royalists to investigate 'crimes against the State'.[10] The methods used by these courts included torture, mutilations and imprisonment, with the accused very often being interrogated on oath prior to charge in the hope that he or she would incriminate themselves. The principle that *nemo tenetur se ipsum prodere* (no one is bound to condemn themselves) arose therefore as a protest against such methods and, although initially meaning only that no one should be obliged to make the first accusation against him/herself, it came to be interpreted as prohibiting the compulsion of an accused in a more general sense. The privilege was invoked in the common law courts after the abolition of the Star Chamber and Commission and gradually gained acceptance by judges. It is important, however, not to overstate the suddenness of this transformation. As Wigmore[11] notes, the tradition of vigorous questioning of an accused did not disappear until the start of the eighteenth century and the English revolution had been firmly established. Further, it is important to note that the accused did not become a competent witness at his or her own trial until the enactment of the *Criminal Evidence Act 1898*[12] and silence was therefore an obligation rather than a right exercised by the accused of his or her own volition. The privilege's main significance until that date was in relation to pretrial examinations and in civil matters. The 1898 Act firmly established that the accused could elect whether to give evidence on oath and if they chose not to, the prosecution were not permitted to make adverse comments about the fact.

With the development of modern police forces, the right of silence in the face of police interrogation also became an issue, although judges varied widely in their attitudes to evidence obtained by such methods. In 1912, the Home Secretary asked the Judges of the Kings Bench Division for clarification on the issue and they subsequently formulated a set of rules relating to the eliciting of statements from suspects which came to be known as the Judges Rules.[13] One of the rules coined the famous caution, 'you do not have to say anything unless you wish to do so, but what you say may be given in evidence', and required it to be administered prior to questioning to every suspect.

No information currently exists as to the number of persons who exercise their right to silence both at the pre trial stage and at trial in Ireland. Statistics from England, however, show that only a small number of suspects, approximately 5 per cent, maintain complete silence in police custody, contrary to the popular image of the recalcitrant criminal staring at the wall of the interrogation room.[14] Further, Leng's[15] research for the Royal Commission on Criminal Justice (Runciman Commission) conducted in the early 1990s also found that in only a tiny percentage of non-prosecuted cases and acquittals was silence exercised and that these outcomes rarely could be attributed to the accused's silence. There is no reason to assume that these figures would be any different in this jurisdiction.

(III) Rationales of the Right to Silence

Much has been written in an attempt to identify justifications for the privilege against self-incrimination and/or right to silence. In the US, the preponderance of the literature seeking a coherent rationale for the privilege has met with difficulty, resulting in many calls for the removal or curtailment of the Fifth Amendment.[16] The merit of such arguments will be taken up below, but for the moment the relevant issue is the rationales advanced for the rule. Such examinations have revealed a wide range of potential justifications. Schulhofer,[17] reviewing the US jurisprudence, proposes six plausible *raisons d'etre* for the privilege which are listed below:

- to preserve a fair balance between the state and the accused;
- to prevent prosecution for crimes of belief and association;
- to avoid what has been called the cruel trilemma of perjury, self condemnation and contempt;
- to prevent use of inhumane methods to extract testimony;
- to reduce the risk of convicting the innocent;
- to protect privacy.[18]

In England, those objecting to the erosion of the right (which has occurred in the *Criminal Justice (Public Order) Act 1994*), have drawn on arguments relating to the right to privacy and autonomy as well as an increased risk of false confessions. Galligan[19] has put forward a strong case in relation to the right to privacy, basing his arguments on the fundamental concepts of personhood and individual autonomy. For instance, he compares the imposition of a requirement to answer questions on pain of adverse inferences, to the compulsory use of a machine for the purposes of extracting information from the human memory. In relation to the increased risk of false confessions, the right to silence has long acted as a protection against what Warren C.J. termed in *Miranda v. Arizona*[20] 'the inherently compelling pressures'[21] of interrogation. It is self-evident that detention in the unfamiliar surrounds of a police station for a prolonged period of time is in itself a disorientating and intimidating experience. In addition, suspects may be exposed to the well-documented psychological pressures of police interrogation. Indeed, it was the danger of an increased number of miscarriages of justice that ultimately led the Runciman Commission[22] to recommend the retention of the right in England:

> [The abolition of the right to silence] might put strong (and additional) psychological pressure upon some suspects to answer questions without knowing precisely what was the substance of evidence for the accusation against them; and in consequence what they needed to tell the police in order

> to allay the suspicion against them. This, in our view might well increase the risk of innocent people, particularly those under suspicion for the first time, making damaging statements.

In her thorough review of the topic, Easton[23] advances the further justification that the right to silence provides an important incentive for the police to search for independent evidence. She recalls the comments of the Indian police to Sir James Stephen when drafting the Indian Code of Criminal Procedure, when asked why they sometimes resorted to the use of force. They replied: 'There is a great deal of laziness in it. It is far pleasanter to sit comfortably in the shade rubbing red pepper in a poor devil's eyes than to go about in the sun hunting up evidence.'[24]

(IV) Silence and the Burden and Standard of Proof

The rationale ostensibly missing from the discussion so far is that relating to the presumption of innocence and its corollary, proof beyond all reasonable doubt. One of the main arguments animating the right to silence remains the presumption of innocence on the basis that placing a burden on the accused to speak through the drawing of adverse inferences offends against the principle that the prosecution prove its case. This is a commonly held view. A leading Irish commentator,[25] for example, has chosen to treat the case law on the right to silence under the rubric 'presumption of innocence' in his book on criminal procedure. He describes the right as 'epitomiz[ing] the fundamental principle that the onus of proof lay on the prosecution which had to discharge the onus without any assistance from the accused. Accordingly, the accused was entitled to remain silent throughout the criminal trial and thereby put the prosecution to its proof.' Morton and Hutchinson[26] in their book on the presumption of innocence go even further:

> The presumption of innocence forms part of the broader privilege against self incrimination. It is enough for an

> accused to plead not guilty. No one is bound to betray himself – *nemo tenetur prodere seipsum*. The Crown cannot secure a conviction until it has proven its case – the Crown cannot rely on any expectation that the accused will testify.[27]

Indeed, the juxtaposition of the right to be presumed innocent with the concomitant right not to incriminate oneself in the Canadian Charter of Rights strongly supports this view.[28] The common thread running through the rights was recognized by Lamer J. in the Canadian Supreme Court in *Dubois v. R*:[29]

> [The presumption of innocence] imposes upon the Crown the burden of proving the accused's guilt beyond a reasonable doubt as well as that of making out the case against the accused before he or she need respond . . . The concept of the 'case to meet' is common to ss.11(c), (d) and 13. In the context of s.11(c) and 13, it means specifically that the accused enjoys 'the initial benefit of a right to silence'. . . and its corollory, protection against self incrimination.[30]

In the United States, too, this argument has purchase in the jurisprudence. Goldberg J., in his famous exposition on the privilege in *Murphy v. Waterfront Commission of New York Harbour*,[31] declared that it 'reflects many of our fundamental values and most noble aspirations', including 'our sense of fair play which dictates a fair state–individual balance by requiring the Government to leave the individual alone until good cause is shown for disturbing him and *by requiring the Government in its contest with the individual to shoulder the entire load*.'[32] Finally, it should be noted that the *Royal Commission on Criminal Procedure* (the Phillips Commission),[33] one of the many bodies established in England to examine the right to silence, decided against its abolition for the reason that to abolish the right to silence would be to subvert the fundamental principle that the prosecution must bear the burden of proof:

> There is an inconsistency of principle in requiring the onus of proof at trial to be upon the prosecution and to be discharged without any assistance from the defence and yet in enabling the prosecution to use the accused's silence in

> the face of police questioning under caution as any part of their case against him at trial.[34]

Despite the frequent association of the two ideas, it is certainly arguable that it is quite simply overestimating the reaches of the presumption to claim that the state must bear the full burden of proof and as a corollary, it is wrong in principle to compel the suspect to be a source of incriminating evidence. Addressing the Society of Public Teachers of Law, the eminent writer on the law of evidence, Professor Cross, saw little difficulty in advocating the abolition of the 'sacred cow' of the right to silence while urging the preservation of the presumption of innocence inviolate.[35] The accused may still enjoy the benefit of reasonable doubt at trial as the drawing of adverse inferences relates only to the means by which evidence is gathered by the state. This is the position which has been taken by the Irish Supreme Court in *Rock v. Ireland*[36] and is also one which is argued for by various legal commentators such as Dennis[37] and Roberts and Zuckerman.[38]

Rock can now be regarded as the seminal decision in this jurisdiction on the right to silence and the presumption.[39] In *Rock* the applicant sought a declaration that sections 18 and 19 of the *Criminal Justice Act 1984* were unconstitutional in that they constituted an unjust attack on the presumption of innocence and right to silence. Section 18 permits inferences to be drawn from an individual's failure or refusal to account for objects, marks or substances in their possession or on their person. Section 19 allows similar inferences to be drawn from a failure to account for one's presence at a place at or about the time when a crime had been committed. Murphy J. rejected the applicant's arguments and, relying on the decision in *O'Leary v. A.G.*,[40] held that the sections were no more than an 'evidence-gathering operation'. The High Court's decision was upheld by the Supreme Court which adopted similar reasoning. As Hamilton C.J. noted:

> It is clear from the provisions of the said section that it does not interfere in any way with the accused person's right to the presumption of innocence or the obligation on the prosecution to establish guilt beyond all reasonable

> doubt. The burden of proof which rests on the prosecution in a criminal charge is not in any way affected by the provisions of the impugned sections, which merely provide a factor which may be adduced in evidence in the course of the trial.[41]

In his 1995 reassessment of the privilege against self-incrimination, Dennis expands somewhat on this approach. He assesses the claim at the level of doctrine and principle respectively. He notes that at doctrinal level basing the right to silence on the presumption clearly fails, as the legal burden of proof is unaffected. At the level of principle, the author concedes the undesirability of allowing inferences of guilt from silence, but for reasons *other than* those relating to the presumption of innocence, such as, *inter alia*, the unreliable nature of such evidence. To rely on the presumption, he claims, is a step too far, being contrary to common sense and the existing English law. He argues, somewhat sweepingly it may be said, that common sense dictates that 'if other evidence yields a *prima facie* inference of guilty, a failure to provide an innocent explanation suggests that one does not exist'.[42]

Dennis' 'common sense' argument (which has shades of the 'innocent have nothing to fear' mantra) misses two important points. The first is that a *prima facie* case is not necessarily a strong case and is certainly very far departed from the high hurdle of beyond a reasonable doubt. The second point relates to the myriad non-criminal reasons which suspects may have for remaining silent. They may not want to disclose personal or embarrassing conduct in order to conceal, for example, sexual activities unknown to family or friends. They may wish to consult personal records or they may simply feel ignorant of the law. (In this regard it is significant that in Irish law a suspect does not have the right to have their solicitor present during interview.) Another reason which should not be lightly dismissed is that they may be trying to protect other people. Ashworth[43] cites a recent study by Bucke and Brown[44] in England which examined cases where the suspects had refused to answer at least some of the questions put to them in police custody. The results showed that 46 per cent of the questions concerned *only* the involvement of others in the offence. This suggests that this desire to shield others could be a powerful factor influencing their decision to remain silent, yet it would be extremely difficult for the defence at trial to advance this as a convincing explanation for the accused's silence.

(a) Altering the Incidence of the Burden of Proof

While, as Dennis argues, it must be conceded that the legal or probative burden at trial is in principle unaffected, this is by no means the end of the matter. The problem with such arguments is that they remain on the level of formality, while failing to recognize the reality of the situation. One of the practical manifestations of the presumption of innocence is that it is incumbent upon the prosecution to prove its case against a defendant. The fact that the burden of proof remains at all times on the prosecution constitutes the tangible fruits of the presumption. If adverse inferences may be drawn from an accused's decision to remain silent, particularly when silence is given evidential significance as a means of corroboration, the balance between the state and the suspect is altered. Although *formally* the burden remains on the prosecution, *in practice* the suspect comes under increased pressure to speak. As Stannard[45] notes: 'They [the prosecution] are using the accused to do their job for them. We are a long way from *Woolmington* here.' It is contended, therefore, that placing a burden on the accused to speak through the drawing of adverse inferences offends against the principle.

Easton[46] provides a useful description of the way in which the burden is altered in practical terms:

> [O]nce comment is permitted on silence, whether in the police station or at trial, then the whole focus of the trial shifts onto the defence and assessment of its arguments rather than on the prosecution's case against the accused so it is hard to sustain the view that the burden of proof is not affected. The defendant becomes the focus of attention and his account, or failure to supply an explanation of his conduct, rather than the strength of the prosecution's case, dominates the trial.

As noted above, the conflict which exists between the drawing of adverse inferences in such a manner and the prosecutorial burden of proof was recognized by the Royal Commission on Criminal Procedure[47] in England, reporting in 1981. Similar conclusions were drawn by Jackson[48] in his examination of the effects of the drawing of inferences from silence at trial. He argues that the traditional conception of the accusatorial criminal trial is that it is not so much in the nature of an inquiry into an accused's guilt as a demonstration by the prosecution of the accused' s guilt. He concludes: '[I]t is arguably inconsistent with the principle that it is for the prosecution to demonstrate the accused's guilt to allow the accused's refusal to participate in the trial by testifying to play a part in this demonstration.'[49] The reality of the situation has also been recognised by McAuley and McCutcheon,[50] who note that the distinction between the placing of the legal and evidential burden is one without a difference as 'this arrangement is clearly intended to work in ease of the prosecution in respect of matters which it is normally required to prove without the assistance of the defence.' It is difficult to draw a distinction in this regard between adverse inferences drawn from the accused's refusal to testify at trial and his or her refusal to answer questions at the pre-trial stage. If anything, the need for protection is greater during police questioning where the accused is unsure of exactly what the case against him or her is.

(b) Altering the Standard of Proof

Another way in which the effectiveness of the presumption can be undermined by the drawing of inferences from silence is through the lowering of the *standard* of proof to be met at trial. This can be done either through the use of silence to establish a *prima facie* case at trial or through bolstering an existing *prima facie* case to the standard of beyond a reasonable doubt. In this regard, it is salutary to note the comments of the English Working Group on the Right of Silence,[51] that '[g]iving silence evidential weight might enable the police to bring charges in some cases where there would otherwise not be a *prima facie* case . . . we do not think that silence should be used to establish a *prima facie* case'.[52] McConville[53] has taken the second view that if silence is used to corroborate other evidence against the suspect, then in cases where there is little evidence against the accused, the *prima facie* case (or case to answer), the lowest threshold of proof, could in effect be elevated to the highest form, that beyond a reasonable doubt

Zuckerman and Roberts dismiss both these arguments in a critique of what they term 'conceptualist rationales'[54] for the right to silence. Silence may be evidentially probative, so their argument runs, without diluting the normative reasonable doubt standard. There is therefore 'no more justification for preventing the prosecutor from relying on probative silence, than for discounting other apparently incriminating evidence'.[55] They also meet the argument that silence may be used to construct a *prima facie* case with the response: 'Silence might *contribute* to a *prima facie* case but could never *constitute* a case to answer. Silence, that is to say, is only ever probative in the context of other incriminating evidence.'[56] As argued above, these claims are open to the objection that while, in principle, the standard of proof remains the same, its practical effect or its 'tangible consequences', to borrow Tribe's term, for the accused have been reduced. While their argument may hold some force in respect of a case where silence only serves to corroborate a substantial body of independent evidence, it rings somewhat hollow in a situation where it serves as the mainstay of a very weak case. A state which is truly committed to a principle which mandates a 'suspension of adverse judgment' necessarily breaches this guarantee in drawing adverse inferences from silence, particularly if this evidence is used as corroboration. The authors also seem to assume, like Dennis, that the silence is 'incriminating' or 'probative', yet as discussed above the reasons motivating silence may not necessarily relate to a guilty conscience. To maintain this view is not, as Zuckerman and Roberts contend, to take an overly literal or 'purist' view of the presumption and the adversarial process, but to insist upon a commitment to the presumption that provides a *real* effect.

Moreover, it is a matter of no small moment that the view taken by the European Court of Human Rights, as evidenced in decisions such as *Murray v. UK*[57] and *Saunders v. UK*[58] is that the privilege against self-incrimination (and the right to silence as a derivative application of it) is founded on a broad conception of the presumption of innocence referred to in Article 6(2) of the European Convention on Human Rights. Although the right to silence is not expressly recognized in the Convention, in *Murray* the Court confirmed that the right to silence was implicit in the fair trial guarantee in Article 6 of the Convention: 'The right to remain silent under police questioning and the privilege against self-incrimination are generally recognized international standards which lie at the heart of the notion of a fair procedure under Article 6.'[59] One year later in *Saunders* the Court identified the origin of the right as the presumption of innocence:

> The right not to incriminate oneself, in particular, presupposes that the prosecution in a criminal case seek to prove their case against the accused without resort to evidence obtained through methods of coercion or oppression in defiance of the will of the accused. In this sense the right is closely linked to the presumption of innocence contained in Article 6(2) of the Convention.[60]

While it should also be noted that the Court made reference to other 'instrumentalist' justifications of the privilege such as 'the avoidance of miscarriages of justice', it is submitted that, as will be discussed in the next section, these are not necessarily inconsistent.

(IV) Further connections between silence and the presumption

For those who remain unconvinced by the above argument in relation to the burden of proof, there remain ways in which the presumption of innocence, in the broadest sense, reinforces the right to silence. The close link of the presumption of innocence with the constitutional right of the innocent in Irish law not to suffer criminal conviction and punishment has already been noted in Chapter One. The right to silence shares a similar *raison d'être* and, indeed, one which according to some commentators provides the primary justification for the right. Schulhofer[61] argues that the only compelling basis for the privilege against self-incrimination is in its function as a practical safeguard, namely as a means of reducing the risks that the trial and investigatory process present to an innocent defendant who would prefer not to speak. He argues: 'The claim is only that the privilege helps many innocent defendants and that acquittal of those defendants is more important than convicting an equal or somewhat larger number of guilty defendants.'[62] Seen, in what may be its original formation, that 'it is better that ten guilty men go free than one innocent be convicted', the presumption chimes precisely with Schulhofer's thesis.

His argument also brings an important air of reality to an increasingly academic debate. He makes the point that most critics of the privilege are in agreement about the role of the right to silence as a constraint on abusive police questioning. Further, in relation to the exercise of the privilege at trial, Schulhofer argues cogently that there are myriad reasons why a defendant may not want to take the stand or (the more likely scenario) why he would be advised by his counsel not to give evidence:

> [H]e may look sleazy. He may be inarticulate, nervous or easily intimidated. His vague memory on some of the details may leave him vulnerable to clever cross-examination. Most ordinary citizens find that being a witness in any formal proceeding is stressful and confusing. The problems are bound to be heightened when the witness appears to be on trial for his life or his liberty. Some people can handle this kind of situation, but others, especially if they are poor, poorly educated or inarticulate, cannot. They may handle the trial experience poorly whether or not they are guilty.[63]

In the absence of empirical data, it is worth noting that anecdotal evidence would suggest that defendants who exercise their right to silence at trial in Ireland (among them a growing number of non-nationals who perhaps may be less articulate than Irish defendants) have done so on the strength of legal advice for precisely the above reasons.

An argument on similar lines, although with a symbolic rather than a practical bent (what Greer[64] terms 'symbolic retentionism' in the debate on the right to silence), is that the right to silence should be retained as a brake on state power. This view maintains that 'the right to silence proclaims an ideology of innocence until proven guilty which is all the more necessary in the face of practices which proclaim an ideology of guilty until proven innocent'.[65] Yet, as noted by Greer, few would argue for retention purely on this basis.

A final way in which the right to silence may overlap with the presumption is through Ashworth's and Redmayne's[66] view of the presumption *qua* protector of an individual's autonomy. They describe the principle 'not,... as a rule about the standard of proof in criminal cases, but as a rule about how the state should treat citizens. The state should not treat its citizens as suspects unless it can provide reasons for doing so; it should treat people with dignity.'

However one chooses to view the relationship between the presumption of innocence and the right to silence, the presumption of innocence, as with many other rationales of the presumption, fails to explain the (widely accepted) distinction drawn in the jurisprudence between forced testimony and compelled bodily samples such as blood, breath or urine samples frequently used in drink driving prosecutions.[67] This point has also been made by Dennis, who argues: 'It is not clear why the theory should be restricted in this way; there seems to be nothing in the premise of the presumption of innocence to justify it.'[68] This is a significant argument given that most countries make provision for the taking of bodily samples in certain types of case and that denial of access to these types of evidence would have great social costs. Yet, the argument presupposes the validity of the distinction currently in place and only retains credibility from this standpoint. It works back from the jurisprudence upholding the distinction to the rationales and endeavours to find a rationale that is consistent with it. It is submitted that this process should be reversed and that the case law should be examined in the light of the rationales for the right to silence, among them the presumption of innocence. This approach invites the conclusion that the principle has had to be compromised on the basis of policy considerations, thereby creating distinctions which are difficult to reconcile with its traditional underpinnings. This is not to contest the policy compromises reached in this area but to recognize that theoretical coherence is not inextricably linked with the boundaries imposed on the privilege by the case law.[69] As Easton[70] argues, the distinction between speech and samples is not set in stone and presents its own problems: 'While the distinction might be justified on grounds of policy or expediency, nonetheless it is artificial and problematic, because both samples and speech are subject to similar considerations and arguments, and because the law already construes actions as a form of speech in certain cases.'[71]

Conclusion

The relationship between the presumption of innocence and the right to silence is a contested one in the academic literature. Yet, it is clear that the two rights are closely connected. In its broadest sense, the right to silence can be seen as the logical extension of the presumption through its symbolic and immensely practical role in preventing wrongful conviction. The right to silence may also be viewed as an expression of the presumption of innocence in its broader guise as a principle requiring that the state respect its citizens. More specifically, the evidential guarantees of prosecutorial proof beyond all reasonable doubt protected by the presumption are compromised, (at least at the level of tangible effect), by adverse inferences drawn from silence. As shall be seen in Chapter Five, this debate is far from academic in light of recent legislative developments.

Notes

1 [1947] 2 All ER 372 at 373–4.
2 Lawton L.J.'s comments in *R v. Yap Chuan Ching* (1976) 63 Cr App R 7 at 11 are telling: 'If judges stopped trying to define that which is almost impossible to define there would be fewer appeals.'
3 G. Williams *The Proof of Guilt* (3rd ed., Stevens, 1963) p.191.
4 (1952) 36 Cr App Rep 14.
5 *R v. Bracewell* (1979) 68 Cr App R 44.
6 See www.jsboard.co.uk/specdir.
7 See L. M. Solan 'Refocusing the Burden of Proof in Criminal Cases: Some Doubt about Reasonable Doubt' (1999) 78 *Texas LR* 105.

8 M. Zander 'The Criminal Standard of Proof – How Sure is Sure?' (2000) 150 *NLJ* 1517.

9 See A. Ashworth *Human Rights, Serious Crime and Criminal Procedure* (London: Sweet and Maxwell, 2002) p.18.

10 For an alternative view see M.R.T MacNair 'The Early Development of the Privilege Against Self Incrimination' [1990] *OJLS* 66 who suggests that the privilege originated in Roman Canon law and was extended to criminal trials with the religious objections to compulsory testimony under oath in the late seventeenth and early eighteenth centuries.

11 J.H. Wigmore *A Treatise on Evidence* (Boston, Little Brown, 1960) Vol. VIII.

12 In Ireland, it was not until the passage of the *Criminal (Evidence) Act 1924* that the accused became a competent witness in his or her own defence.

13 These Rules are also considered part of Irish law. The full text of the Judges' Rules is set out in *People v. Cummins* [1972] IR 312 at 317–8.

14 P. Roberts and A. Zuckerman *Criminal Evidence* (Oxford University Press, 2004) p.394.

15 R. Leng *The Right to Silence in Police Interrogation*, RCCJ Research Study No.10 (London: HMSO, 1993).

16 See, by way of example, D. Dolinko 'Is there a Rationale for the Privilege Against Self Incrimination?' (1986) 33 *University of California Law Review* 1063; H.J. Friendly 'The Fifth Amendment Tomorrow: the Case for Constitutional Change' (1968) 37 *University of Cincinnati Law Review* 671.

17 S.J. Schulhofer 'Some kind words for the privilege against self incrimination' (1991–2) 26 *Valparaiso University Law Review* 311.

18 *Ibid.* p.317.

19 D. Galligan, 'The Right to Silence Reconsidered' (1988) *Current Legal Problems* 69.

20 384 US 439.

21 *Ibid.* at 467.

22 Report of the Royal Commission on Criminal Justice, Cmnd 2263 (London: HMSO, 1993).

23 S. Easton *The Case for the Right to Silence* (2nd ed., Aldershot: Ashgate, 1998).

24 Sir James Stephen, *A History of the Criminal Law of England* (London: Macmillan, 1883) p.441

25 D. Walsh *Criminal Procedure* (Dublin: Thomson Round Hall, 2002) p.913.

26 J.C. Morton and S.C. Hutchinson *The Presumption of Innocence* (Carswell, 1987).

27 *Ibid.* p.112.

28 Sections 11 and 13 of the Charter read:

> 11. Any person charged with an offence has a right
>
> ...
>
> (c) not to be compelled to be a witness in proceedings against that

person in respect of the offence;
(d) to be presumed innocent until proven guilty according to law in a fair and public hearing by an independent and impartial tribunal.
13. A witness who testifies in any proceedings has the right not to have any incriminating evidence so given used to incriminate that witness in any other proceedings, except in a prosecution for perjury or for the giving of contradictory evidence.

29 [1985] 2 SCR 350.
30 *Ibid.* at 356–8.
31 378 US 52.
32 *Ibid.* at 55. Emphasis added.
33 *Report of Royal Commission on Criminal Procedure*, (London, HMSO, 1981) (Cmnd. 8092).
34 *Ibid.* para. 4.51.
35 A.R.N. Cross 'The Right to Silence and the Presumption of Innocence – Sacred Cows or Safeguards of Liberty?' (1970–1) 11 *Journal of the Society of Public Teachers of Law* p.66.
36 [1997] 3 IR 484; [1998] 2 ILRM 35.
37 I. Dennis 'Instrumental Protection, Human Right or Functional Necessity? Reassessing the Privilege Against Self-Incrimination' (1995) 54(2) *CLJ* 342. See also I. Dennis 'Reconstructing the Law of Criminal Evidence' (1989) *Current Legal Problems* 21.
38 P. Roberts and A. Zuckerman *op. cit.* pp.414–16.
39 The precedential value of another key decision on the issue, *Heaney v. Ireland* [2000] 1 ILRM 191, has been considerably weakened by the subsequent conflicting judgment of the European Court of Human Rights in *Heaney v. Ireland* (2001) 33 EHRR 264. For discussion of these cases see Chapter Five.
40 [1995] ILRM 259.
41 [1997] 3 IR 484 at 498.
42 Dennis, *op. cit.* p.356.
43 A. Ashworth *The Criminal Process* (Oxford University Press, 1998).
44 T. Bucke and D. Brown *In Police Custody: Police Powers and Suspects' Rights under the Revised PACE Codes of Practice* Home Office Research Study 174, (HMSO, London, 1997).
45 J.E. Stannard, 'A Presumption and Four Burdens' (1994) 51(4) *NILQ* 560 p.574.
46 S. Easton *op. cit.* p.182.
47 *Op. cit.*
48 J. Jackson 'Inferences from Silence: From Common Law to Common Sense' [1993] 44(2) *NILQ* 103.
49 *Ibid.* p.108.
50 F. McAuley and P. McCutcheon, *Criminal Liability: A Grammar* (Round Hall Sweet and Maxwell, 2000) p.41.
51 *Report of the Working Group on the Right of Silence*, (London: HMSO, 1989).
52 *Ibid.* para. 84.

53 M. McConville 'Silence in Court' (1987) *NLJ* 1169.
54 *Viz* arguments that the right to silence is conceptually implied by other well-established features of the criminal justice system such as the presumption of innocence.
55 *Op. cit.* p.415.
56 *Ibid.*
57 (1996) 22 EHRR 29.
58 (1996) 23 EHRR 313.
59 (1996) 22 EHRR 29, para. 45.
60 (1996) 23 EHRR 313, para. 68.
61 *Op. cit.*
62 *Ibid.* p.329.
63 *Ibid.* p.330.
64 S. Greer 'The Right to Silence: A Review of the Current Debate' (1990) 53(6) *MLR* 709.
65 *Ibid.* p.724.
66 A. Ashworth and M. Redmayne *The Criminal Process* (3rd ed. Oxford University Press, 2005) p.134.
67 For a discussion see A. Ashworth *Human Rights, Serious Crime and Criminal Procedure op. cit.*, pp.20–23.
68 *Op. cit.* p.355.
69 For an alternative view see D. J. Seidmann and A. Stein 'The Right to Silence helps the innocent: a game-theoretical analysis of the Fifth Amendment Privilege' (2000) 114 *Harvard L.R.* 431 who claim that they have developed a theory which justifies and coherently explains the Fifth Amendment jurisprudence. This theory which has been termed an 'anti-pooling' rationale argues that the privilege assists the innocent by preventing the pooling of statements by guilty and innocent persons alike. If the privilege were removed the guilty would lack an incentive to exercise the right to silence, there would be an increase in the number of false and misleading statements given to the police, and the credibility of all statements made by suspects and defendants would decrease. Given that the theory rests on the opportunity for dissimulation, it only applies to oral testimony rather than bodily samples and in this way, it is claimed, 'imposes order on the self incrimination doctrine'. It should be noted that this theory is linked with the requirement of proof of guilt beyond all reasonable doubt as silence will only assist a guilty defendant to obtain an acquittal in a system based on reasonable doubt.
70 *Op. cit.* Chapter 8.
71 An example is the law on hearsay evidence. *Op. cit.* p.218.

Chapter Four

Criminal Justice (Public Order) Act 1994

It will be recalled from Chapter Two that the Supreme Court in *King v. Attorney General*,[1] in striking down the offence of loitering with intent created by s.4 of the *Vagrancy Act 1824* as unconstitutional, held that the presumption of innocence applied equally to all persons and that criminal behaviour must be defined by reference to behaviour rather than the condition or character of the accused. The Court found that the impugned section was unconstitutional due to its vagueness and contravention of 'the basic concept inherent in our legal system that a man may walk abroad in the secure knowledge that he will not be singled out from his fellow citizens and branded and punished as a criminal unless it has been established beyond reasonable doubt that he has deviated from a clearly prescribed standard of conduct . . . '.[2]

The Irish Supreme Court is not alone is its appreciation of the threat posed to due process rights by arbitrary conceptions of 'public order' such as loitering. Ashworth[3] has identified 'public order', along with 'public safety', as a concept used 'as a means of introducing wide discretionary powers and offences defined in ways that disadvantage the defence' and as a 'difficult to contest reason for introducing sweeping powers that ignore sound principle'. In a similar vein, it is the burden of this chapter that the *Criminal Justice (Public Order) Act 1994*, and subsequent amending legislation, represents a serious attack on the right of Irish citizens to be presumed innocent.

(I) BACKGROUND TO THE ACT

The 1994 Act was conceived in response to a perceived problem of urban crime and disorder, particularly acts committed by groups of intoxicated young males. Although the need for reform had been recognized some time before the introduction of the Bill,[4] the impetus for the legislation was provided by increased media reportage of the problem. The preoccupation with youthful miscreants permeates the Dáil debates on the Bill which are replete with references to the terrorism of peaceful citizens by 'delinquents' and 'thugs'. Indeed, it is submitted that the following passage from the Senate debates on the Bill accurately captures the public mood:

> What is the human dimension of this Bill? Unfortunately there are all too many examples: the old woman who is terrified to leave her house because of the taunting behaviour of a *group of youths* outside or that same old woman who is terrified inside because of the taunts of the group outside; the young couple who are harassed by a *group of delinquents* as they return from a night out; the young mother who cannot let her children out to play through fear of the *congregation of gangs* in the vicinity; the shopkeeper whose trade suffers because *youths loiter* at his door, scaring off customers; and, worst of all, the families on urban housing estates whose daily lives are made an absolute misery by *gangs of roving thugs*.[5]

Fears about such activity, moreover, centred around specific incidents such as a number of attacks on tourists in Dublin city centre and a fatal attack on a young Donegal GAA supporter which received considerable media attention. Carey[6] has described how the media were instrumental in the debate preceding the Act with deputies citing media reports on incidents coming within the scope of the Bill in aid of their arguments. The impact of the media coverage on the debate is obvious when one compares the heated exchanges in the Dáil at the time with the more moderate approach of the Inter Departmental Group on Urban Crime and Disorder.[7] This Group, which reported on the problem two years earlier, laid considerable emphasis on a multi-faceted and holistic approach to the problems of deprivation and under-privilege in Dublin suburbs, while also recommending that legislation should be considered 'as a matter of priority'. Further, as Carey[8] notes, the relevance of the climate of opinion in which the Bill was passed is highlighted by the fact that a Bill containing similar provisions – the *Criminal Justice Bill 1967* – had in the past been defeated in the face of public opposition.

This is not to say that the Bill enjoyed an easy passage through the Oireachtas. The President convened a meeting of the Council of State with a view to referring the Bill to the Supreme Court in light of her concerns about its constitutionality (although she ultimately decided against this course of action) and the Bill was the subject of considerable criticism and amendment. The reactionary nature of the debate, however, may account for some of the more egregious provisions contained within it as well as possible drafting errors discussed below.[9]

(II) 'MOVE ON' POWERS: SECTION 8

In light of the decision in *King*, the obvious starting point for any legal critique must be the provisions contained in s.8 of the 1994 Act on loitering. It is important to note at this juncture that, as noted by the Court in *King*, prior to arrest a person is protected by the assumption that he is innocent and free from blame, as well as by the constitutionally protected freedom of movement. In this regard, Thayer[10] has noted that 'the presumption of innocence is simply the application of the rule of sense and convenience, running through all the law, that in the absence of evidence to the contrary people are presumed to be good, honest and free from blame'.

Section 8 provides as follows:

> (1) Where a member of the Garda Síochána finds a person in a public place and suspects, with reasonable cause, that such person –
> (*a*) is or has been acting in a manner contrary to the provisions of *section* 4, 5, 6, 7 or 9, or

(*b*) without lawful authority or reasonable excuse, is acting in a manner which consists of loitering in a public place in circumstances, which may include the company of other persons, that give rise to a reasonable apprehension for the safety of persons or the safety of property or for the maintenance of the public peace, the member may direct the person so suspected to do either or both of the following, that is to say:

(i) desist from acting in such a manner, and

(ii) leave immediately the vicinity of the place concerned in a peaceable or orderly manner.

The section goes on to provide that failure to comply with the order of a member of the Gardaí to desist or to move on, without reasonable excuse, constitutes a criminal offence punishable in the District Court by a maximum fine of €650 or six months' imprisonment. In relation to the behaviour which triggers the 'move on' powers of the Gardaí, the section firstly refers to sections 4–7 and 9. These are offences of intoxication in a public place (s.4); offensive conduct (s.5); breach of the peace (s.6) and wilful obstruction (s.9), some of which are discussed in more detail below. It is sufficient to note here that in relation to sections 5, 6 and 7, concerns have been expressed as to their constitutionality given the nebulous offences which they seek to create. The second form of behaviour is loitering which gives rise to a 'reasonable apprehension for the safety of persons or the safety of property or for the maintenance of the public peace'.

The introduction of a replacement offence of loitering was considered by the Law Reform Commission in its *Report on Vagrancy and Related Offences*[11] and ultimately rejected owing to both the difficulty of drafting an offence in harmony with the Constitution and the fact that there did not appear to be a pressing need for such powers. In relation to the latter point, the Commission remarked that in the four-year period following the decision in *King*, the existence of what they termed an 'unacceptable hiatus' in the criminal law in dealing with persons or gangs who may be loitering had not been brought to the attention of the Commission. They noted that situations where such legislation may be desirable, such as loitering with a view to stealing a car, would already appear to be criminalised in Irish law.[12] If, in the Commission's view, the lacuna left in the law by *King* was more apparent than real, doubt must be cast on the need for the police powers contained in section 8.

The Commission's legal analysis of legislative provisions on loitering from other common law jurisdictions also raises questions as to the constitutionality of section 8. The Commission considered legislation along the lines of section 250.2 of the US Model Penal Code which provides that: 'A person commits a violation if he loiters or prowls in a place, at a time, or in a manner not usual for law-abiding individuals under circumstances that warrant alarm for the safety of persons or property in the vicinity.' They found, however, that the section suffered 'from vagueness and potential arbitrariness of application and would in practice almost certainly involve some consideration of antecedent conduct in some cases'.[13] The Commission thus dismissed the section as a possible model for Irish law despite the safeguards contained in the section, such as (i) the circumstances outlined in the section to guide the police officer in the exercise of his discretion, such as the fact that the person took flight, refused to identify themselves, etc (ii) the requirement that the police officer must give the individual in question the opportunity to provide an explanation for their presence and/or conduct, which is a condition precedent to a conviction under the section and (iii) the defence afforded the defendant under the section to the effect that the court cannot convict if a satisfactory explanation is given for his or her presence and/or conduct. In line with the Commission's analysis of s.250.2, it is submitted that in some regards section 8 is a more draconian provision than the section from the Model Code. There are no safeguards in the former equivalent to those outlined above save to the extent that the defendant must be proved to be acting 'without lawful authority or excuse' and the apprehensions of the police officer must be 'reasonable'. Indeed, the courts have taken it upon themselves to imply safeguards into the legislation. In *DPP v. Galligan*,[14] Laffoy J. held that a valid conviction for failure to comply cannot be obtained unless there is evidence of the arresting Guard formally warning the defendant that a failure to comply could result in prosecution.

The Commission also found that section 28(1) of the New Zealand *Summary Offences Act 1981* suffered from similar constitutional infirmities. This section provides that: 'Every person commits an offence who is found in any public place behaving in a manner from which it can be reasonably inferred that he is preparing to commit a crime.' This section is similar in form to section 8 in that the inference drawn must be 'reasonable'. In light of the foregoing analysis, it is questionable whether the drafters of the 1994 Act succeeded in achieving what the Law Reform Commission considered could not be done in light of *King*, namely devising a legislative formula for a loitering offence which would pass constitutional muster. In this regard, it is likely that any constitutional infirmity cannot be cured by the fact that the criminal conduct in section 8 is conditioned on the failure to obey the directions of a member of the Garda Síochána. This argument was rejected by the US Supreme Court in *Shuttlesworth v. City of Birmingham*,[15] and by the Supreme Court of Illinois in *City of Chicago v. Morales*:[16]

> Merely adding the element of refusing to obey an order by police to disperse does not elevate the gang loitering ordinance to such a level that it provides adequate notice of proscribed conduct. See *State v. Hudson*, 111 NNH at 26, 274 A.2d at 879 (merely loitering cannot be made criminal, even if the statute requires refusal of police's order to disperse)... [I]f the underlying statute itself is impermissibly vague... then a conviction based upon the failure to obey the order of a police officer pursuant to that statute cannot stand.

While the Dáil debates do not shed much light on parliamentary intention in this relation, the speech of the then Minister for Justice (Mrs Máire Geoghegan Quinn) contains some suggestion that the fact that the offence committed is not loitering itself, but rather a failure to obey directions of the Gardaí, shields it from constitutional difficulties:

> In drafting this Bill we looked at the possibility of creating a new loitering with intent offence but we concluded that any replacement type of offence would be unlikely to

> withstand constitutional challenge on similar ground to those used in the King case. We recognised, however, that there was a need for some provision to assist the Garda in this area and what we now propose, while not making loitering of itself an offence, will give the power to the Garda to 'move on' people loitering in the circumstances which I have outlined.[17]

As Hogan[18] notes, in the final analysis it is important to remember that the provisions of the 1994 Act will be read narrowly by the courts, in order to ward off any constitutional challenges. In this regard, it will be significant that, unlike the section in *King*, section 8 is not restricted to conduct 'by a suspected person or reputed thief' and requires the Garda's initial suspicion to be 'reasonable'. On the other hand, as noted in the *King* case itself, the presumption of constitutionality does not permit the legislature to 'ignore the fundamental norms of the legal order postulated by the Constitution' including the presumption of innocence. It is also significant that the majority of the Supreme Court in *King* rejected the submission of the DPP that the removal of words 'suspected person or reputed thief' would cure the section of any unconstitutionality, therefore indicating that the problem was not confined to the defendant's antecedent behaviour.

Before proceeding to examine the other sections of the Act, it is worth examining how the section has been applied in practice. One of the grounds on which the Law Reform Commission objected to the US and New Zealand provisions was that they 'would in practice almost certainly involve some consideration of antecedent conduct in some cases'.[19] From the limited information available concerning the operation of the Public Order Act, it would appear that section 8 is, in some instances at least, being applied in line with Garda perceptions of the area and persons being policed.

This is one of the conclusions drawn by a study on public order offences in Ireland commissioned by the National Crime Council which reported in 2003.[20] As part of the study, researchers were allowed to accompany the Gardaí on duty at two sites, one in Dublin city centre ('Liffeyside') and one in the Dublin suburbs ('Parkway'), in order to observe public order incidents as they occurred. 'Parkway' had an established negative history and had been the site of difficulties in previous years. 'Liffeyside', in contrast, was perceived by the Gardaí to be frequented by young, fairly affluent adults who were on the whole more 'respectable' than the residents of 'Parkway'. The researchers found that the negative perceptions of the area formed by the Gardaí in 'Parkway' manifested themselves in their treatment of the residents and a more confrontational approach was generally adopted by Gardaí in 'Parkway' than by their colleagues in 'Liffeyside'.

In relation to section 8, the researchers note that in 'Parkway' strong language was frequently employed to move people on. Significantly, the report notes that 'the threatened use of section 8 of the CJPOA, as well as its actual citation, were also more common occurrences in "Parkway"' leading to 'a discernible air of resignation among the young people in this area . . . the mere sighting of a Garda was enough to cause them to move on'.[21] The report was critical of the Garda approach in light of the fact that most of the young people involved resided in the area. There is also a clear implication in the research that the 'Parkway' youths were automatically being treated as suspected persons by virtue of geographical assessment rather than any suspected individual misconduct, and the section was thus being applied in the arbitrary manner impugned by the Supreme Court in *King*. The research also raises doubts about the effectiveness of 'reasonable cause' and 'reasonable apprehension' without further definition as thresholds for suspicion in the Act. As the report notes: 'The nature of their work gives police officers considerable scope for making their accounts of incidents the authoritative ones.'[22]

(III) Strict Liability Offences under the Public Order Act

The relationship between the presumption of innocence and the presumption of *mens rea* has already been noted in Chapter One. The two are interrelated in that, once the requirement for the prosecution to prove *mens rea* or the mental element is removed, as in offences of strict and absolute liability, if the accused adduces evidence raising a reasonable doubt as to his or her mental culpability, the judge must nevertheless convict. It will be recalled that strict liability offences are criminal offences which do not require proof of any type of fault, although a defence of reasonableness may be available to a defendant, while absolute liability offences are offences which do not require proof of any type of fault but in respect of which no such defence is available. Both strict and absolute offences fly in the face of the *Woolmington* principle as they result in the conviction and punishment of the morally innocent where there is a reasonable doubt about the moral culpability of the accused.

The 1994 Act adopts a cavalier approach to the principles of *mens rea* and fault. Sections 4 and 5, which create the offences of intoxication in a public place and disorderly conduct in a public place respectively, do not require any proof of fault on behalf of the accused such that, for example, the defendant's failure to take reasonable care ('negligence') will suffice for conviction. While the proliferation of offences of strict liability must be a source of concern, particularly in the context of public order offences with only vague and ill-defined *actus reus* definitions, it is some comfort at least that both these offences do not attract a term of imprisonment.

(a) Riot

Greater cause for concern in this regard is provided by the mental elements of the offences of riot and violent disorder which both attract a maximum penalty of ten years' imprisonment following conviction on indictment in addition to an unlimited fine. Taking the offence of riot first, it would appear that the offence is bereft of any fault element[23] requirement at all. Riot may be described as use of unlawful violence by one or more persons in a group of at least twelve persons who are using or threatening violence. It reads:

> (1) Where –
> (a) twelve or more persons who are present together in any place (whether that place is a public place or a private place or both) use or threaten to use unlawful violence for a common purpose, and
> (b) the conduct of those persons, taken together, is such as

would cause a person of reasonable firmness present at that place to fear for his or another person's safety,

then, each of the persons using unlawful violence for the common purpose shall be guilty of the offence of riot.

(2) For the purposes of this section –

(a) it shall be immaterial whether or not the twelve or more persons use or threaten to use unlawful violence simultaneously at any place;

(b) the common purpose shall be inferred from conduct;

(c) no person of reasonable firmness need actually be, or be likely to be, present at that place.

The failure to provide for *mens rea* for the offence is highly anomalous given that, save for this critical omission, the section closely mirrors the English legislation on riot contained in section 1 of the *Public Order Act 1986* and also given the incorporation by the Irish legislature of *mens rea* in the sister offence of violent disorder.[24] The issue has been considered in some detail by Carey[25] in a recent article which explores whether the omission was by accident or design and whether riot was intended to be a strict liability offence and therefore one to which the common law presumption of *mens rea* does not apply. He concludes that 'Ultimately, while the failure to include a *mens rea* requirement under Irish law with regard to riot is not easily explained . . . the offence, in spite of the lack of a *mens rea* requirement, attracts sufficient reasons to justify displacing the presumption of *mens rea* otherwise applicable.'[26]

In arriving at this conclusion, Carey relies on *dicta* of Lynch J. in *Maguire v. Shannon Regional Fisheries Board*[27] to the effect that the presumption of *mens rea* can be rebutted where (i) this is clearly or by necessary implication the effect of the statute (ii) the statute is concerned with an issue of public safety and (iii) the creation of a strict liability offence will promote the aims of the statute. Applying this test to riot, he argues that, despite the silence of the Dáil debates on the issue, the fact that the section departs from both the English legislation and the closely allied offence of violent disorder in this regard could lead to the necessary implication that liability is strict and the fact that riot is a serious public order offence may justify the creation of a strict liability offence. Carey notes that the old common law offence of riot was an offence of strict liability and in construing the 1994 Act the courts may well have regard to the previous state of the law.

While Carey's arguments have merit, there are factors militating against such a conclusion. First, it beggars belief that the Oireachtas intended, without any discussion on the issue, to take the unprecedented step of introducing into Irish law a strict liability offence which attracted a penalty of up to ten years' imprisonment. To date, offences of strict liability have been for regulatory type offences with minimal punishments. The one notable exception to this rule used to be the offence of unlawful carnal knowledge (which attracts a maximum penalty of imprisonment for life) yet the law in this area has since been radically overhauled.

On the 23rd May 2006 the Supreme Court held in the case of *CC v Ireland*[28] that the provisions creating the offence[29] are inconsistent with the Constitution The *dicta* of the Supreme Court in that case strongly support an argument that the offence of riot created by the 1994 Act is, by extension, unconstitutional. Hardiman J., delivering the judgment of the court, refers to the severe penalties faced by the accused charged with statutory rape and, interestingly, also relies on the concept of mental guilt. He argues:

> 'It appears to us that to criminalise in a serious way a person who is mentally innocent is indeed "little more than a means to an end", in the words of Wilson J. quoted earlier in this judgment. It appears to us that this in turn, constitutes a failure by the State in its law to defend and vindicate the right to liberty and good name of the person so treated, contrary to the State's obligations under Article 40 of the Constitution."[30]

This recent judgment is perfectly in accord with authority in Canada to the effect that statutes which create offences of absolute liability which attract *any* term of imprisonment breach the Charter's guarantees of fundamental justice.[31] Carey considers the presumption of *mens rea*, as well as the presumption against changes in the common law, yet fails to weigh in the balance the constitutionally protected guarantee to a trial in due course of law and the presumption of innocence.

Rather than a deliberate omission, it is submitted that the absence of *mens rea* was, on this occasion, a legislative oversight testifying more to the casual attitude adopted by politicians to fundamental principles of criminal law rather than a deliberate policy to curtail them. As Carey[32] himself observes, the provisions in the Act concerning the more serious public disorder offences had a different genesis than the provisions concerning lesser forms of urban disorder in that they were included pre-emptively rather than in response to any perceived existing crisis. The opportunity was taken to abolish the common law offences of riot, violent disorder and affray and replace them with statutory offences along the English model. Unlike England, however, Ireland has been remarkably free of mass public disorder connected with industrial or political issues and this was recognized by the Minister for Justice in the Dáil: 'It is wrong to suppose that we are dealing with the sort of problems that existed in Britain . . . however, legislation should be in place in advance of such problems arising.'[33] The context in which the offence of riot was enacted therefore makes it highly improbable that the political will existed to press home vigorously the objects of the offence by way of dispensing with *mens rea*. The lacuna in all likelihood provides an excellent example of what Glanville Williams[34] has described as, '[parliamentary] departures from the cherished principle . . . done through carelessness and lack of subtlety' rather than expediency.

(b) Prosecutorial Requirements and the Negation of Mens Rea

Violent disorder is generally perceived to be a less serious offence than riot, involving as it does only three persons, however, in Irish law it carries the same ten year sentence. The essence of the offence is the use of or the threat of violence in a group of at least three persons who are using or threatening violence in a manner which would cause a reasonable person present at that place to fear for their safety. As observed above, *mens rea* for the offence has been written into the Act, namely, the provision in section 15(3) 'A person shall not be convicted of the offence of violent disorder unless the person intends to use or threaten to use violence or is aware that his conduct may be violent or threaten violence.' In his annotations on the 1994 Act, Hogan[35] describes this as an 'additional safeguard' in relation to this offence which is not present in the definition of riot and the possible reasons for distinguishing between the two offences in this way have been discussed above. The question which remains to be examined, however, is the extent to which the mental element in the violent disorder definition acts as a true safeguard in light of the newly introduced restrictions on what the prosecution need prove.

In respect of both the offences of riot and violent disorder, for example, the prosecution need not prove that all the persons involved were using or threatening to use violence simultaneously. Given the small number of people which must be involved for the offences to be committed (twelve and three respectively), this extends the range of situations to which the offence could be applied considerably. Even more significant is the reform of the law so that the 'person of reasonable firmness' referred to in the sections does not actually have to be present or be likely to be present.[36] This allows for an assessment of the defendant's behaviour on a purely hypothetical basis, and comes close to calling into question the whole rationale of these crimes as public order offences. As noted by Ashworth,[37] if one regards public order offences as offences of 'creating fear' which shore up the law on assault, it is nonsensical to dispense with the tangible requirement that someone actually is put in fear by the defendant's actions. The rationale of the offences is further undermined by the fact that, despite the label '*public order* offences', both violent disorder and riot can be committed either in public or on private property. Finally, violence is not defined in the Act, unlike the comparable English legislation, although there is Irish authority to the effect that, at common law, a hard stare may be sufficient to constitute 'force'.[38] If this authority is followed in relation to the new offences of violent disorder and riot, taken in combination with the other factors outlined above, the two offences will have an intolerably wide scope.

In light of the above, it is unlikely that the *mens rea* requirement will afford a defendant much protection. As Ashworth notes, the effect of the changed definitions is that the 'odds are stacked in favour of the prosecutor'.[39] The legislation is drafted in such a way as to sideline the issue of the moral culpability of the defendant. Whether the defendant had the requisite *mens rea* is to be inferred from his or her conduct and this depends on the context. In a situation where there has been a gathering of a controversial political group, who have been associated with violence in the past, this is particularly problematic. As argued by Lacey *et al.*:

> The test in terms of the reactions of a hypothetical reasonable person acts as a positive invitation to the tribunal to interpret the situation in terms of what their own perceptions and judgment would have been. Can such a tribunal distinguish between the person who was defending herself in a disordered situation, one who was fighting with the police, or one who was simply trying to remove herself from the situation . . . in a context where initial presence may already invoke the court's opprobrium and a willingness to interpret a defendant as having certain predispositions?[40]

(IV) Amendments to the 1994 Act by the Criminal Justice Act 2006

Section 184 of the *Criminal Justice Act 2006* amends the 1994 Act by creating two new sections to be known as sections 23A and 23B. Under s.23A a member of An Garda Síochána who has reasonable grounds for believing that a person is committing or has committed an offence under section 5 of the 1994 Act may serve on the person either in person or by post a notice stating that the person upon whom it is served is alleged to have committed the offence at a stated time and place. The individual will also be informed that a prosecution will not be instituted if within twenty-eight days they pay to a member of the Gardaí, at a specified Garda station, a prescribed amount of money. Should the person fail to comply within this deadline, he or she will become liable for an additional 50 per cent of the original sum which must be paid within a further twenty-eight days. Failure to pay the fine within two months will lead to the person being prosecuted. Section 23B applies this same 'fixed charge' procedure to offences committed under s.4 of the 1994 Act.

The use of this fixed charge procedure, albeit in respect of minor offences such as being intoxicated in a public place to the extent that there can be a reasonable fear of danger to the person or another person in the vicinity (s.4) and offensive conduct in a public place between the hours of midnight and 7am (s.5), demonstrates once again the lack of confidence within the political establishment in the criminal justice system. As evidenced by the adoption of anti-social behaviour orders and civil confiscation orders,[41] the Government has recently demonstrated a preference for non-criminal methods of dealing with offenders. A similar sentiment drives the provisions on fixed penalties for criminal offences. No doubt the declared aim of the legislation is to enhance efficient use of court time by diverting 'clearly guilty' offenders away from the District Courts, but the idea that offenders who enjoy the presumption of innocence are wasting court time by exercising their right to a trial in due course of law should be challenged. The 'solution'[42] presented by the Act offends the presumption of innocence at least on a symbolic level. As Tribe[43] notes the presumption mandates a refusal to acknowledge prosecutorial omniscience, yet under the Act the Garda becomes 'judge, jury and executioner'. In this altered framework the presumption of innocence does not exist for, as noted by Joe Costello TD: 'The suspect has no right to due process as there is no due process.'[44]

The procedure also carries a clear risk that offenders will pay a small fine rather than run the risk of going to court, even in cases where they are clearly not guilty of any wrongdoing. As will be discussed in Chapter Eight, there is a considerable body of research to suggest that some innocent defendants with the full benefit of protections afforded them by the criminal justice system (including access to legal advice) plead guilty in light of the sentencing discount offered for a guilty plea or in response to a prosecutorial plea bargain. An innocent defendant who has been accused of a public order offence is in many respects in a much weaker position given (i) the nebulous definition of 'offensive conduct' in section 5 of the 1994 Act,[45] (ii) the absence of any due process safeguards and (iii) the huge incentive which is implicit in avoiding the possibility of a criminal conviction by simply making a small payment. In addition to this, as Binchy[46] notes, there is an implicit threat in that individuals, particularly those with previous criminal convictions, may be wary of the judge taking a dim view of the court's time having been expended unnecessarily.

Conclusion

The legislative powers granted members of An Garda Síochána under the *Criminal Justice (Public Order) Act 1994* have gone a considerable way towards undermining the tangible benefits of the presumption of innocence for certain Irish citizens. A teenager hanging around a street corner of a deprived Dublin suburb who is constantly being moved on by the Gardaí may (not unreasonably) consider his right to be presumed innocent prior to arrest to be more apparent than real. These problems are compounded by amendments to the Act which allow the Gardaí to usurp the functions of the courts in respect of certain public order offences, thereby consolidating a trend whereby due process protections such as the presumption of innocence are circumvented. Parliamentary oversight of the *mens rea* requirement for the serious offence of riot also demonstrates the lack of esteem in which fundamental principles such as the presumption of *mens rea* and presumption of innocence are held and may provide an illustration of what Kilcommins *et al.*[47] have described as the 'politics of neglect' in Irish law. Overall, one may wonder whether those charged with public order offences form a category of offenders which have been somewhat sidelined from procedural protections. Lacey *et al.*'s[48] argument in relation to those charged with drink and drugs offences finds an equal application here: 'This area further demonstrates ways in which a general commitment to the [presumption of innocence] obscures the social marginalisation of certain groups; beyond the curtain of golden threads, a less well scripted play takes place, which involves fewer procedural props.'

NOTES

1 [1981] IR 233.
2 *Ibid.* at 257.
3 A. Ashworth *Principles of Criminal Law* (4th ed. Oxford University Press, 2003) p.332.
4 Law Reform Commission *Report on Offences under the Dublin Police Acts and Related Offences* (LRC 14–1985); *Report of the Inter Departmental Group on Urban Crime and Disorder* (Dublin: 1992).
5 Senator Crowley, Seanad Debates, Vol 138, 8 December 1993, Col 1192. Emphasis added.
6 G. Carey 'The Performative Character of Media Presentation of Crime' (1999) 47 *ICLJ* pp.66–7.
7 *Op. cit.*
8 *Op. cit.* p.69.
9 On the relationship between instances of disorder and moral panics see N. Lacey, C. Wells, and D. Meure *Reconstructing Criminal Law* (Weidenfield and Nicolson, 1990) pp.105–13.
10 J. Thayer 'The Presumption of Innocence in Criminal Cases' in *A Preliminary Treatise on Evidence at the Common Law* (1989) p.553 cited in J. Thaler 'Punishing the Innocent: The Need for Due Process and the Presumption of Innocence Prior to Trial' (1978) *Wis. L. Rev* 441 p.442, fn 7.
11 LRC 11-1985.
12 Section 113, *Road Traffic Act 1961* – unlawful interference with the mechanism of a vehicle.
13 *Op.cit.* paragraph 15.7.
14 Unreported, High Court, Laffoy J., 2 November 1995.
15 382 US 87.
16 177 Ill.2d 440 (1997).
17 *Dáil debates*, Vol 433, 2 July 1993, Cols. 952–3.
18 G. Hogan 'Criminal Justice (Public Order) Act 1994', *ICLSA*, R.34 (Round Hall, 1994).
19 Law Reform Commission *op. cit.* paragraph 15.7.
20 National Crime Council *Public Order Offences in Ireland: a Report by the Institute of Criminology, Faculty of Law, University College Dublin for the National Crime Council* (Dublin, 2003).
21 *Ibid.* p.68.
22 *Ibid.*
23 A fault element of an offence comprises the level of fault required in order to ensure a conviction. It incorporates *mens rea* or mental elements such as intention or recklessness but also includes negligence. Offences with little or no fault elements are known as offences of strict or absolute liability.
24 Section 15(3) 'A person shall not be convicted of the offence of violent disorder unless the person intends to use or threaten to use violence or is aware that his conduct may be violent or threaten violence.'

25 G. Carey 'Mens Rea and the Irish Riot' (2000) 10(4) *ICLJ* 4.
26 *Ibid.* p.10.
27 [1994] 3 IR 580.
28 Unreported, Supreme Court, 23 May 2006.
29 Section 1(d), *Criminal Law (Amendment) Act 1935.*
30 Unreported, Supreme Court, 23 May 2006 at pp.24–5 of the unreported judgment.
31 *Ref. re s.94(2) of the Motor Vehicle Act (B.C).* [1985] 2 SCR 486 (SCC).
32 Carey *op. cit.* p.4.
33 *Dáil debates*, Vol 433, 2 July 1993, Col. 968.
34 G. Williams *The Proof of Guilt* (3rd ed, Steven S 1963) pp.184–5.
35 Hogan *op. cit.* para. 2–11.
36 Section 15(2). For the purposes of this section:

……

(b) no person of reasonable firmness need actually be, or be likely to be, present at that place.'

37 *Principles of Criminal Law op. cit* p.331.
38 *ÓFaoláin v. Lord Mayor of Dublin* Unreported, High Court, 10 December 1996.
39 *Op. cit.* p.331.
40 *Op. cit.* p.113.
41 See Chapters Five and Six.
42 There is no indication that the problem of overcrowded lists in the District Courts merited such a drastic intervention in the first place. As noted by the Irish Human Rights Commission in their *Final Observations on the Criminal Justice Bill 2004*, November 2004: 'The Commission is not satisfied that the Government has demonstrated the need for this measure.'
43 L. Tribe 'Trial by Mathematics: Precision and Ritual in the Legal Process' (1971) 84 *Harvard Law Review* 1329.
44 *Dáil debates*, Vol 598, 17 February 2005.
45 Section 5(3) of the 1994 Act defines 'offensive conduct' as 'any unreasonable behaviour which, having regard to all the circumstances, is likely to cause serious offence or serious annoyance to any person who is, or might reasonably be expected to be, aware of such behaviour'. This definition has been described by the Irish Human Rights Commission as:

> vague and open to subjective judgments. Under Article 7 of the ECHR the criminal law is required to be sufficiently precise to ensure that it satisfies the requirement that it is 'in accordance with the law'. This condition is satisfied where the individual can know from the wording of the relevant provision, and if need be, with the assistance of the national court's interpretation of it, what acts and omissions will make him or her liable. In the view of the Commission it is questionable whether the wording of section 5 of the *Criminal Justice (Public Order) Act* meets the standard required by Article 7 of the ECHR.

See further Irish Human Rights Commission *op. cit.* Professor Binchy has also expressed concerns about the lack of specificity in the section, noting: 'There is indeed an issue on the constitutional validity of section 5 from the standpoint of its vagueness of definition.' W. Binchy 'Offences Conduct, Intoxication, Section 29 and the Constitution', address given to a conference on the Criminal Justice Bill 2004: Implications for Human Rights and Legal Practice, Trinity College Dublin, 20 April 2005 p.11.

46 *Ibid.* p.3.

47 S. Kilcommins, I. O'Donnell, E O'Sullivan and B. Vaughan *Crime, Punishment and the Search for Order in Ireland* (IPA, 2004) p.199–200. They attribute this state of affairs to 'a backdrop of low crime and incarceration rates, the lack of a developed criminological discourse, and the disinterest shown by political parties in law and order issues.'

48 N. Lacey, C. Wells and D. Meure *Reconstructing Criminal Law* (Weidenfield and Nicolson, 1990) p.175.

Chapter Five

Panic and the Presumption

At around 1pm on the evening of 26 June 1996, a white motorcycle pulled up alongside the car of investigative journalist, Veronica Guerin, while she was stationary at the traffic lights on the Naas dual carriageway in Dublin. The pillion passenger opened fire on the journalist, shooting her several times in the upper body. She was believed to have died instantly. Her killers were suspected to be among a group of major Dublin criminals who had been linked to illegal drugs trafficking and were led by a man named John Gilligan.[1] This killing took place against the background of the murder of policeman Jerry McCabe who had been shot by the IRA during a robbery in Adare on 7 June.

The period following the death of these two figures can be viewed as a watershed in Irish criminal justice policy. As O'Donnell and O'Sullivan[2] note: 'These killings were defining moments in the debate about law and order in Ireland. They were the catalyst for a hardening in political attitudes. Crime control became a national priority and it was almost as if a state of emergency had been declared . . . This was a textbook case of "moral panic".' Indeed, the following brief summary of the media–political discourse at the time appears to support the authors' description of the period as a time of 'moral panic' (a disproportionate social reaction to a given threat or behaviour).

Ireland as Little Italy?

The idea that the murderers were 'godfathers' who considered themselves beyond the law was ubiquitous in media coverage of the murder right from the outset. The angry cry that rose from the *Irish Independent* on 27 June began: 'We know who killed her and he's untouchable.' The view was evocatively captured by a writer in the *Evening Herald* who wrote: 'Not even in the worst days of gangsterdom in Chicago did the Capones, the Legs Diamonds or the Bugsy Morans order a hit on the journalists who covered their activities.'[3] More subtle links were made with headlines such as 'Could Ireland go the Colombian way?'[4] or 'Italy leads the way in the fight against the Mafia.'[5] Another theme emphasized the perceived 'weakness' of the state in the face of organized crime which must be addressed by strengthening state powers. The *Irish Independent* surmised: 'The gangs feel they are beyond the reach of the law. They realize that our criminal laws are totally inadequate and the Gardaí have very little leverage when it comes to solving crime.'[6]

The media themes and images were quickly seized upon by those in Leinster House. Indeed, the view that the killers were 'untouchable' found particular favour with the Fianna Fáil and Progressive Democrats deputies, then in opposition, and the term was extravagantly used in their debates. In a relatively short commentary on the Organised Crime Bill, Progressive Democrat Liz O'Donnell used the term 'untouchable' no less than six times;[7] Fianna Fáil leader, Bertie Ahern, referred to the criminals with 'vast and unexplained wealth who consider themselves to be untouchable, and who to date have been untouchable';[8] and another Fianna Fáil TD called on the Government to 'end the phenomenon of untouchability in this society'.[9] Comparisons were drawn between Irish criminals and the Mafia in Italy,[10] despite the huge discrepancies in the scale and complexity of the criminal gangs, and indeed, analogies were drawn between the IRA[11] and organized crime. Statements were made by politicians that there were only twelve major godfathers in Dublin, and then it was claimed that there were fifty. No one seemed exactly sure of the facts, yet all seemed willing to accept that organized crime was endemic within Irish society.

Indeed, the hyperbolic language employed by TDs, especially opposition deputies, during the initial debates on 2 July is striking. It is not an exaggeration to say that some of the speeches made by TDs were indistinguishable in both their content and style from articles in the tabloid press. The threat was defined as one to democracy and to the security of the state: 'one of the gravest this State had ever faced',[12] a 'shadow over our democracy',[13] and a 'calculated attack on the freedom of each and every person in this country'.[14] Intimidation was 'rife', organized crime 'had a grip on the country', Dublin had been reduced to 'a sense of helplessness and fear', and we were in the midst of a 'crime wave' or 'epidemic'. Further, the problem was presented as such that it merited extreme bellicosity. Bertie Ahern spoke of 'a war to row back the level of crime. That war must be waged relentlessly and must be won'.[15]

In relation to the instant study, the significance of the finding of moral panic lies in its role in bringing about an attenuation of the presumption of innocence. The fruits of this particular 'war on crime' have left a clear mark on the Irish legal landscape. In a remarkably short space of time after the journalist's murder, the Government of the day had met public concern with a summer 'anti-crime package', described by the *Bar Review* as 'the most radical single package of alterations to Irish criminal law and procedure ever put together'.[16] The basic principles underlying bail were to be revised,[17] the right to silence curtailed for those charged with serious drugs offences,[18] and a novel civil process introduced to facilitate the seizure of the proceeds of crime.[19] The purpose of this chapter is therefore to examine the effect of these legislative provisions on the presumption of innocence.

Prior to embarking upon an examination of the legislation, the obvious cause for public concern at this unprecedented murder should be acknowledged. The fact that a professional, a *journalist*, had become the victim of a contract killing in broad daylight on a public highway and in all likelihood for reasons related to her work, deeply shocked the public. A journalist had not been murdered on home soil in the history of the state. It is easy to see how the public concluded that organized criminals were taking over the country. Further, the pathos of the story cannot be denied. A family deprived of its key figure, leaving a young child without a mother, packs a particular emotional punch and strikes a universal chord. The difficulty arises when public outrage and empathy is automatically translated into demands for draconian measures. The way in which the issues were framed in the media has already been noted with the result that little space was devoted to rational discussion of the alternatives to 'get tough' measures. Few column inches were devoted to discussions on the equally, if not more effective, measures concerning refocusing Garda activity, reducing the demand for drugs through proper treatment for heroin addicts or reducing the allure of such criminal organizations for young men in disadvantaged areas. As O'Donnell and O'Sullivan[20] note: '[These measures] could all have occurred in parallel with finding the killers and bringing them to justice. However, the response was swift, harsh, uncompromising and skewed towards punishment.'

The Summer Anti-Crime Package of 1996

The £54 million 'summer anti-crime package' as it came to be known, provided for the recruitment of 400 extra Gardaí; the increased 'civilianization' of the force; more prison spaces; a new remand prison at Wheatfield; increased supervision of prisoners granted early release; and new powers to provide for the eviction of known drug dealers from housing estates.[21] The core of the package, however, was formed by six Acts, namely, the *Disclosure of Certain Information for Taxation and Other Purposes Act*; the *Courts Act*; the *Criminal Justice (Miscellaneous Provisions) Act*; the *Criminal Assets Bureau Act*; the *Proceeds of Crime Act*; and the *Criminal Justice (Drug Trafficking) Act*. In a very real sense the *Bail Act 1997* is also attributable to the period, as a firm commitment to a constitutional referendum on bail was only finally secured from the Rainbow Coalition in the wake of Veronica Guerin's murder, and this was subsequently held in November 1996. The positive result in that referendum paved the way for the enactment of the *Bail Act 1997* and with it the introduction of preventative detention. While important procedural changes were effected by most of these Acts – the appointment of three extra High Court judges,[22] for example, and improved inter-agency co-operation between the Gardaí and the Revenue officials[23] – it is only proposed to examine here those Acts which have potentially made an impact on the presumption of innocence and the rights which flow therefrom. For this reason, only the *Bail Act 1997*, the *Proceeds of Crime Act 1996* and the *Criminal Justice (Drug Trafficking) Act 1996*, (or more correctly the amendment thereto pertaining to the right to silence), fall to be examined here.

(a) The Bail Act 1997

The approval of the principle of preventative justice by the people in the referendum in November 1996 led to the insertion of Article 40.4.7 into the Constitution, which Article provides:

> Provision may be made by law for the refusal of bail by a court to a person charged with a serious offence where it is reasonably considered necessary to prevent the commission of a serious offence by that person.

The *Bail Act 1997* was introduced in order to implement the above amendment to the Constitution.[24] It was signed into law by the President on 5 May 1997 but did not come fully into operation until 15 May 2000. The main effect of the legislation is that bail may be refused on the ground that the accused might commit an offence while on bail. The primary provision in this regard is contained in section 2(1) of the Act which provides as follows:

> Where an application for bail is made by a person charged with a serious offence, a court may refuse the application if the court is satisfied that such refusal is reasonably considered necessary to prevent the commission of a serious offence by that person.

It will be noted that bail can only be refused on this ground to those persons charged with a 'serious offence.' This is defined in the Act as an offence which is listed in the Schedule to the Act and one which attracts a sentence of five years imprisonment or more. The Schedule includes a wide range of offences, some of them relatively minor in character. Therefore, even petty thefts which are classified as indictable offences or fairly minor assault charges fall within this definition.[25] It is important to bear this in mind when examining the effect of the substantive provisions.

(I) Bail and the Presumption of Innocence

The fundamental right to liberty is jeopardised by the possibility of an unsuccessful bail application and the deprivation of a suspect's liberty is moreover heightened when it is viewed in the context of the presumption of innocence. The defendant has not yet been convicted and is entitled to be presumed innocent until proved otherwise at trial. Preventative detention, which seeks to prevent the accused from committing further offences pending trial, offends the presumption in two possible ways. First, through reliance on the present charge as an indicator of a predisposition to commit offences and secondly, through the claim that he or she will be guilty of future, as yet unidentified offences. Indeed, it is of interest to note that prior to the 'crime crisis' of July 1996, the Tanaiste and leader of the Labour Party, Dick Spring, had expressed serious misgivings about the concept of preventative detention[26] on the basis that 'everyone is innocent until proven guilty'.[27]

It may be argued that the public's right to protection from serious offences committed by those on bail should override such considerations. The rejoinder must be that there are numerous restrictions which can be placed on an offender as part of the conditions of bail in order to ensure that he or she does not reoffend. These include measures such as signing-on daily at a Garda station; forfeiture of passport; restrictions in relation to his or her place of residence and his or her association or communication with specified persons; curfews; and restrictions on the use of specified substances. One very practical solution which is thoroughly in accord with the rights of the accused is to ensure an expeditious trial after arrest and charge. The final point is that the research to support the change in the bail laws had not been done. Given that little reliable information as to the percentages of people who would be denied bail was produced by the Government, the projected gains in terms of crime control were necessarily speculative and reliant on media reporting.

Some of the strongest defences of the right to bail, as grounded on the right to be presumed innocent, can be found in the decisions of the former Supreme Court in the *O'Callaghan*[28] case, later reaffirmed in *Ryan*.[29] Prior to the enactment of s.2, this case law formed the basis for the test for bail applications. Thus, the two grounds on which bail could be denied were those relating to the evasion of justice, namely:

(i) that it was thought the accused might abscond and not stand trial; and
(ii) that it was thought that the accused might interfere with witnesses or evidence.[30]

While these two grounds formed the basis for the decision as to bail, the Court also held that other factors could be taken into account. Ten criteria were approved in all, such as the nature and seriousness of the offence charged and the weight of evidence against the accused.

The *O'Callaghan* case firmly established Ireland's 'liberal' position on bail, anchored in the view that the presumption of innocence is a principle governing *all* stages of the criminal process until a verdict of guilty is reached. Indeed, the decision has been described by O'Mahony as a 'powerful affirmation of the principle of the presumption of innocence and resolute refusal to compromise this principle any more than is absolutely essential in order to ensure that an accused stands trial'.[31]

The facts of O'Callaghan were that the defendant had been refused bail in both the District and High Courts. One of the grounds on which he had been refused bail was on the basis that the Superintendent in charge of the case had indicated that were he to be released on bail he believed that there was a serious risk that the applicant would commit further offences. The Supreme Court in considering the defendant's bail application set out the basic principles which underlie the law on bail as outlined above, namely bail can only be denied for the purpose of ensuring that the accused stands trial and that the accused would not interfere with witnesses. The main judgments rejecting denial of bail on the basis of the likelihood of commission of further offences were delivered by ÓDálaigh C.J. and Walsh J.

Walsh J. was unequivocal in his view that the presumption of innocence is not merely a procedural rule at trial but that it operates at the pre-trial stage also. To quote him once again, the presumption was 'a very real thing and is not simply a procedural rule taking effect only at the trial'.[32] He described the refusal of bail on the grounds of putative offending in the following terms:

> This is a form of preventative detention which has no place in our legal system and is quite alien to the true purpose of bail...In this country it would be quite contrary to the concept of personal liberty enshrined in the Constitution that any person should be punished in respect of any matter upon which he has not been convicted or that in any circumstances he should be deprived of his liberty upon only the belief that he will commit offences if left at liberty, save in the most extraordinary circumstances spelled out by the Oireachtas and then only to secure the preservation of the state in a time of national emergency or some situation akin to that.[33]

ÓDálaigh C.J. also took a principled stance on the basis of the right to be presumed innocent. He stated that to remand an accused in custody in respect of future charges would constitute a denial of the whole basis of our system of law, as grounded on the presumption of innocence:

> It transcends respect for the requirement that a man shall be considered innocent until he is found guilty and seeks to punish him in respect of offences neither completed nor attempted. I say 'punish' for deprivation of liberty must be considered a punishment unless it can be required to ensure that an accused person will stand his trial when called upon... *The Courts owe more than verbal respect to the principle that punishment begins after conviction, and that every man is deemed to be innocent until tried and duly found guilty.*[34]

While the reasoning followed by the Supreme Court in *O'Callaghan* has been criticised for failing to sufficiently explain why it is so unfair to refuse bail on grounds of predicted future offending while there are no such difficulties with predicting that the applicant might abscond or seek to interfere with witnesses,[35] Walsh J.'s 'necessity test' goes some way towards resolving this difficulty. This was outlined by Walsh J. thus: 'From time to time necessity demands that some unconvicted persons should be held in custody pending trial to secure their attendance at the trial but in such cases "necessity" is the operative test.'[36] Walsh J. recognized that some *limited* concessions, involving minimal interference with the right to be presumed innocent, had to be made to pragmatism.[37] Most importantly, as Tribe has written, assessments as to whether the accused is likely to abscond or interfere in any way with the trial process do not entail any assumptions of guilt.[38] They serve only the purpose of ensuring that the accused will stand trial and in no way reflect on a defendant's guilt or innocence in relation to the offence charged.

Over twenty years on, in *Ryan v. DPP*,[39] a differently constituted Supreme Court was provided with an opportunity to overrule the *O'Callaghan* principles, but declined to do so. The facts were that the respondent was charged with two alleged offences of malicious damage and larceny. He was brought to the District Court and was remanded in custody following Garda objections that he would be likely to commit further offences if admitted to bail. This was reversed by the High Court, however, relying on *O'Callaghan*. Subsequently, the respondent was arrested and charged with other offences. Having obtained bail in respect of these offences in the District Court, he successfully sought a reduction in the amount of bail fixed in the High Court. The DPP appealed against the two High Court orders on the basis that the High Court had a discretion at common law to deny bail and that the constitutionally protected rights to life, bodily integrity and property which would be affected by the commission of crime conferred a right and duty on the High Court to exercise this discretion against granting bail.

The Supreme Court dismissed the appeal and upheld the *O'Callaghan* decision. Finlay C.J. rejected the arguments on a number of grounds. First, if the discretion vested in the courts in relation to granting bail were to be exercised in an attempt to prevent the apprehended commission of crime, it would constitute an abuse of power. Second, a mere intention to commit a crime does not constitute a crime and an adequate basis on which to detain. In this relation, the questions posed by Finlay C.J. are germane to our new bail regime:

> An intention to commit a crime, even of the most serious type, is not in our criminal law a crime itself unless it is furthered by overt acts of preparation or converted by an agreement with another into a conspiracy. The courts cannot create offences or crimes, though the Oireachtas may. Are they, however, to be permitted to detain a person because he is suspected of an intention, which even if proved in a full criminal trial, could not lead to his punishment? If such a power did exist in the courts, why should its exercise be confined to cases where the suspect is an applicant for bail? Why should the courts' prevention of the apprehended harm cease in the event of the determination without a sentence of imprisonment of the original charge, which charge may in its character and seriousness bear no resemblance at all to the feared offence? How can such an intention be proved, and by what standard of proof must it be established? Could there be any grounds on which an accused person suspected of such an intention would be afforded less comprehensive notice of the evidence to be offered against him of the grounds for such suspicion and less opportunity to prepare and be represented to contest such allegations as he is afforded in relation to the presenting of a criminal charge against him? Would every applicant for bail accordingly in which this ground was advanced as the substantial ground of opposition, take on the nature and necessary requisites of a criminal trial?[40]

The then Chief Justice further observed that the criminalizing of intention in such a manner was 'usually the badge of an oppressive or unjust legal system'. The proper methods of crime prevention were rather 'the long established methods of police surveillance, speedy trial and deterrent sentences'.[41]

McCarthy J. delivered a judgment with which Walsh J. also agreed. He held that if an accused person were to be denied his liberty merely because of his accuser's suspicion that if released he might cause grievous harm, this would be far from a balancing of constitutional rights – it would be a recalibration of the scales of justice. He went on to say that if a person were to be denied his liberty because of a well-founded suspicion, there was no reason why another citizen not so charged might not be detained upon a similar suspicion.

It is interesting to compare the judgments in *O'Callaghan* and *Ryan* to the seminal decision of the United States Supreme Court on bail in *US v. Salerno*.[42] As noted above, the majority of the Supreme Court upheld the constitutionality of the *Bail Reform Act 1984* which provided for pre-trial preventive detention on the basis that it was regulatory rather than punitive in nature. The minority judgments, delivered by Marshall J., however, take an equally broad view of the presumption of innocence, if not broader. He opined: 'The very pith and purpose of this statute is an abhorrent limitation of the presumption of innocence. The majority's untenable conclusion that the present Act is constitutional arises from a specious denial of the role of the Bail Clause and the Due Process Clause in protecting the invaluable guarantee afforded by the presumption of innocence.'[43] His judgment can be distinguished from those in *O'Callaghan* and *Ryan*, however, on the basis that he perceived the violation of the presumption of innocence to stem from an assumption of guilt in relation to the current charge, rather than future offences. In this regard, he based his reasoning on the fact that the Government would not be permitted to detain someone who had been shown to be dangerous but had subsequently been acquitted. An indictment would be necessary. This led the judge to conclude that 'The indictment has been turned into evidence, if not that the defendant is guilty of the crime charged, then that left to his own devices he will soon be guilty of something else.'[44]

These decisions expressly disapprove in the strongest possible terms the concept of preventative detention as inimical to the presumption of innocence. The former Supreme Court's uncompromising adherence to the principle is difficult to reconcile with the law as it now stands. As O'Mahony noted prior to the referendum: 'It is difficult to see how any amendment to allow preventative detention would not introduce a note of self-contradiction and so undermine the integrity and credibility of the Constitution.'[45] While it is of course constitutionally mandated that the will of the Irish people as expressed in the referendum should prevail over the opinions of the Supreme Court, the *Bail Act* nevertheless remains a significant attack on the presumption of innocence as previously interpreted by the courts. The judiciary now find themselves in the invidious position of having to work a system of bail which they have consistently declared incompatible with the provisions of the Constitution. As O'Mahony observes: '[This] less than harmonious end result must be both an erosion of the fundamental principle of the presumption of innocence and a diminution of the Supreme Court's ability to uphold such fundamental principles.'[46]

Further, the attack on the presumption of innocence which section 2 represents is compounded by s.2(2)(f) which provides that in exercising its jurisdiction under s.2(1), a court shall take into account and may receive evidence and submissions concerning 'any other offence in respect of which the accused person is charged and is awaiting trial'. The relevance and fairness of this provision has been questioned by several commentators.[47] These are also charges in respect of which the applicant for bail supposedly enjoys the presumption of innocence – they are as yet unproven – yet they may influence the court's decision. As Liston[48] asks: 'How can an untried and unproven charge be of any relevance to an accused person's bail application in respect of a different charge?'. The only answer to the question rests on an assumption of guilt. It is significant that this provision is not included in the corresponding sections of the English *Bail Act 1976*, although there is considerable overlap with regard to the rest of the criteria. Should this factor prove influential in any particular case, it leads to the conclusion that the more charges that are levelled against the accused, the lesser his or her chances of being granted bail. This allows a procedural decision, in respect of which the prosecution has almost complete discretion, to hold sway over the accused's right to bail.

(b) Section 7, Criminal Justice (Drug Trafficking) Bill, 1996

The *Criminal Justice (Drug Trafficking) Bill* had been in gestation since March 1996 and thus the main provision of the Act allowing for a seven day period of detention for those charged with drug trafficking offences can in large part be divorced from the panic which ensued in July 1996, although this period of heightened alarm did form the backdrop for its passage. Therefore, although the concept of seven-day detention without charge in itself raises serious concerns,[49] it is proposed to confine the current discussion to the impact of section 7 of the Act on the right to silence. It should be emphasized that this section was not a pre-planned provision, having been introduced as an amendment to the *Drugs Trafficking Act* by means of a guillotined legislative procedure and in the absence of any debate. Media images of the professional criminal staring obstinately at the police station wall were used to justify an amendment to the Bill on the eve of its passage in the Dail which effectively removed the accused's right to silence in the context of criminal proceedings for drug trafficking offences.[50]

Section 7 of the Act allows a court, in any proceedings against a person for a drug trafficking offence, to draw inferences from the failure of an accused to mention certain facts when being questioned or on being charged where the accused later relies on those facts in his or her defence and where the court considers that he or she could reasonably have been expected to mention certain facts when being questioned or on being charged but did not do so. That failure may be used as corroboration, but a person shall not be convicted of an offence solely on an inference drawn from such failure or refusal.

The restriction on silence applies to all those charged with 'drug trafficking' offences. As with the *Bail Act*, the net cast by the legislation is very wide, covering not only persons suspected of importing or manufacturing large quantities of drugs, but also those suspected of supplying, distributing or transporting drugs or possessing them for the purpose of supply.[51] Thus, anyone who is suspected of possessing a quantity of drugs larger than that which can be shown to be 'intended for immediate personal use'[52] could be held under the Act.

The relationship between the right to silence and the presumption have been outlined in detail in Chapter Three. In the context of the detention period permitted under the 1996 Act, moreover, the incursion of the right merits particular concern, particularly in terms of its compatibility with the ECHR. As noted above, it has been affirmed in cases such as *Murray* and *Saunders* that the right to silence inheres in Article 6 of the Convention and in particular Article 6(2). More recent decisions such as *Heaney and McGuinness v. Ireland*[53] and *Condron v. UK*[54] give rise to the cautious hope that the incorporation of the Convention into Irish law will afford a detainee under the 1996 Act a greater measure of protection than is provided under Irish law.

The *Heaney* case concerned s.52 of the *Offences Against the State Act 1939*, a legislative provision which makes it an offence punishable by six months' imprisonment for someone detained for an offence under the 1939 Act or for a number of other offences to refuse to account for his or her movements when required to do so. Costello J. in the High Court held that the modification of the right to silence introduced by s.52 of the *Offences against the State Act 1939* was a permissible encroachment on public interest grounds and this decision was upheld by the Supreme Court on appeal. The decision is significant in that while the constitutionality of the section was upheld domestically on this proportionality test, the European Court adopted a stricter approach to the interpretation of the right. It held that the 'degree of compulsion' imposed on the applicants destroyed the 'very essence' of the right to silence and could not be justified as proportionate to the public interest. It would appear, therefore, that the Strasbourg Court's 'very essence' test imposes a higher standard with regard to any legislative qualifications of the right to silence.

Of particular relevance to the 1996 Act, moreover, is the decision in *Condron*, which concerned the drawing of adverse inferences under s.34 of the English *Criminal Justice and Public Order Act 1994*. The section is similar in its wording to s.7. The trial judge had invited the jury to draw an inference from the fact that the applicants had failed to mention certain facts in custody which they later sought to rely on in their defence, despite the fact that the applicants had only acted on the advice of their solicitor who was concerned that they were suffering from the effects of drug withdrawal. The European Court held that there had been a breach of the right to a fair trial under Article 6(1) in that the trial judge's direction to the jury had left them at liberty to draw an adverse inference notwithstanding that it might have been satisfied as to the explanation put forward by the applicant for his silence. While the Court made it clear that it did not find the right to silence provisions *per se* to be incompatible with Article 6, it nevertheless established that strict safeguards will have to be followed, and that compatibility will depend on the circumstances of each case.

It is easy to envisage a situation identical to that in issue in *Condron* arising under the 1996 Act. As has been noted, the detainees under the Act may in all likelihood be drug abusers themselves, who, as observed by Farrell,[55] will be 'strung out or desperate for their next fix and ready to sign anything put in front of them'. Moreover, there are fewer safeguards for a detainee under the 1996 Act than for the applicant in *Condron*, an obvious difference being that the inferences drawn under the 1996 Act are capable of amounting to corroboration and may therefore be given probative value. Detainees under the Drug Trafficking Act, unlike English suspects detained under the *Police and Criminal Evidence Act 1984* (PACE), will also be denied the presence of their solicitor in the interview room with them during interrogation, a restriction which will presumably apply regardless of their fitness for questioning. It is of interest that the Court in *Condron* sought to emphasise the importance of legal advice as a safeguard:

> It must also be observed that the applicants' solicitor was present throughout the whole of their interviews and was able to advise them not to volunteer any answers to questions put to them. *The fact that an accused person who is questioned under caution is assured access to legal advice, and in the applicants' case the physical presence of a solicitor during police interview, must be considered a particularly important safeguard* for dispelling any compulsion to speak which may be inherent in the terms of the caution.[56]

The fact that under Irish law the interview with the detainee will not necessarily be tape recorded, nor notes from the interview given to the solicitor or to the individual, is also a relevant consideration. In this regard, it is noteworthy that Ashworth[57] has raised doubts about the compatibility of s.34 with Article 6(1) in circumstances where the police have failed to provide the legal adviser with sufficient information on the case against the accused. The same logic could easily be applied when assessing the compatibility of s.7 with the Convention. It has been held by the Supreme Court in *Lavery v. Member in Charge, Carrickmacross Garda Station*[58] that solicitors do not have a right to interview notes despite the fact that access to notes is necessary to allow the individual and his solicitor the opportunity to make an informed legal assessment of the information the detained person should volunteer.

At the very least, the decision in *Condron* will ensure that Irish judges are scrupulous in explaining to juries that inferences may be drawn from an accused's silence *only* in circumstances where they have rejected the explanation given by an accused for his silence.

(c) The Proceeds of Crime Act 1996

The *Proceeds of Crime Bill 1996* was hurriedly enacted in the summer of 1996,[59] together with its sister Bill, the *Criminal Assets Bureau Bill,*[60] in order to establish a multi-agency body with powers to forfeit the proceeds of crime. It is the statutory framework of the former, however, which governs the novel *civil* asset confiscation procedure whereby applications can be made to the High Court by a Garda Chief Superintendent or a Revenue Officer to seize assets which are believed to constitute directly or indirectly the proceeds of crime. This is a new departure for law enforcement in Ireland. While the *Offences Against the State Act 1985* authorizes the freezing of bank accounts that are believed to be held on behalf of unlawful organizations and the disposal of moneys to the benefit of the Exchequer, the Act only applied to subversive crime. The 1996 Act applies to the proceeds of *all* kinds of crime. Similarly, while the *Criminal Justice Act 1994* made provision for the making of an order by the trial court for the confiscation of goods on the conviction of an offender, such confiscation only took place *after* a conviction.

The 1996 Act can be outlined briefly thus.[61] Under section 2 an interim order can be obtained on an *ex parte* basis freezing the proceeds of crime for twenty-one days, at which stage an interlocutory order may be sought under section 3. 'Proceeds of crime' is defined in section 1 of the Act as meaning 'any property obtained or received at any time (whether before or after the passing of the Act) by or as a result of or in connection with the commission of an offence'. The total value of the property must not be less than £10,000 (€13,000). The interlocutory order granted under section 3 will remain in place *unless* the respondent can show that the property is not the proceeds of crime or that its value is under £10,000 (€13,000). After this interlocutory order has been in place for seven years a final disposal order may be sought under section 4. Section 8 states that the standard of proof required to determine any question arising under the Act shall be the civil standard, namely, the balance of probabilities.

The Act holds obvious implications for the presumption of innocence in that through its civil label its provisions may circumvent the whole gamut of due process protections normally afforded a defendant in criminal proceedings. Certainly, this civil label has assured the survival of the Act through two constitutional challenges in the High Court and a joint appeal to the Supreme Court. The judicial affirmation of its civil nature has meant that defendants to proceedings under the Act are not entitled to the presumption of innocence, nor are they entitled to assert that the prosecution must prove its case beyond a reasonable doubt. The main concern therefore centres around the question of whether the proceedings under the Act are in reality criminal and that, simply by flashing its civil identity tag at the courts, the state has been able to shrug off the safeguards of the criminal law.

(I) Ersatz Civil Law?

The constitutionality of the *Proceeds of Crime Act 1996* has been upheld in a number of decisions by our superior courts. The first ruling on this issue came from McGuinness J. in *Gilligan v. Criminal Assets Bureau*[62] which case was brought by John Gilligan, the gang leader who was charged with and subsequently acquitted of the murder Veronica Guerin.[63] The principal argument advanced on behalf of the appellants in this case was that the provisions of the 1996 Act essentially formed part of the criminal law and not the civil law and that the persons affected by those provisions were deprived of some of the most important safeguards which were historically a feature of the criminal law. Specifically, the presumption of innocence was reversed, the standard of proof was on the balance of probabilities rather than beyond reasonable doubt, and there was no provision for a trial by jury in respect of any of the issues. The High Court held that since the confiscation procedure introduced under the 1996 Act was labelled and operated as a civil process, it did not have 'all the features of a criminal prosecution' and so Article 38.1 did not apply.

This decision was followed by O'Higgins J. in *MF Murphy v. GH*[64] and both these decisions were upheld by the Supreme Court in a joint appeal.[65] Like the High Court, the Supreme Court focused on the trappings of criminal procedure and held that the *indicia* that rendered proceedings criminal in character – the provision for the detention of the person concerned, the bringing of him [or her] into custody to a Garda station, the searching of the person detained, his [or her] admission to bail, the imposition of a pecuniary penalty with liability to imprisonment in default, the reference in the statute to a party having been 'convicted of an offence' and the provision for the withdrawal of proceedings by the entry of a *nolle prosequi* – were conspicuously absent in the 1996 Act. This meant that the courts refused to allow the safeguards of Article 38.1 of the Constitution, which include the presumption of innocence, to apply to this procedure. These decisions have been criticized by Meade,[66] among others, on the basis that the state has been permitted to disguise as civil a process which imposes a sanction on the basis of criminal conduct, but without any criminal conviction having been obtained.

Although it must be acknowledged that *using these criteria as a guide*, a finding that the 1996 Act is civil in nature is inescapable, it must also be questioned whether this test is entirely satisfactory. As Meade has noted, this is a test with a very narrow focus, 'rooted in an understanding of the labels and procedures of confiscation procedure itself, having no regard to the purpose or result of such procedure'.[67] The author also observes that the Act sets a dangerous precedent. By choosing a test which focuses on the trappings and procedural intricacies of the criminal law, to the neglect of its substance, one is permitting the state to pursue with immunity its crime control aims by recourse to ostensibly civil legislation, thereby by-passing due process protections. The narrow definition of 'criminal' adopted by the courts has allowed the state to infer that an individual is guilty of complicity in (a) criminal act(s), with the consequent confiscation of his or her property, while sidestepping essential procedural safeguards such as the presumption of innocence.

By broadening somewhat the scope of the test for criminality, a completely different conclusion may be reached. A list of features may be compiled which would militate against the conclusions reached by the High and Supreme Courts:

(i) The *Proceeds of Crime Act* is a law of general application – it applies to all citizens. That a law should apply generally is one of the *indicia* of criminal legislation outlined in the case of *Melling v. ÓMathghamhna*[68] and in the case law of the European Court of Human Rights.
(ii) The aims of the Act are punitive or retributive, not remedial. It was enacted as part of the state's 'war on crime'.
(iii) 'Crime' is the key word in the title and the main emphasis in the long title.
(iv) Relief may not be granted under ss.2–4 of the Act unless it is shown to the satisfaction of the Court that the assets are derived from crime. The commission of an underlying criminal offence is the central focus of the provisions.
(v) The plaintiff under the Act is usually a senior Garda officer.
(vi) Although an individual's liberty is not in jeopardy, a 'sanction' is imposed on the basis of criminal conduct through the confiscation of assets. The consequences of a successful application for an individual are actually far more serious than the imposition of a heavy fine subsequent to conviction.

In addition, because actions brought under the Act are seen as an indicator that an individual is in some way complicit in criminal activity, the opprobrium which may attach to a respondent under the Act must be considered. The property owner risks the stigma associated with engaging in or being connected to criminal activity. As McCutcheon and Walsh[69] have noted in this regard: 'If a disciplinary charge of plagiarism against a student is "criminal in nature", is the case for the same conclusion not as compelling, if not more so, in criminal assets proceedings?'[70] Although McGuinness J. in *Gilligan* approved the classification of proceedings under the Act as an action *in rem* (against the property) rather than *in personam* (against a specific person), she also noted that the main aim of the Act, simply put, is to deprive '*major criminals* of their ill-gotten gains'.[71] Inadvertently, therefore, the judge laid bare the reality of the situation. The courts may be able to draw a clear line between the 'guilt' of the assets and the property owner in law, but in reality, the initiation of proceedings under the Act gives rise to an implication that the respondent has engaged in wrongdoing, or at least has been negligent with regard to criminal activity. Legal fictions aside, this is the position in which respondents under the Act are placed.

It is noteworthy that the Supreme Court in *Murphy* appeared to take the view that proceedings under the Act were remedial rather than retributive in nature. Keane C.J. (delivering the judgment of the Court) states unequivocally 'In general such a forfeiture [of property which is shown to be the proceeds of crime] is not a punishment and its operation does not require criminal procedures.'[72] Proceedings under the asset forfeiture legislation in the United States are defined in this way. This is premised on the belief that they simply facilitate the restitution to the state of the profits of crime, which are viewed as rightfully belonging to the state. However, as Meade[73] has observed, recent decisions of the U.S. Supreme Court would appear to qualify this view of forfeiture as a purely remedial process.[74] In particular, the decision in *Austin v. Texas*[75] represents an important shift in the Court's thinking about forfeitures. In that case, the Court held that forfeiture was subject to the Eighth Amendment which prohibits the imposition of excessive fines. The importance of the decision lies in its belated recognition that the aims of forfeiture may be *retributive*, if only in part. As Cheh[76] comments: 'The Court pierced a central fiction of forfeiture and acknowledged the reality that many forfeitures are forms of punishment.'[77] It is instructive that in reaching this conclusion the Court eschewed a formalistic approach and had regard to other factors such as the character of the punishment, the intent of the legislature in enacting the law, and its operation in practice.

It is submitted that a similar, broader approach should be adopted by the courts here. Even a cursory examination of the origins of the 1996 Act would indicate that its aims were retributive: to punish those 'godfathers of crime' against whom sufficient evidence could not be gathered to bring a criminal prosecution. Further, as Meade[78] has observed, the schema of the Act supports this conclusion. The definition of 'proceeds of crime' in s.1 is very broad, extending to 'any property obtained or received at any time (whether before or after the passing of this Act) by or as a result of or *in connection with* the commission of an offence.' This brings within the ambit of the Act more than mere *profits* of crime, but also, for example, a 'start-up' fund amassed for the purpose of buying narcotic drugs. No profit may yet have been made, and indeed no crime yet committed, yet this money will be liable to forfeiture. The broad scope of the section belies any claims in relation to the purely remedial nature of the proceedings and thereby its civil vestiture.

(III) THE POLICE INVESTIGATION

While the discussion above has focused on the effect of Ms Guerin's murder on the criminal justice system, in a more immediate sense the murder placed tremendous pressure on the Gardaí to bring her murderers to account. On the morning after the murder of the journalist, John Bruton, then Taoiseach, announced: 'The full resources of the state are being applied to finding and bringing to justice those who committed this murder and those who inspired and directed it.'[79] The investigation was the most extensive ever launched by the Irish police force and involved a number of novel departures such as the institution of a new Witness Protection Programme. Unfortunately, as will be seen below, the investigation was characterized by what O'Mahony has termed 'an unhealthy

Garda culture, focused exclusively on getting the man regardless of the method.'[80] In respect of some of the men suspected of involvement in the murder, the police engaged in practices which cannot be reconciled with respect for the right to be presumed innocent.

Charles Bowden, who was given immunity from prosecution for his role in the murder and was therefore the state's first 'supergrass', had admitted preparing and loading the gun used to kill the journalist. In 1997, he was sentenced to six years for drugs and firearms offences, which amounts to a considerable reduction on the sentence he would have received without his co-operation with the prosecution. Moreover, he did not serve all of this sentence and was released in April 2001 in order to begin a new life abroad. His evidence was pivotal to the prosecutions brought against the members of the gang suspected of murdering the journalist, helping to convict not only Paul Ward but another gang member, Brian Meehan, for the journalist's murder. Brian Meehan was convicted as an accessory before the fact to the murder by the Special Criminal Court on 29 July 1999. He received a life sentence and concurrent sentences of twenty and twelve years for drug offences. Bowden also testified against John Gilligan, the man suspected of being the ringleader of the criminal gang. On 15 March 2001 Gilligan was acquitted of the murder of Ms Guerin at the Special Criminal Court, although he was sentenced to twenty-eight years' imprisonment for the importation of cannabis resin. This sentence was later reduced to twenty years on appeal.[81]

Paul Ward was accused of disposing of the motorcycle and gun used to kill the journalist and was, again on Bowden's evidence, convicted as an accessory before the fact to the murder by the Special Criminal Court on 27 November 1998.[82] He received a life sentence. His conviction, however, was subsequently overturned on 22 March 2002 by the Court of Criminal Appeal on the grounds of the unreliable nature of the accomplice evidence.[83] The Ward judgment merits particular attention given the judicial scepticism expressed therein about interrogative practices engaged in by members of An Garda Síochána.

The case against Ward essentially comprised two main planks of evidence: first, the evidence of state witness Bowden as to his involvement in the murder and secondly, admissions allegedly made by Ward in Garda custody. Ward had maintained silence for many interview sessions since his detention under s.30 of the *Offences Against the State Act 1939* until meetings with his partner and his elderly mother who had also been arrested and detained. These admissions were excluded by Barr J., delivering the judgment of the Court, as having being obtained in breach of Ward's constitutional right to fair procedures and treatment while in custody. The learned High Court judge was satisfied that the visit from Ward's mother was 'not arranged for any humanitarian purposes but was a cynical ploy which it was hoped might break down the accused and cause him to make what was perceived to be crucial admissions regarding what had happened the weapon'. Similarly, he accepted that Ward's girlfriend, Vanessa Meehan, had been placed under considerable psychological pressure to assist in breaking Ward down. Overall, the Court was severely critical of police actions in the case, which the judge described as 'deliberate gross violations of the fundamental obligation which the interrogators and their superiors had of conducting their dealings with the accused in accordance with the principles of basic fairness and justice.'[84]

Further, it is possible to infer from certain conclusions drawn in the judgment that the police may have fabricated evidence. The alleged admissions made by Paul Ward were supposedly made late on 17 October 1996 though, strangely, two separate teams of detectives who interviewed Ward the next day were not aware of the breakthrough as there was no memorandum or note on the custody record to that effect. This contradicted the evidence of interviewing officers in court to the effect that the memorandum was drawn up contemporaneously with the interview. In this relation Barr J. observed: '[This] indicates either incredible disorganization in the murder investigation, despite the fact that there was a continuously manned incident room at Lucan Garda station or there was no memorandum of the interview at the time and it came into existence later.' Such practices do little to dispel the cloud of suspicion which has hung over interrogative police practices in Ireland since the Sallins Train Robbery and Kerry Babies cases.[85]

It is also worth noting that on the morning of the arrest of

Patrick Holland, who was subsequently convicted of drugs trafficking on the evidence of Bowden, Holland's solicitor was arrested and thereby effectively prevented from providing legal advice to his client while he was in Garda custody. It must be viewed as more than just a coincidence that his solicitor was released at the same time that Holland was charged. Further, as with Ward, no tape or video recording was made of Holland's interviews with Gardaí during which it was alleged that crucial admissions in relation to drugs dealing had been made. The final troubling aspect of the trial of Patrick Holland is that Garda Marion Cusack, who arrested Holland at Dun Laoghaire, gave evidence that she believed he was the man who shot dead Veronica Guerin at the Naas Road on 26 June 1996. It must be noted that Garda Cusack gave this evidence in order to explain the basis for Holland's arrest, *viz* suspicion of having a firearm at the junction of the Naas Road and Boot Road on 26 June 1996, and that the highly legally trained judges in the Special Criminal Court will no doubt have confined its relevance to this aspect of the case. However, it must also be conceded that evidence as to suspected involvement in a high-profile murder is undeniably prejudicial evidence to introduce at a trial for the separate and distinct charge of drugs trafficking. As will be discussed in Chapter Nine, evidence of bad character shifts the focus of the trial away from the prosecution case and 'conjures up a highly suspicious prejudicial atmosphere in which the presumption of innocence tends to be replaced with a presumption of guilt'.[86]

Conclusion

The cumulative impact of the three legislative developments discussed above on the presumption of innocence must be viewed as very serious indeed. The tangible benefits of the presumption in the form of a right to bail, to remain silent and even to remain free of punishment (in the form of property confiscation) until a finding of guilt by a court, are no longer available to the citizen in certain circumstances. It is of particular concern that the provisions on civil forfeiture appear to deny the protection afforded by the presumption to persons accused of substantive criminality. This trend towards the evasion of the criminal law and its safeguards appears to have been consolidated with the proposed introduction of ASBOs in this jurisdiction (discussed in Chapter Six) and raises serious questions about the role of the criminal law in crime control. One may pose the question, as Ashworth has done in England, as to whether the criminal law can now be regarded as a lost cause.[87]

The significance of the outbreak of moral panic in the period following Veronica Guerin's death lies in the effective dilution of the presumption of innocence discussed in this chapter. It raises the possibility that another tragedy or sequence of tragedies such as occurred in the summer of 1996 could lead to further inroads into one of our most fundamental rights. As has been observed, it is also of note that the excesses of the legislature in their rush to the statute book found a parallel in the police investigation.

NOTES

1 Paul Ward was convicted as an accessory before the fact to Ms Guerin's murder by the Special Criminal Court on 27 November 1998. He received a life sentence. His conviction, however, was subsequently overturned on 22 March 2002 by the Court of Criminal Appeal on the grounds of the unreliable nature of the accomplice evidence. John Gilligan was acquitted of her murder at the Special Criminal Court on 15 March 2001. He was, however, sentenced to twenty-eight years' imprisonment for the importation of cannabis resin, a sentence which was later reduced to twenty years by the Court of Criminal Appeal. A final appeal to the Supreme Court against this conviction was rejected in a judgment handed down on 23 November 2005. Brian Meehan therefore stands as the only individual convicted in connection with the murder. He was convicted as an accessory before the fact to the murder by the Special Criminal Court on 29 July 1999. He received a life sentence and concurrent sentences of twenty and twelve years for drug offences.

2 I. O'Donnell and E. O'Sullivan *Crime Control in Ireland: The Politics of Intolerance* (Cork: Cork University Press, 2001) pp.2–3.

3 'Law unto themselves', *Evening Herald*, 27 June 1996, p.6.

4 *Irish Times*, 29 June 1996, p.7.

5 *Irish Times*, 28 June 1996, p.7.

6 *Irish Independent*, 27 June 1996, p.11.

7 *Dáil debates* vol. 467, 2 July 1996, Cols. 2365 *et seq.*

8 *Dáil debates* vol. 467, 2 July 1996, Col. 2374.

9 *Dáil debates* vol. 467, 2 July 1996, Col. 2464, (Mr O'Dea).
10 *Dáil debates* vol. 467, 2 July 1996, Cols. 2476–2477.
11 *Dáil debates* vol. 467, 2 July 1996, Cols. 2457 and 2473.
12 *Dáil debates* vol. 467, 2 July 1996, Col. 2378.
13 *Dáil debates* vol. 467, 2 July 1996, Col. 2379.
14 *Dáil debates* vol. 467, 2 July 1996, Col. 2405.
15 *Dáil debates* vol. 467, 2 July 1996, Col. 2379.
16 Editorial, *Bar Review*, July 1996 at p.5.
17 *Bail Act 1997.*
18 Section 7, *Criminal Justice (Drug Trafficking) Act 1996.*
19 *Proceeds of Crime Act 1996.*
20 *Op cit.* p.78.
21 See '500 Gardai drafted for the crime war' *Irish Independent*, 2 July 1996, p.1.
22 *Courts Act 1996.*
23 *Disclosure of Certain Information for Taxation and Other Purposes Act 1996.*
24 *Sixteenth Amendment of the Constitution Act 1996.*
25 The fact that some of the 'serious offences' in the schedule of the Act may in reality be quite minor was even acknowledged by the then Minister for Justice, Nora Owen. See Vol. 477 *Dáil debates* Col. 1425.
26 The Labour Party had hitherto indicated that they were firmly opposed to a referendum on bail and the possibility of preventative detention for those suspected of committing serious offences while awaiting trial. Indeed, Labour's opposition had been widely viewed as the main reason for the Government's vacillation on bail reform, which had been under consideration since 1995. The political cost of such principles was obviously seen as too high, however, in the atmosphere of heightened concern, and the party was forced to stage a major U-turn on the issue. The party issued a statement the day following the killing urging the Government to bring forward its proposals on the reform of the bail laws. See *Irish Times*, 29 June 1996, p.6.
27 *Irish Times*, 28 June 1996, p.1.
28 *People (AG) v. O'Callaghan* [1966] IR 501.
29 *Ryan v. DPP* [1989] IR 399.
30 No mention is made of the *O'Callaghan* guidelines in the Act, so it must be assumed that they continue to apply alongside the new s.2. Indeed, the constitutional guidelines set out therein will continue to provide the test for bail in other non-serious cases.
31 P. O'Mahony, 'The Proposed Constitutional Referendum on Bail: An Unholy Grail?' [1995] *ILT* 234 p.237.
32 [1966] IR 501 at 513.
33 *Ibid.* at 517.
34 *Ibid.* at 508–9. Emphasis added.
35 O'Mahony has highlighted the criticisms of Ashworth in this regard. (P. O'Mahony *op. cit.* pp.237–8); and O'Malley has noted the observations of Professor Daniel Freed, a leading expert on bail, in the context of a

conference to discuss the earlier American legal position on bail, which then corresponded largely to our pre-1997 position. As O'Malley notes:

> [The Professor] put it to the conference that irrespective of whether the reason for refusing bail was the prevention of flight or the prevention of injury to persons or property, it still amounted to (a) a prediction of the defendant's conduct on the basis of past conduct; (b) a prediction that, if released, the defendant will do something illegal i.e. jump bail or do some other unlawful act; and (c) detention of a man who is presumed innocent of the present charge against him. He maintained that both purposes of restraint could be regarded as equally violative of the due process clause in that they both deprive a man of his liberty by imposing a prior restraint to guard against future misconduct.

See T. O'Malley 'Bail and Predictions of Dangerousness' [1989] *ILT* 41 p.43.

36 [1966] IR 501 at 513.

37 For a discussion on the problems posed by remands before trial, see A. Ashworth *The Criminal Process*, (2nd Edition, London: Oxford University Press, 1998), Chapter 7.

38 L.H. Tribe 'An Ounce of Detention: Preventive Justice in the World of John Mitchell' (1970) 56 *Virginia Law Review* 371 p.404 as cited in O'Malley, *op. cit.*

39 [1989] IR 399.

40 *Ibid.* at 407.

41 *Ibid.*

42 481 US 739 (1987).

43 *Ibid.* at 763.

44 *Ibid.* at 764.

45 P. O'Mahony *Criminal Chaos: Seven Crises in Irish Criminal Justice* (Dublin: Round Hall Sweet & Maxwell, Dublin, 1996) p.18.

46 P. O'Mahony 'The Constitution and Criminal Justice' in P. O'Mahony (ed.) *Criminal Justice in Ireland*, (Dublin: IPA, 2002).

47 See M.P. O'Higgins, 'Bail – A Privilege or a Right?' (1998) *Bar Review* 318 p.319 and also J. Liston 'Bail Act, 1997' (1997) *Irish Current Law Statutes Annotated 1997*, para. 16-01–16-08.

48 *Ibid.*

49 For a development of the arguments raised against the Bill, see M. Farrell 'The Criminal Justice (Drug Trafficking) Bill 1996 – the Seven Day Detention Bill', Irish Council for Civil Liberties, Briefing Paper No.2.

50 It is noteworthy that Ashworth (*The Criminal Process*, *op. cit.* p.101) observes that similar arguments based on the 'professional criminals' claim (the argument that the right to silence is abused by professional criminals) were also used to aid the passage of the English *Criminal Justice Public Order Act 1994*, (which seriously eroded the right to silence in English law), despite these arguments having been considered and emphatically rejected by the Royal Commission on Criminal Justice.

See *Report of the Royal Commission on Criminal Justice* (London: HMSO, 1993 (Cmnd, 2263)).

51 Section 1, *Criminal Justice (Drug Trafficking) Act 1996*.

52 Section 15, *Misuse of Drugs Act 1977*.

53 [2001] 33 EHRR 264.

54 [2000] 31 EHRR 1.

55 *Op. cit.*

56 [2000] 31 EHRR 1, paragraph 60. Emphasis added.

57 A. Ashworth, *op. cit.*, p.108: 'The submission here, then, is that section 34 of the 1994 Act probably does breach 6.1 of the ECHR, and that... where the police had failed to give the legal adviser sufficient information on the case against the accused, and English court (applying the ECHR, once the Human Rights Bill is in place) ought not to permit adverse inferences and ought to hold that section 34 is incompatible with the ECHR.'

58 Unreported, Supreme Court, 23 February 1999.

59 The Bill was introduced into Parliament on 2 July, and it went immediately to Committee stage, where it was subsequently amended. It was passed by the Dáil at the special one-day debate on organized crime on 25 July, and was passed by the Seanad the following day. The Bill was promulgated by the President on 4 August 1996. The entire legislative process therefore only spanned a five-week period, and this was achieved *despite* the fact that for much of this time, the two Houses of the Oireachtas were out of session.

60 The *Criminal Assets Bureau Bill* was not passed at the special Dáil debate on 25 July, but was referred to Select Committee. It was, however, set up on an *ad hoc* basis on 1 August 1996 and was finally established under statute on 15 October 1996.

61 For an in-depth overview of the Act, see J. Meade 'The Proceeds of Crime Act, 1996: An Overview' 4 (1998) *ILT* 52.

62 [1998] 3 IR 185.

63 John Gilligan has also brought various challenges to the confiscation of his assets under the *Criminal Justice Act 1994* and in these proceedings he has met with more success. On 21 December 2005, the Supreme Court upheld the earlier finding of the High Court (McCracken J., 8 November 2002) that the Special Criminal Court had no jurisdiction to make an order for the confiscation for assets under s.4 of the 1994 Act.

64 Unreported, High Court, O'Higgins J., 4 June 1999.

65 *Murphy. v. GM, PB, PC Ltd, GH, Gilligan v. CAB* Unreported, Supreme Court, 18 October 2001.

66 J. Meade 'The Disguise of Civility: Civil Forfeiture of the Proceeds of Crime and the Presumption of Innocence in Irish Law' (2000) *Hibernian Law Journal* 1.

67 *Ibid.*, p.20.

68 [1962] IR 1.

69 J.P. McCutcheon and D. Walsh, (1999) 9 *ICLJ* 127.

70 *Ibid.* p.131.

71 [1998] 3 IR 185 at 217.

72 *Murphy v GM, PB. PC Ltd, G.H. Gilligan v CAB*. Unreported, Supreme Court, 18 October 2001, para. 124.

73 J. Meade (2000) *op. cit.*

74 *Austin v. Texas* 509 US 602 and *US v. James Daniel Good Real Property* 114 S. Ct. 492 in which the US Supreme Court held that forfeitures of property must comply with procedural due process requirements with regard to notice and an opportunity to be heard before property is seized.

75 *Ibid.*

76 M. Cheh 'Can something this easy, quick and profitable also be fair? Runaway Civil Forfeiture stumbles on the Constitution' (1994) 39 *New York School Law Review* 1.

77 *Ibid.* p. 20.

78 J. Meade, (2000) *op. cit.*.

79 *Dáil debates* vol. 467, 2 July 1996, Col. 1737 *et seq.*

80 P. O'Mahony 'Ward judgment gives rise to concerns on Garda behaviour' *Irish Times* 3 December 1998.

81 *People v. Gilligan* Unreported, Court of Criminal Appeal, 12 November 2003 (McCracken, Quirke and Peart J.J.). The Court of Criminal Appeal found that, in sentencing Gilligan for the drugs offences, the Special Criminal Court had 'overstepped the line between considering surrounding circumstances and in effect sentencing for criminal activities of which the applicant had not been convicted'. Gilligan's appeal against conviction was rejected by the Court of Criminal Appeal on 8 August 2002. An appeal to the Supreme Court on points of law of exceptional public importance (relating mainly to the Witness Protection Programme) was also unsuccessful (23 November 2003).

82 *People v. Ward*, Unreported, Special Criminal Court, 27 November 1998.

83 *People v. Ward* Unreported, Court of Criminal Appeal, 22 March 2002 (Murphy, Ó Caoimh and McKechnie J.J.). The court said that it was 'questionable whether one could be confident of eliminating all factors which would motivate and encourage liars, such as Mr Bowden, so as to justify a belief beyond all reasonable doubt in any evidence given by him'. The evidence did not support the conclusion that Ward was involved in the murder.

84 *Ibid.* p.13.

85 See further P. O'Mahony 'The Psychology of Police Interrogation: The Kerry Babies Case' in P. O'Mahony (ed.) *Criminal Justice in Ireland* (IPA, 2002) p.520.

86 *R v. Perry* (1982) 150 CLR 580.

87 A. Ashworth 'Is the Criminal Law a Lost Cause?' (2000) 116 *LQR* 225.

Chapter Six

Police Powers

It will be recalled that, in line with the jurisprudence of the European Court of Human Rights and the Irish Supreme Court, it is proposed to place a broad interpretation on the presumption of innocence throughout this book. From this ontological standpoint, the presumption applies equally to the pre-trial stages of a criminal prosecution as at the trial and imposes limitations on powers exercised by the police in their investigation of offences. Indeed, it is arguable that the following rights flow from the presumption:

- Detention should be within reasonable limits and justified by substantial objective evidence against an individual;
- Suspects should not be required to give evidence of innocence or to answer the case for the prosecution;
- The police should not be able to require suspects to answer questions;
- Police methods of extracting confessions should be viewed sceptically;[1] and
- In line with Packer's[2] analysis of the presumption, 'qualifying and disabling doctrines', such as evidentiary exclusionary rules, should be applied.

Taking the above as a guide, the purpose of this chapter is to assess the impact on the presumption of the major criminal justice statutes in Irish law enhancing the powers of the police. In this jurisdiction, significant advances in the powers of An Garda Síochána can be traced back to the *Criminal Justice Act*

1984 which, in the words of one leading commentator, 'effected a fundamental re-alignment in our criminal justice system by introducing for the first time a general police power to detain suspects for investigation and by imposing restrictions on the individual's centuries-old right to silence, among other things.'[3] Since 1984, there has been considerable legislative activity augmenting police powers of arrest, detention, interrogation, search and seizure, stop and question and stop and search,[4] particularly, as has been seen in the previous chapter in the period following the murder of journalist Veronica Guerin. With the possible exception of the anti-crime package of 1996, however, a series of reforms on a scale commensurate with those effected in the 1984 Act have not been seen in this jurisdiction until the enactment of the most recent *Criminal Justice Act*. Given its potential, therefore, for 'completing a crime control model of criminal justice'[5] in Irish law, its provisions provide an important focus for the current chapter.

(I) CRIMINAL JUSTICE ACT 1984

Although most people today take the power of detention for granted, it should be remembered that prior to the enactment of the *Criminal Justice Act 1984* members of An Garda Síochána enjoyed no general power of arrest and detention for the purpose of interrogation. At common law, the view taken as to the purpose of an arrest was that it was a process to secure the attendance of the suspect in court to answer a charge. It was not permitted 'for the purpose of interrogation or the securing of evidence from that person'.[6] The only exception to this common law rule was the power of arrest and detention in respect of subversive offences under the *Offences Against the State Act 1939*. Section 30 of this Act permitted detention for a period of 24 hours, which period could be extended for a further 24 hours at the direction of a Chief Superintendent or superior officer.[7] The provisions of the Act had a clear interrogative purpose. Indeed, the section expressly provided for the release of suspects without charge.[8] This inevitably resulted in the use by the police of the s.30 detention provision to detain individuals suspected of ordinary crime, a dubious practice which was curiously upheld by the Supreme Court.[9]

The impetus for change was provided by the speech of former Garda Commissioner, Patrick McLaughlin, who criticized the law governing arrest and detention and suggested a power of detention of between six and twenty-four hours.[10] Section 4 of the 1984 Act in fact authorized detention for six hours, with provision for extension of that period on the authorization of a member of An Garda Síochána of the rank of Superintendant or above. The Act also introduced for the first time into the ordinary criminal law penalties for remaining silent in response to police interrogation. Section 18 of the Act permits inferences to be drawn from an individual's failure or refusal to account for objects, marks or substances in their possession or on their person. Similarly, section 19 refers to a failure to account for one's presence at a place at or about the time when a crime had been committed and allows inferences to be drawn from this failure. As has been discussed in Chapter Three, the constitutionality of these sections was upheld by the Supreme Court in *Rock v. Ireland*,[11] which took the view that the presumption was not affected by the changes. It is noteworthy that, despite these incursions on the right to silence, the Act, unlike its English counterpart, the *Police and Criminal Evidence Act 1984*, did not introduce the important safeguard of legal representation during interrogation.

(II) CRIMINAL JUSTICE ACT 2006

(a) Background to the Act

The latest Criminal Justice Act contains a plethora of reforms on disparate elements of the criminal justice system which have given rise to considerable criticism in civil libertarian quarters.[12] It is undoubtedly one of the most extensive pieces of legislation dealing with criminal and judicial matters in recent years and is a clear response by the Government to rising crime rates, in particular deaths from organized crime.[13] Introducing the Bill to the Dáil, Minister McDowell adopted the, by now familiar, language of 'balance':

> Time and time again one hears repeated voicing of disquiet that the rights of society to be protected take second place

> in the quest to ensure fairness to the suspect – *in other words that the balance has shifted too far in favour of the accused.* I believe this is a legitimate concern which must be addressed and I am doing so in this Bill...[14]

The Minister was clearly of the opinion that the dramatic reforms initiated since the enactment of the *Criminal Justice Act 1984* (discussed in Chapters Four and Five above) had had little or no impact on the orientation of the criminal justice system and state-accused relations. Moreover, the language employed suggests that criminal justice is a 'zero-sum game' and places the rights of 'society' in direct opposition to the rights of accused persons with no recognition that society has a considerable interest in observing the rights of suspects as well as pursuing prosecutions. This is misleading as it suggests that one of the main ways to reduce crime is to cede the rights of accused persons. Indeed, the dubious gains to be made in ceding same are obscured by the language of balance.

Among other provisions, the Act bestows a power on the Gardaí to issue search warrants to themselves without the important safeguard of judicial supervision[15] and to admit witness statements in evidence without allowing the accused person the right to cross-examine, a clear breach of the hearsay rule.[16] In addition, the Minister introduced a number of significant amendments to the Bill after it was initiated. The amendments treated *inter alia*, the following issues:

- A provision to deal with participation in organized criminal gangs;
- Provisions to strengthen the existing sentencing provisions for drug trafficking and firearms offences;
- New offences of supplying drugs to prisoners;
- Provisions in relation to a Drug Offenders Register;
- Provisions to allow for the electronic tagging of offenders; and
- New provisions to deal with anti-social behaviour.

These amendments have changed the original Bill beyond recognition, extending its scope from the extension of Garda powers to matters as disparate as organized crime, sentencing and anti-social behaviour. Serious concerns must be expressed about the way in which important changes to the Bill were made *after* its introduction to the Oireachtas. This procedure is not conducive to a full debate on the weighty issues outlined above and represents a clear departure from standard legislative processes. However, given the specific concern of this book with the presumption of innocence, it is proposed to examine here only the following measures:

- the detention provisions of the Act;
- the proposals in relation to the reclassification of saliva as a non-intimate sample;
- the provisions allowing a prosecution appeal in certain circumstances; and
- the provisions on behaviour orders.

(b) Detention

Given that individuals charged with criminal offences enjoy a presumption of innocence, it is arguable that detention should be confined to those periods which are strictly necessary for the investigation of offences. Indeed, as the Human Rights Commission have noted. 'Prolonged periods of pre-trial detention... ha[ve] the potential to detrimentally affect other fundamental human rights including the right to be presumed innocent until proven guilty, the right to silence and the privilege against self incrimination'.[17] Section 8 of the *Criminal Justice Act* doubles the maximum period during which a person suspected of having committed an arrestable offence can be detained from 12 hours to 24 hours. As occured under the previous legislative regime, investigations will be suspended between midnight and 8am, subject to the consent of the suspect, and this rest time will therefore not be included in calculating the detention period. When allowance is made for these rest periods, the reality for a suspect, therefore, may be detention for up to forty hours in a Garda station.

This provision constitutes an extraordinary quantum leap in the period of time for which a person can be detained without charge in respect of ordinary criminal offences. A vital point in relation to this reform is the inadequacy of the existing safeguards in place to protect the suspect and to guard against miscarriages of justice. The most obvious protection for a detainee in the isolation of Garda custody is access to legal advice. Under the existing law, a suspect has a constitutional right to reasonable access to a legal advisor and to consult with them privately[18] but unlike detainees in England this does not extend to a solicitor being present during interview.[19] The presence of a solicitor during interviews, moreover, was recognized as long ago as 1978 by the O'Brian Committee[20] as 'essential', and was only eschewed by the Martin Committee[21] in the light of the new provisions as to audio-visual recording. This is particularly important in a situation where adverse inferences may be drawn from the failure to mention certain facts, which, as discussed in Chapter Three, is the case under sections 18 and 19 of the *Criminal Justice Act 1984*.

Another problem relates to the issue of recording of interviews, which has yet to be satisfactorily resolved. Regulations providing for the recording of interviews have been introduced into law in 1997.[22] These contain important loopholes, however, which deprive them of much of their effect. For example, recording is only mandatory in stations in which the appropriate equipment has already been installed[23] and, even then, there is a saver to the effect that recording does not have to take place where it is not practicable to do so.[24] It is now over twenty years since the passage of the 1984 Act, and recording of statements is not yet standard practice, despite many Garda stations having installed the necessary electronic equipment. This is despite the strong recommendations of the Martin Committee that 'as a safeguard towards insuring that inculpatory admissions to the Garda Síochána are properly obtained and recorded . . . the questioning of suspects take place before an audio-visual recording device'.[25]

The main objection to the proposed extension of the existing detention period, however, is that a case has not been made out for it. Persons whose guilt has not been proved to a standard beyond a reasonable doubt are entitled to their liberty save where empirically justified. No independent research has been commissioned by the Minister for Justice into the need for such a measure. Rather the proposal has as its genesis the Garda Strategic Management Initiative (SMI) Report[26] and the subsequent Report of the Expert Group appointed to consider the SMI recommendations,[27] which both found that the available period of detention is inadequate for the proper investigation of serious crimes such as rape and murder and for complex offences such as fraud.

Assuming a case has been made (despite the absence of *independent* evidence to that effect) for an increased detention period in respect of such offences, it does not follow, as argued by the Human Rights Commission, that this should apply to *all* arrestable offences. The proposal represents a significant incursion on the liberty of those presumed to be innocent, and its provisions should therefore only apply to those charged with offences involving a substantial threat to personal security or property. By extending s.8 to all arrestable offences, defined as offences which attract a penalty of five years or more, even relatively minor offences are brought within its ambit, such as petty thefts or less serious assault charges. This argument is supported by research in England where, until recently, the police could extend detention without charge up to thirty-six hours in respect of serious arrestable offences.[28] Home Office research conducted in 2000[29] showed considerable disparity between the average detention periods for minor and moderately serious offences (at four and seven hours respectively) and serious offences such as murder and rape (twenty-two hours). Overall, the average time for which people were held without charge was six hours and forty minutes and prolonged detention (over eighteen hours) was rare.

(c) Prosecution Appeals

Section 21 of the Act makes a number of changes to the existing law in respect of prosecution appeals. The avenues for such appeals have traditionally been limited owing to the common law rule against double jeopardy which provides that no one should be tried twice for the same offence. The provisions in respect of cases tried on indictment are contained in s.34 of the *Criminal Procedure Act 1967* which provides for a prosecution right of appeal to the Supreme Court on a point of law arising from a judge-directed acquittal. This is a 'without prejudice' appeal, however, which can't interfere with the decision to acquit the accused and the consequences of the appeal are strictly limited to the point of law at issue in the direction.

The changes introduced by s.21 have broadened the scope of the appeal under s.34, although it remains without prejudice to the acquittal of the accused on a point of law only. First of all, the procedure may now apply where there has been an acquittal by the Special Criminal Court, not simply an acquittal by a jury. The second, more significant change, is that the appeal can now be taken against any acquittal, not simply an acquittal arising by virtue of a direction by the trial judge.

The justification offered by the Minister for the new provisions is that some channel needed to be created so that rulings unfavourable to the prosecution of crime can be appealed, particularly in light of legal issues which may arise during criminal trials subsequent upon the incorporation of the European Convention on Human Rights. The provisions raise concerns, however, as to the impact of such an appeal on the presumed innocence of an acquitted party. While the defendant is at no risk of conviction and the presumption of innocence will remain intact in a formal sense that does not dispose of the issue. It must be acknowledged that a successful prosecution appeal detracts from the 'moral force' of an acquittal and has the potential to undermine the good name of the individual in question. As noted by the Irish Human Rights Commission: 'Where the appellate court overrules the legal basis for their acquittal this could create the public perception that their acquittal was hollow, and based on a mere technicality. The acquitted person does not have a further avenue to clear their good name.'[30] Indeed, the Commission questions the compatibility of s.21 with the Convention, in light of authority that the presumption of innocence contained in Article 6(2) extends to any proceedings relating to the accused's guilt or innocence. In the case of *Hammern v. Norway*,[31] for example, the European Court found that compensation proceedings for pre-trial detention prior to the applicant's acquittal were sufficiently related to the criminal charge to attract the protection of Article 6(2). In holding that the applicant was entitled to compensation in respect of the detention, the Court reiterated that Article 6(2) embodied a general rule that following a final acquittal even the voicing of suspicions regarding an accused's innocence was no longer admissible.

The section does contain certain safeguards for the protection of the acquitted person. Section 21(3), for example, provides that the Supreme Court can hear argument by counsel on behalf of the acquitted person or by that person if the court agrees. If the accused person does not wish to be represented, the Supreme Court is required to assign counsel to argue in support of the decision and, indeed, the Supreme Court may assign counsel to argue in support of the decision even if the accused is represented. In this regard, there are provisions within the section for free legal aid for the acquitted person if it appears that the person's means are insufficient to obtain legal aid. An important protection is also contained in s.21(5) which provides that the identity of the acquitted person should not be disclosed unless that person agrees otherwise.

It has been argued, in light of these safeguards, and the 'without prejudice' nature of the appeal that 'the changes invoked... are not particularly troubling from a human rights perspective'[32] and it is certainly true that the provisions fall far short of the more far-reaching prosecution appeal model recommended by the Law Reform Commission,[33] amongst other bodies. However, consideration of the traditional arguments underpinning the rule against double jeopardy reveals that they may still have application, even in this limited context. Choo[34] lists them as follows:

> To put a person in double jeopardy may increase the chances of his or her being convicted even though innocent and will also undermine the moral integrity of the criminal process. The accused may, as a result of having revealed his complete defence at the first trial be at a greater disadvantage at the second trial, and thus less able to defend him or herself effectively. *Irrespective of this*, it is in any event morally objectionable to subject someone to the embarrassment, expense and anxiety of a second prosecution, with the possibility that a verdict might be returned which is inconsistent with that reached the first time.

While it is clear that objections concerning the danger of convicting the innocent or the prosecution's attempt to mend their hand on a second attempt cannot be raised, there remains the strong likelihood that an appeal by the prosecution to the Supreme Court will expose the accused to further 'embarrassment, expense and anxiety' considering the potential of the outcome to undermine the moral authority of their acquittal. If an accused opts to be legally represented in the Supreme Court, and given the natural inclination to clear one's name it is likely that they will, the possibility that they may be ineligible for legal aid must be considered. Without legal aid, it is improbable that a person of ordinary means, yet not indigent, could afford the cost of legal representation in lengthy proceedings in the Supreme Court. The mental strain caused by the proceedings must also be considered. Further, it must be questioned whether the prospect of maintaining the accused's anonymity is a realistic one, particularly in high profile cases.

(d) DNA and Bodily Samples

Section 14 of the Act extends the powers of the Gardaí to take DNA samples from suspects. These increased powers allowing members of the Gardaí to have increased access to bodily samples are with a clear view to the establishment of a DNA database. Indeed, in the Minister's presentation of the Bill to the Dáil, he indicated that it was his intention 'to draw up proposals for that purpose which would, having regard to constitutional requirements and the requirements of the European Convention on Human Rights, permit as extensive a database as possible'.[35] The section amends s.2 of the *Criminal Justice (Forensic Evidence) Act 1990* in the following ways:

- it reclassifies saliva and mouth swabs as a non-intimate bodily sample;
- it clarifies that a sample of hair, other than pubic hair, may be taken by cutting or individually plucking hairs by their roots, provided that the amount of hair plucked is reasonably considered necessary to constitute a sufficient sample;[36]
- it increases the penalty where a person obstructs a garda in

seeking to obtain a non-intimate sample from £1,000 to €3,000; and
- it increases the period of time for which the sample may be retained by the Gardaí in the event that proceedings are not instituted.

Of these changes the first is clearly the most significant. Under the existing regime consent is required for intimate samples such as blood, pubic hair and urine, while for non-intimate samples consent is not required if a member of An Garda Síochána not below the rank of Superintendent authorizes the taking of the sample on a reasonable belief that the person from whom the sample is being taken has committed the crime under investigation and the sample will confirm or disprove the involvement of that person. The proposal to bring saliva within the category of samples which may be taken without consent raises issues in relation to the right to privacy, the right to bodily integrity[37] and also the privilege against self-incrimination. Given that the privilege, as discussed in Chapter Three, is closely allied to the presumption, some consideration is given here to the question of whether compulsorily obtaining a DNA profile from a suspect constitutes an infringement.

At first blush, the authorities on this issue would suggest a negative response to the question. The Law Reform Commission in their *Consultation Paper on the Establishment of a DNA Database*[38] cite English,[39] American[40] and European authority[41] to the effect that the taking of bodily samples does not breach the privilege against self-incrimination. In all these decisions the various courts drew a distinction between oral or testimonial evidence and real or physical evidence. In *Saunders v. UK*,[42] for example, the European Court of Human Rights stated that the right not to incriminate oneself is primarily concerned with respecting the will of the accused person to remain silent. The Court drew a distinction between the right of the accused person to remain silent, and the use in criminal proceedings of material which might be obtained from the accused through the use of compulsory powers, but which has an existence independent of the will of the suspect, such as documents acquired pursuant to a warrant, breath, blood and urine samples, and bodily tissue for the purpose of DNA testing. In the opinion of the Court the right not to incriminate oneself does not extend to the use in criminal proceedings of these materials as is commonly understood within the legal systems of the State Parties to the ECHR and elsewhere.

As argued in Chapter Three, this distinction may be a necessary one in policy terms and there can be little doubt that in many cases of compelled testing of bodily features that the public interest in obtaining the evidence will outweigh the sacrifice of rights made by the accused. However, this does not detract from the argument that the distinction drawn by the courts may be artificial and fails to recognize grey areas such as body language and physical features revealing a person's lifestyle or occupation. Further, it is clear that the effect of refusing a sample has a similar effect to remaining silent in that attention is focused on the defence and their reasons for non-compliance rather than on the strength of the prosecution's case. The existence of forensic or DNA evidence may also act as a disincentive for the police to search for other independent evidence. Assuming the privilege applies to the new provisions, it is questionable whether the inclusion of the mouth was necessary if DNA can be extracted from hair without consent. As with the detention provisions, the Minister has failed to justify his decision to resort to the compulsory taking of mouth swabs, a decision moreover which raises human rights concerns as force may be necessary in the event of non-co-operation.

Before leaving this topic, a cautionary note should be sounded in relation to two aspects of DNA profiling in light of the Minister's declared intention to provide for a DNA databank. First, it should be remembered that, although DNA evidence can produce extremely accurate results, like speech it is subject to problems of interpretation and human error. These include accidental contamination in the process of collection, mistakes in the labelling and recording of samples as well as the way in which the comparison is made to the rest of the population. In the latter regard, Easton[43] cites a German case where a conviction was overturned because the DNA evidence collected from the accused was compared with a random sample of German citizens, rather than a sample of Serbians, the defendant's own nationality. The court felt that the genetic make-up of the German population could differ to that of the

Serbian population. Given that defence solicitors and barristers do not have the necessary expertise to analyse such subtleties in the evidence, it is crucial that defence legal teams are granted access to laboratories and experts in DNA evidence and that this is adequately funded through legal aid. It will be recalled that misinterpretation or inaccuracies in the forensic evidence, although not DNA evidence, was a critical factor in the spate of British miscarriages of justice of the late 1980s and 1990s.[44]

Secondly, caution must be exercised in relation to a technique known as DNA request surveillance which is difficult to reconcile with the privilege against self-incrimination. This can be described as a tactic whereby the authorities may rely on the reaction of a suspect to a request for a DNA sample to support an inference that he or she is guilty of the offence in question. As noted by the Law Reform Commission,[45] this particular method differs from compulsory DNA surveillance (coercively gathering genetic material from a person for potential use in incriminating the person) as 'there is no real choice here. This is different to a case where a suspect is compelled to submit a sample as the recipient of this coercive request is not revealing anything by his or her reluctance to give a sample'. In this regard, it has been convincingly argued by Gans[46] that 'the potential for DNA request surveillance to breach the privilege against self-incrimination in unprecedented ways is clearest in its unique ability to prompt self-incrimination by non-suspects'.

(e) Civil Orders

In addition to increased police powers, the Minister for Justice has made provision in the 2006 Act for 'civil orders' which are in fact first cousins to the English Anti Social Behaviour Order (ASBO). A 'civil order' is an order made by the court to protect the public from anti social behaviour, defined in the English legislation as 'harassment, alarm or distress' but given a slightly narrower definition in the Irish Criminal Justice Act: [behaviour] in a manner that caused or, in all the circumstances, was likely to cause to one or more persons not of the same household:

(a) harrassment
(b) significant or persistent alarm, distress, fear or

(c) significant or persistent impairment of their use or enjoyment of their property.

As with so many other criminal justice 'innovations' in this jurisdiction, it is a concept borrowed from our English neighbours, transplanted wholesale into Ireland without any thought to the very different cultural factors obtaining. As O'Mahony[47] has noted recently:

> We are, most significantly, a very small nation with just one large city; with a very different demographic mix to Britain and with a different education system, a generally weaker welfare state and an improving but far less developed infrastructure. Reflecting these and other differences our crime problem is distinctive and less severe and requires a culturally specific approach.

Although the order is civil in nature, its breach does not invoke the normal contempt of court procedure for breach of a civil order, but in fact constitutes a criminal offence punishable by a maximum penalty of five years' imprisonment. ASBOs were first introduced in England in 1999 in the *Crime and Disorder Act 1998* and were adopted by New Labour as a deliberate policy choice to 'mix the best of the criminal and the civil law'[48] in order to more effectively target anti-social behaviour perpetrated primarily by young people and groups of young people. One of the main benefits of this hybrid structure (which has been described as 'sailing as close to the wind as possible')[49] was that the civil rules of evidence and procedure applied so that hearsay evidence from frightened and intimidated people within the community could be adduced in court, without such persons giving direct evidence. Another benefit clearly intended by New Labour was the assessment of evidence according to the civil standard of proof, that is, on the balance of probabilities, thereby circumventing the presumption of innocence and the beyond a reasonable doubt standard. Given that a similar structure has been adopted by the Minister in the 2006 Act, hard questions must be asked concerning whether the procedure is being used as a means of subverting the strictures of the criminal law, including the presumption of innocence.

The issue is far from a mere academic quibble. It is salutary to note that while concerns in England originally centred around 'net widening' and the use of imprisonment for minor, non-criminal behaviour, six years of practice has shown that the orders are primarily being used for acts which already fall within the statutory definition of criminal behaviour, such as burglary, criminal damage, theft and various forms of threatening and abusive behaviour.[50] The argument becomes even more compelling when it is considered that defendants without the benefit of the presumption of innocence in civil order proceedings can face penalties of up to six months imprisonment.

This question was considered recently by the House of Lords in *R (on the application of McCann) v. Manchester Crown Court*[51] who rejected the contention that ASBO proceedings were, 'in reality and in substance',[52] criminal, albeit with the concession that the criminal standard of proof should apply. The four issues which fell to be considered by their Lordships were:

- whether as a matter of domestic classification proceedings leading to the making of an anti social behaviour order were criminal in nature;
- whether under Article 6 of the ECHR such proceedings involved a 'criminal charge';
- whether under s.1 of the Act hearsay evidence was admissible in proceedings seeking such an order; and
- what the standard of proof was in such proceedings.[53]

The Court held that the proceedings under the *Crime and Disorder Act* were civil, not criminal, both for the purposes of domestic and Convention law. This conclusion was based on various factors: proceedings were not brought by the Crown Prosecution Service; there was no formal accusation of a breach of the criminal law; ASBOs did not appear on criminal records; and there is no immediate imposition of imprisonment. In this latter regard, the House held that proceedings for breach of an order, though undoubtedly criminal in character, should be considered separately from the initial application. As Lord Steyn noted: 'These are separate and independent procedures.

The making of the order will presumably sometimes serve its purposes and there will be no proceedings for breach. It is in principle necessary to consider the two stages separately.'[54] Perhaps most significantly, however, for the purposes of determining compatibility with the Convention, the Law Lords held that ASBOs, unlike ordinary criminal penalties, are designed to *prevent* anti-social behaviour rather than to *punish* the offender. Lord Steyn held that 'the true purpose of the proceedings is preventative ... It follows that the making of an anti-social behaviour order is not a conviction or condemnation that the person is guilty of an offence. It results in no penalty whatsoever.'[55] Lord Hope was similarly of the view that 'an anti-social behaviour order may well restrict the freedom of the defendant to do as he wants and to go where he pleases. But these restrictions are imposed for preventative reasons, not as punishment'.[56]

In light of the above classification of the proceedings as civil, it was held that hearsay evidence was admissible pursuant to the *Civil Evidence Act 1995*. In the Law Lords' estimation, the admission of such evidence is critical if magistrates were to be adequately informed of the scale of anti-social behaviour and the measures of control required. Indeed, as Lord Hutton noted, this has been key to their effectiveness:

> [T]he courts have held that proceedings under section 1 [of the *Crime and Disorder Act 1998*] are civil proceedings and not criminal proceedings. Therefore it has not been necessary for those who allege that they have suffered as a result of anti-social behaviour on the part of the defendant to go into the witness box to give evidence against him, because hearsay evidence can be given of their complaints and allegations pursuant to section 1 of the *Civil Evidence Act 1995*.[57]

In relation to the standard of proof, it is an interesting feature of the judgment that the Court held that it is the criminal standard which applies in ASBO proceedings. This standard should be met, in the interests of fairness, when the allegations of criminal or quasi-criminal behaviour were made owing to the 'seriousness of matters involved'.[58]

A superficial reading of the legislation supports the Law Lords' conclusion. As Tausz[59] notes, sections 1–9 of the 1998 Act 'contain... many clear pointers to civil proceedings... The application must be made by complaint, which is a civil process; it may not be made by the usual prosecuting authority or a member of the public; and a successful application does not have any of the types of outcome that normally follow criminal proceedings'. It is submitted, however, that many of the above elements, such as the absence of a formal charge and criminal record, focus on form rather than substance and as such should not have influenced the decision of the Lords. Moreover, on closer examination, it is clear that the original application for an ASBO cannot be so conveniently separated from its criminal counterpart in the event of a contravention of the order.

One of the main reasons for this, as cogently argued by McDonald,[60] is that findings of fact from the initial application may have a bearing on the sentence which will be ultimately imposed. A person sentenced for breach of an ASBO will be punished, not just for one act of defiance of the order, but for the previous anti-social acts committed by that person which led to the imposition of the order. Thus, to give McDonald's example, a 'Rowdy Roger' who insists on playing his heavy metal music late at night and who is subsequently made the subject of an ASBO will be punished, in the event of his breach, not just for one night of loud music in defiance of the order but for the effect of all the preceding nights of loud music. McDonald supports his argument with comments made by Labour spokesperson, Alun Michael, in the Commons Standing Committee on the 1998 Bill. Mr Michael was asked to explain the maximum five year term of imprisonment for breach of an ASBO in light of the fact that the maximum sentence for affray is only three years under the *Public Order Act 1986*. He explained that affray 'involves one incident' whereas breach of an ASBO involves 'a pattern of behaviour that is damaging people's lives over a considerable period of time'.[61] The fact that the behaviour proven at the initial hearing contributes towards the criminal penalty finally imposed would clearly suggest that a global approach should be taken to the issue of the characterization of the proceedings and would suggest that they do have a punitive element.

Other commentators have taken issue with the narrow focus of the House of Lords in *McCann* on the purpose of the proceedings under the 1998 Act. Bakalis[62] notes that 'the House of Lords, was...rather selective in the parts of the Strasbourg judgment it chose to apply' through its excessive focus on the preventative/punitive distinction. She cites two decisions of the European Court of Human Rights, *Ozturk v. Germany*[63] and *Lauko v. Slovakia*,[64] which place an equal emphasis on factors such as the existence of a deterrent element, whether the offences were aimed at the world at large, and whether the aim of the proceedings was to stop any interference with the world at large. In a similar vein, Ashworth[65] has questioned the approach of the English courts to the issue and has drawn attention to the robust case law developed by the European Court in this area. The Court has held on several occasions that, in order to prevent subversion of the procedural safeguards guaranteed in the fair trial provisions of Article 6 of the Convention, the term 'charged with a criminal offence' should be given an autonomous meaning which looks to the substance rather than the form. This is known as the anti-subversion doctrine and exists to prevent states simply reclassifying criminal proceedings as civil in order to avoid the protections attaching to defendants in criminal proceedings.[66] In light of this approach, it is to be expected, as Ashworth notes, that the Strasbourg Court will subject the new ASBO hybrid to much closer scrutiny than that undertaken by the House of Lords.[67]

Interestingly, Ashworth also contrasts the approach of the House of Lords in *McCann* with the leading case of *Welch v. UK*.[68] In *Welch* a confiscation order imposed upon the applicant subsequent to his conviction for drug trafficking offences[69] was successfully challenged on the basis that it amounted to the application of a retrospective criminal penalty under Article 7 of the Convention. The significance of the decision in the current context is its designation of the confiscation order as a 'penalty'. The Government's submission related solely to the aims of the Act, which were partly confiscatory and partly preventative. The Court, however, relied on a number of elements of the order in reaching its decision, such as the power of the Court to take into account the defendant's culpability when fixing the amount of order; the wide ranging statutory assumptions about the origins of the money and the provision for imprisonment in default. As Ashworth notes, applying the principles adumbrated in *Welch* to the 1998 Act would require consideration of the seemingly unlimited extent of the orders[70] (the applicant in *McCann* was prohibited from entering the area in which he lived), as well as consideration of the substantial penalties in the event of default or breach. Such an analysis did not feature prominently in the Lords' decision in *McCann*: '[The decision] places the emphasis on the purpose of the order and appears to give far less weight to the impact and consequences of the order than did the Strasbourg Court in *Welch*. Purpose is important but, if the effects of an order are far-reaching, there must surely come a point at which they may fairly be held to override the purpose.'[71]

It must also be noted that the judgment appears contradictory in its conclusion that the 'seriousness of the matters involved' mandate a higher standard of proof, yet similarly exacting standards are not required in relation to the admission of hearsay evidence. Indeed, it is a point of concern that the leading of hearsay evidence in proceedings for an ASBO may subvert the application of the criminal standard of proof by the House of Lords and deprive it of any practical effect. The House of Lords justified the use of hearsay evidence on the basis of the rights of the community: 'The general interest of the community... represented by vulnerable people...[balanced against] the protection of the defendants' rights requires the scales to come down in favour of the protection of the community and of permitting the use of hearsay evidence.'[72] Yet, this argument could equally be made in relation to burglary and armed robbery which are also endemic in some deprived areas. In line with the House of Lords' logic, should not a reduced standard of proof apply here also?[73]

This point was taken up by the Human Rights Commissioner Alvaro Gil-Robles[74] in his recent report on his visit to the UK: 'For my part, I find the combination of a criminal burden of proof with civil rules of evidence rather hard to square; hearsay evidence and the testimony of police officers or "professional witnesses" do not seem to me to be capable of proving alleged behaviour beyond reasonable doubt.' Significantly, he further notes that the use of professional witnesses and hearsay evidence (and therefore the poorest quality evidence) is unduly encouraged in the Home Office Guidelines on ASBOs. Even commentators more disposed to the ASBO concede that 'with the right evidence, an application based solely on hearsay may well succeed.'[75] The Commissioner's argument would appear to be borne out by statistics which show an overwhelming success rate for authorities in obtaining ASBOs. Of the 2,035 ASBO applications notified to the Home Office up to 30 June 2004, only forty-two applications were refused, which constitutes a success rate of ninety-eight per cent.[76] As observed by one commentator: 'This suggests that the added protection of a higher standard of proof... [has] not made any *practical* difference to the control of the state over the individual's freedom.'[77]

(f) The Compatibility of the ASBO with Irish law

Section 115(9) of the Act states clearly that the standard of proof required is the civil standard of the balance of probabilities. In relation to the cognate issue of the admissibility of hearsay evidence, the Bill as enacted is silent on this issue, however, given that the proceedings are civil in nature, it would appear that hearsay evidence may be admitted to the extent that it is permitted in civil proceedings. It should be noted that in practice the rule is applied with less vigour in civil rather than criminal matters, however. *McCann* may certainly prove persuasive authority for the Irish Courts should issues arise in relation to the compatibility of the legislation with Article 6 of the ECHR[78] subject, of course, to a ruling by the European Court of Human Rights on the issue.[79] On the other hand, s115(9) is difficult to reconcile with the *dicta* of their Lordships in *McCann* as to the standard of proof.

It remains to consider the constitutionality of the legislation in the light of Article 38.1 which enshrines certain procedural protections, among them the presumption of innocence, for persons charged with a criminal offence. Should the courts find that the legislative provisions introduced by the Minister were in reality criminal and the necessary safeguards had therefore been avoided, they would be struck down as unconstitutional.

Key to such a determination is the issue of whether the courts will consider the initial application for an ASBO as capable of separation from the later proceedings for breach. Despite the reasoning of their Lordships in *McCann*, there are compelling reasons for finding that they are inextricably linked: the initial hearing defines the scope of the order and therefore determines the extent of the defendant's criminal liability, indeed, it is impossible to defend proceedings for breach without harking back to the terms of the original order. As argued by Prof. William Binchy at a recent conference on ASBOs:

> ...this rigorous segregation between the two stages of the ASBO process is less than convincing. There is an integration between each stage: the civil element is a necessary precondition of the criminal element: it defines the outer limits – and indeed may well define the full scope – of the conduct that can constitute a crime. There may turn out to be further interconnections, such as placing the onus on a defendant accused of breach to show that any breach was based on 'just cause or reasonable excuse'.[80]

It must be said, however, that cause for optimism that the courts will adopt an approach of 'substance over form' would not be derived from a brief survey of the Irish case law on the characterization of proceedings as civil or criminal. As will be recalled from Chapter Five, the High Court in *Gilligan v. Criminal Assets Bureau*[81] held that since the confiscation procedure introduced under the *Proceeds of Crime Act 1996* was labelled and operated as a civil process, it did not have 'all the features of a criminal prosecution'. This decision was followed by O'Higgins J. in *MF Murphy v. GH*[82] and both these decisions were upheld by the Supreme Court in a joint appeal.[83] The crux of the Supreme Court's reasoning was that the indicia of criminal proceedings such as arrest, detention and admission to bail were not present. The narrow interpretation of 'criminal' adopted in these decisions, focusing on the labels and procedures of the procedure itself, is redolent of the House of Lords' approach in *McCann*, and would suggest that the hybrid structure of which ASBOs are comprised may well pass the constitutional litmus test.[84]

While concerns surrounding anti-social behaviour are not to be minimised, there are more effective[85] means of meeting this social problem which address the underlying causes of the behaviour[86] and which do not seek to undermine fundamental values such as the presumption of innocence and the criminal standard of proof. It is perhaps symptomatic of the casual attitude towards these core legal concepts in England[87] that the 1998 Act was silent as to the standard of proof required to obtain an ASBO and indeed, that judicial legislation by the House of Lords was required to resolve the issue.[88] The entrenchment in Irish law of this hybrid concept, however, is indicative of much more than laxity towards the presumption of innocence, but represents a deliberate blurring of the lines between civil and criminal process at the expense of due process protection and the presumption.

Conclusion

The provisions of the *Criminal Justice Act 2006* reflect the state's weakening commitment to the rights of the accused person including the cardinal right to be presumed innocent. The summary doubling of the detention period for all arrestable offences, without distinction, and other incremental developments towards the creation of a DNA database and prosecution appeals reflect an assumption of guilt. Most worrying of all, however, is the creation of a shadow legal system in which an individual may be accused of criminal activity on pain of imprisonment yet denied the traditional protections of the criminal law.

Notes

1 See further A. Sanders and R. Young *Criminal Justice* (2nd ed., Butterworths, 2000), Chapter 5 'Police Questioning' pp.245–6.

2 H. Packer. *The Limits of the Criminal Sanction* (London: OUP, 1969).

3 D. Walsh 'The Criminal Justice Bill: Completing a Crime Control Model of Criminal Justice?' paper delivered at Conference on the Criminal Justice Bill 2004: Implications for Human Rights and Legal Practice, Trinity College Dublin, 20 April 2005.

4 Walsh *ibid.* estimates that there have been twenty-seven major criminal justice enactments substantially enhancing the powers of the police and/or prosecution at the expense of the individual.

5 *Ibid.*
6 *DPP v. Shaw* [1982] IR 1 at 29.
7 Part V of the *Offences Against the State Act 1939* was brought into force by a Government Proclamation in May 1972, thereby reactivating the s.30 power of arrest and detention. The 48 hour period under s.30 has since been extended to 72 hours by the *Offences Against the State (Amendment) Act 1998*.
8 Section 30(4).
9 *People (DPP) v. Howley* [1989] ILRM 629.
10 McLaughlin 'Legal Constraints in Criminal Investigation' (1981) 16 *Irish Jurist* 217. See also *Irish Times* 27 April 1982.
11 [1997] 3 IR 484.
12 See, for example, Irish Council of Civil Liberties *Submission to Joint Oireachtas Committee on Justice, Equality, Defence and Women's Rights* (February 2005).
13 See comments of B. Ahern who said that almost €1 billion was being spent on criminal justice in 2004, and noted: 'Of course, there is crime. There is too much crime. That is why we have continued to strengthen our law,' *Irish Times*, 7 April 2004.
14 Michael McDowell, Second Stage Speech, Criminal Justice Bill 2004, *Dail Debates*, Vol. 597, 15 February 2005. Emphasis added.
15 Section 6.
16 Section 16.
17 Irish Human Rights Commission, *Observations on the Scheme of the Criminal Justice Bill 2003*, 14 January 2004, p.14.
18 *DPP v. Healy* [1990] 2 IR 73.
19 *Lavery v Member in Charge, Carrickmacross Garda Station*, Unreported, Supreme Court, 23 February 1999.
20 *Report of the Committee to Recommend Certain Safeguards for Persons in Custody and for Members of An Garda Síochána* (Dublin: Stationery Office, 1978).
21 *Report of the Committee to Inquire into Certain Aspects of Criminal Procedure* (Dublin: Stationery Office, 1990).
22 *Criminal Justice Act, 1984 (Electronic Recording of Interviews) Regulations, 1997.* (S.I. No. 74 of 1997).
23 Article 3(1).
24 Article 4(3)(b).
25 *Op. cit.*
26 Garda SMI Implementation Steering Group *Final Report* (Dublin: Stationery Office, 2004) available at www.justice.ie.
27 *Report of the Expert Group Appointed to Consider Changes in the Criminal Law which were recommended in the Garda SMI Report* (Dublin: Stationery Office, 2004) available at www.justice.ie.
28 This detention period was extended by s.7 of the *Criminal Justice Act 2003*.
29 M. Ayre *et al. Arrests for Notifiable Offences and the Operation of Certain Police Powers under PACE* (Home Office Statistsical Bulletin 19/01 (2001).

30 *Op. cit.* p.40.
31 *Hammern v. Norway* [2003] ECHR 75.
32 Dr N. Cox 'Appeals and Fixed Charge Offences under the Criminal Justice Bill 2004', paper delivered at at Conference on the Criminal Justice Bill 2004: Implications for Human Rights and Legal Practice, Trinity College Dublin, 20 April 2005.
33 Law Reform Commission *Consultation Paper on Prosecution Appeals in Cases brought on Indictment* (*LRC* 19-2002).
34 A.L. Choo 'Halting Criminal Prosecutions' [1995] *Crim LR* 866.
35 Michael McDowell, Second Stage Speech, Criminal Justice Bill 2004, *op. cit.*
36 As indicated by the Minister for Justice in his Dáil speech *ibid*, the purpose of this provision is to clarify that 'hair follicles may be taken without consent. Currently, a sample of hair (other than pubic hair) may be taken without consent and the 1990 Act is silent on whether a hair follicle may be so taken. Hair follicles are a useful source of DNA.'
37 In this regard, it should be noted that both the Irish Human Rights Commission and the Irish Council of Civil Liberties have expressed concerns that the powers conferred on the Gardaí may lead to them taking bodily samples as a matter of routine, rather than necessity. See Irish Human Rights Commission *op. cit.* pp.19–35 and Irish Council of Civil Liberties *op. cit.* pp.10–11.
38 LRC CP 29-2004 pp.70–5.
39 *R v. Smith* [1985] Crim LR 590.
40 *Holt v. US* (1910) 218 US 245.
41 *Saunders v. UK* (1996) 23 EHRR 313.
42 *Ibid.*
43 S. Easton *The Case for the Right to Silence* (2nd Edition), (Aldershot: Ashgate, 1998) p.223.
44 For a thorough discussion of this topic, see S. Easton *ibid.*, Chapter 8.
45 Law Reform Commission, *op. cit.* p.75.
46 J Gans 'Something to Hide: DNA, Surveillance and Self-Incrimination' (2001) *Current Issues in Criminal Justice* 168 p.178.
47 P. O'Mahony 'ASBOs: Another pig in the poke and backward step for Juvenile Justice:' paper delivered at conference on 'Anti-Social Behaviour Orders: Social Policy and Human Rights', Trinity College Dublin, 22 June 2005 p.4.
48 Jack Straw, HC Debates Vol 287 Col 791 16 December 1996.
49 A. Ashworth 'Social Control and "Anti Social Behaviour": The Subversion of Human Rights?' [2004] 120 *LQR* 263 p.289.
50 See N. Padfield 'The Anti-Social Behaviour Act 2003: the Ultimate Nanny State Act?' [2004] *Crim LR* 712 p.713: 'In practice, the complaint is not that the law is unduly oppressive on "sub-criminal" behaviour but that the ASBO is being used to avoid the due process protections of the criminal justice system in genuinely criminal cases.'
51 [2003] 1 AC 787.
52 D. Tausz 'Anti Social Behaviour Order: Whether Proceedings are Civil or Criminal in Nature' [2003] *Crim LR* 269 p.270.

53 *Ibid.* at pp.269–70.
54 [2003] 1 AC 787 at 808.
55 *Ibid.*
56 *Ibid.* at 824.
57 *Ibid.* at 832.
58 It should be noted that the criminal standard of proof is only to be applied to the first part of the test to be satisfied in ASBO proceedings, namely whether the applicant has 'acted . . . in a manner that caused or was likely to cause harassment, alarm or distress to one or more persons not of the same household as himself' (s.1 (1)(a)) and not to the second part of the test concerning whether the order is necessary. Lord Steyn said: 'The inquiry under section 1(1)(b), namely that such an order is necessary to protect persons from further anti-social acts by him does not involve a standard of proof: it is an exercise of judgment or evaluation.'
59 Tausz *op. cit.* p.270.
60 S. McDonald 'The Nature of the Anti-Social Behaviour Order – *R (McCann & Others) v. Crown Court at Manchester*' (2003) 66 *MLR* 630.
61 House of Commons Standing Committee B Col 138 5 May 1998. See S. McDonald *ibid.* p.633, fn 6.
62 C. Bakalis 'Anti-Social Behaviour Orders – Criminal Penalties or Civil Injunctions?' [2003] *CLJ* 583.
63 (1984) 6 EHRR 409.
64 (1998) 33 EHRR 994.
65 *Op. cit.*
66 See for example *Konig v. Germany (*1978) 2 EGRR 170 and *Engel v. Netherlands* (1976) 1 EHRR 647.
67 Ashworth (2004) *op. cit.* p.278.
68 (1995) 20 EHRR 247.
69 *Drug Trafficking Act 1986.*
70 Section 1(4) of the English Act allows a court to make an order 'prohibiting the defendant from doing anything described in the order' and does not therefore have to relate to the behaviour proved in court.
71 Ashworth, *op. cit.*, p.281.
72 [2003] 1 AC 787 at 835.
73 A. Ashworth, J. Gardner, R. Morgan, A.T.H. Smith, A. Von Hirsch, M. Wasik 'Overtaking on the Right' (1995) 145 *NLJ* 1501 p.1502.
74 *Report by Mr Alvaro Gil-Robles, Commissioner for Human Rights, on his Visit to the United Kingdom*, 4–12 November 2004 for the attention of the Committee of Ministers and the Parliamentary Assembly, Strasbourg, 8 June 2005, paragraph 115.
75 A. Pema and S. Heels *Anti-social Behaviour Orders: Special Bulletin* (Bristol: Jordans, 2004) p.41.
76 House of Commons Written Answers Col 1143W, 4 February 2005.
77 K. Beattie 'Control Orders and ASBOs: taking liberties?' *Legal Action* April 2005 7 p.8. Emphasis added.

78 Under s.2 of the *European Convention on Human Rights Act 2003*, Irish courts are bound to interpret Irish law in the light of the ECHR and the corresponding case law.

79 An application has been made to the European Court of Human Rights in the McCann case.

80 W. Binchy 'Anti-Social Behaviour Orders and the Constitution': paper delivered at Conference on 'Anti-Social Behaviour Orders: Social Policy and Human Rights', Trinity College Dublin, 22 June 2005 p.15.

81 [1998] 3 IR 185.

82 Unreported, High Court, O'Higgins J., 4 June 1999.

83 *Murphy. v. GM, PB, PC Ltd, GH, Gilligan v. CAB* Unreported, Supreme Court, 18 October 2001.

84 For a critical analysis of the case law see J. Meade 'The Disguise of Civility: Civil Forfeiture of the Proceeds of Crime and the Presumption of Innocence in Irish Law' (2000) *Hibernian Law Journal* 1.

85 Home Office statistics show that 42% of ASBOs were breached up to December 2003 (an increase of 36% on the previous year) and 55% of those persons who breached their ASBO were immediately imprisoned. See Home Office Press Release 042/2005, 1 March 2005.

86 See, for example, NAPO's (The Trade Union and Professional Association for Family Court and Probation Staff) criticism of ASBOs in H. Fletcher *Anti Social Behaviour Orders: Analysis of the First Six Years* (7 April 2005) which concludes at p.11: 'Certain local authorities are using ASBOs to clear sink estates of problematic families and individuals. This appears to avoid dealing with wider environmental problems on those estates and also avoids putting in place wider social policies that would deal with the underlying problems of anti social behaviour.'

87 For a more general discussion on the casual treatment of the presumption of innocence and burden of proof, see A. Ashworth and M. Blake 'The Presumption of Innocence in English Criminal Law' [1996] *Crim LR* 306.

88 Beattie *op. cit.* p.7 contrasts this with the detailed discussion of standards of proof in relation to the controversial control orders under the *Prevention of Terrorism Act 2005*.

Chapter Seven

The Rights of Remand Prisoners

In 1963 Glanville Williams went so far as to argue that the treatment meted out to remand prisoners in Britain amounted to a repudiation of the presumption of innocence. He criticized the conditions in which pre-trial prisoners were detained as persons to whom the presumption of innocence attaches:

> We should, however, do everything possible to treat such a man as if he were innocent, consistent with the demands of the public safety and due trial of the charge. If we were serious in this endeavour we would do much to ameliorate the position of defendants, by improving the conditions of those in prison on remand, improving the cells of the court in which the accused person may be detained overnight... and, except for violent prisoners, no longer requiring them to occupy the dock.[1]

Since Williams wrote in the early 1960s, some advances have been made in relation to the treatment of prisoners on remand or awaiting trial who enjoy the right to be presumed innocent. The purpose of this chapter is to assess the extent to which the prison regime to which remand prisoners are currently subject in this jurisdiction adequately reflects their legal status as unconvicted prisoners.

(I) Background

As outlined in Chapter Five, the right to bail in Ireland was restricted in the moral panic which ensued in the period following the murder of journalist, Veronica Guerin. Given that under the *Bail Act 1997* defendants could now be refused bail on grounds of the likelihood of their re-offending, it was anticipated that the (traditionally low) remand population in Ireland would increase as courts began to exercise their wider discretion to refuse bail.[2] The *Bail Act* came into effect in May 2000 and since then the remand population has indeed increased. On 1 June 2000, remand prisoners comprised around 10 per cent of the prison population and in the 2004 Annual Report on Prisons this figure had climbed to 16.5 per cent.[3]

A related issue is the length of time which unconvicted prisoners are spending on remand, which has also increased significantly. Information on the amount of time spent in pre-trial detention is not routinely available from the Prison Service. However, this writer has been fortunate enough to have sight of a recent study conducted by a senior member of the Prison Service which sheds some much-needed light on the area.[4] This study sought *inter alia* to compare pre-trial detention in 1993 with that in 2003 and to probe the reasons for the changes in the use of such detention. It concluded that both the average daily population of pre-trial prisoners in 2003 had substantially increased (512 compared to 200 in 1993) and that the average length of time spent in custody had also increased threefold (37.39 days as compared to 12 days in 1993). Given that the number of pre-trial *committals* had fallen in the same period, the study concluded that the increase in the average daily population or 'stock' figure should be attributed to an increase in the average period of time spent in custody rather than a change in the number of persons remanded. In explaining this trend, the study considers: 'The principal reasons underpinning this increase are legislative change in the form of the *Bail Act 1997*, the increased numbers of prosecutions of serious crime in the higher courts and increased waiting time for trial in the Central Criminal Court.'[5] It is worth citing the report's recommendations in full in considering the implications these shifts in prison demographics have for prison management:

- Improve living conditions for remand prisoners at Cork and Portlaoise Prisons

- Use of the three-man cells at Cloverhill Prison as cells for no more than two people at the earliest possible time. If this cannot be done quickly, those cells should be used to accommodate only persons identified as likely to be released on bail within a few days of committal;
- Bring the new Education Unit at Cloverhill Prison into operation so as to provide necessary facilities for long-term pre-trial prisoners; and
- Further improve conditions for non-national prisoners, especially for those prisoners who are not English speaking.[6]

Many of these issues will be discussed in further detail below. The general point, however, is that the increasing significance of the remand population within the prison estate serves to underline the importance of meeting their entitlements and needs. It is salutary to note that in England a substantial number of remand prisoners were involved in the prison riots of April 1990 wishing to protest about their conditions and, indeed, the Woolf Report vindicated many of their complaints.[7] Moreover, the cynical may also wish to take note of statistics in the 1994 *Annual Report on Prisons* (the most recent in which this information is available) which show that approximately half of the prisoners who had been remanded in custody were not recommitted to prison on sentence.[8] This statistic appears to be confirmed by the study on remand discussed above which found that only 23.4 per cent of pre-trial committals in 2003 were 'recommitted on conviction', with the remainder either being released on bail from prison (having met the conditions stipulated by the court) (24.3 per cent) or being 'brought up and not recommitted' (52.3 per cent).[9] This latter category refers to cases where the prisoner is released by being granted bail, the charges being withdrawn, or following an acquittal or the imposition of a non-custodial sentence. Given this is the outcome for approximately half of the prisoners remanded in custody, it is particularly difficult to justify poor conditions of detention for this category of prisoners.

There are a number of international provisions which deal with the distinction between convicted and unconvicted prisoners. Article 10(2) of the International Covenant on Civil and Political Rights provides that 'accused persons shall, save in exceptional circumstances be separated from convicted persons and shall be subject to separate treatment appropriate to their status as unconvicted persons'. Further, the UN's Standard Minimum Rules, number 84(2) declares that 'unconvicted prisoners are presumed to be innocent and shall be treated as such'. Rule 95 of the *European Prison Rules 2006*[10] also provides that 'the regime for untried prisoners may not be influenced by the possibility that they may be convicted of a criminal offence in the future.'

(II) Accommodation and Segregation

Both the Irish and European Prison Rules[11] acknowledge that unconvicted prisoners should be kept out of contact with convicted prisoners, although this is only guaranteed under the Irish Rules 'as far as is practicable and subject to the maintenance of good order and safe and secure custody'.[12] Prior to 1999, remand prisoners in Dublin shared a prison regime that was little different from that of convicted prisoners. The opening of a separate prison in 1999 to house remand prisoners at Cloverhill in the western suburbs of Dublin has allowed the state to segregate remand prisoners from convicted prisoners and to honour its international obligations under Article 10(2) of the International Covenant on Civil and Political Rights. The prison became fully operational in 2000 and, despite being regarded as a remand prison, also houses a small number of convicted prisoners. It should be added, however, that these prisoners are trustees who had volunteered to return to the prison, who are engaged in the kitchen and grounds work and who are housed separately in a stand alone prisoner block.[13]

Although separate, the accommodation provided to remand prisoners in Cloverhill is inadequate and overcrowded. Three prisoners share a cell which measures eleven square metres. The limited space afforded prisoners in Cloverhill has been criticized both by the Irish Prisons Inspectorate[14] and the Committee on the Prevention of Torture.[15] Further, female remand prisoners in the Dóchas centre on the Moutjoy Prison site and prisoners outside Dublin do not have the benefit of separate accommodation. Remand prisoners in Cork, Portlaoise and Limerick prisons are accommodated together with convicted prisoners in cramped conditions in some of the oldest prisons in the state. Remand prisoners in the old A and B blocks in Limerick prison still 'slop out' with chamber pots in their cells, a practice which is clearly degrading for all prisoners.[16] The practice of slopping out is also prevalent in Cork prison where prisoners are forced to use a chamber pot without any dignity screen or barrier and without adequate in-cell ventilation.[17] Numbers of remand prisoners in Portlaoise Prison are small but there are no sanitary facilities within the prison and prisoners 'slop out' after each unlock.[18] Overcrowding is a problem in all these prisons. Finally, visits by the Prisons Inspectorate to St Patrick's Institution for juveniles have also revealed that remand prisoners are not kept separate from convicted inmates, a situation which is particularly worrying given the particular vulnerability of remand prisoners (see section below on mental health) and St Patrick's' reputation for bullying.[19]

The failure to make arrangements for the separation of remand prisoners in these institutions is in breach of both our own Prison Rules and falls far below the standard set by Rule 96 of the *European Prison Rules 2006*. This Rule provides that: 'As far as possible, untried prisoners shall be given the option of accommodation in single cells, unless they may benefit from sharing accommodation with other untried prisoners or unless a court has made a specific order on how a specific untried prisoner should be accommodated.' It is to be hoped that the Minister will keep such requirements in mind when designing the new prisons planned in North Dublin and Cork and constructing new wings in Limerick and Portlaoise. The two new major prisons in Cork and Dublin will incorporate separate wings for remand prisoners, including female prisoners, a move which represents an improvement on current practice. Serious concerns remain, however, as to the impact the location of the new prisons (which are to be built some distance away from the respective city centres) will have on the right of remand prisoners to maintain contact with friends, family and their legal representatives, a right which is discussed below.

(III) Communications and Visits

Prison Rule 37(3) provides that: 'Subject to the provision of these Rules, an unconvicted prisoner shall be entitled to receive one visit per day from relatives or friends of not less than 15 minutes in duration on each of six days of the week, where practicable, but in any event, on not less than on each of three days of the week.' This compares favourably with the rights of convicted prisoners who are entitled to one visit per week of at least thirty minutes duration.[20] In practice, remand prisoners are allowed one visit daily from friends or relatives from Monday to Saturday in addition to legal visits which may take place at any reasonable time.

In relation to letters, unconvicted prisoners are entitled in common with all inmates to send up to seven letters a week at the state's expense. There are no restrictions on outgoing letters at their own expense, although both outgoing and incoming mail may be censored on one or more of the various grounds listed under Rule 47.[21] In addition to letters to friends and family, an unconvicted prisoner is 'entitled to send such number of letters to persons (other than persons referred to in that paragraph) as are reasonably necessary for the purposes of the management of his or her property or business affairs, and to receive such number of letters as are sent to him or her for that purpose by persons (other than persons referred to in that paragraph)'. This is crucial to allowing a prisoner to maintain his or her employment and legitimate business interests, if same exist, while on remand.

Despite the advantages afforded remand prisoners discussed above, there is evidence that prisoners are still experiencing difficulties in maintaining contact with the outside world. The *Report of the Prisons Inspectorate on Cloverhill Prison*[22] noted that prisoners complained about the length of time allowed for the use of the telephone, which is restricted to six minutes. They indicated that no warning was given that the time limit had been reached and as a result prisoners were cut off mid-way through a conversation. Complaints as to the short duration of these calls were also heard from detainees in Cloverhill interviewed for a recent report on immigration-related detention in Ireland[23] which recommended time spent speaking to a solicitor should not be included in this allocation. Given that prisoners have rights *both* to the necessary facilities to prepare their defence[24] and to contact with family and friends[25] it would appear inappropriate that time spent speaking to a solicitor is deducted from the overall time allocated. As noted by the report, this situation is particularly unsatisfactory for third-country nationals who are further isolated from friends and family and who, if they are not English speaking, may be experiencing real difficulties in communication. Other problems concern the fact that visiting arrangements are closed and prisoners have complained that visits are very inhumane due to the fact that they were forced to shout at visitors through the screens.[26]

(IV) WORK AND EDUCATION

Remand prisoners cannot be required to work but according to Prison Rule 80(1) they may join in with the structured activity in the prison should they indicate a desire to do so and subject to the Governor's consent. With regard to Cloverhill Prison this would seem to afford unconvicted prisoners little advantage given that there is little by way of structured activity in place. Prisoners can avail of the gym, exercise yard and library but outside these activities there is very little to do. While a small number of prisoners are offered work, this is mostly in the line of cleaning duties as most of the inmates employed in the kitchen are convicted prisoners who are pursuing an officially recognized qualification. The recent *Report of the Committee for the Prevention of Torture*[27] (CPT) noted that, aside from cleaning duties:

> No other organized activities were being offered to inmates, although the delegation was informed of plans to build facilities for education activities. The majority of prisoners at Cloverhill spent their time talking to other inmates or playing games (snooker, etc) and reading or watching television in their cells; in short, they were left to their own devices for weeks and on occasion for months on end.

The comments made by the CPT find a resonance in the recent report of the Prisons Inspector on Cloverhill Prison, where he candidly notes that '[T]he main problem with Cloverhill Prison is sheer boredom'.[28] The problem is compounded by the fact that the prisoners are locked in their cells for seventeen and a half hours a day. This seems an unduly restrictive regime to impose on remand prisoners who benefit from the presumption of innocence. As the only available statistics appear to suggest that only half of these prisoners eventually receive a custodial sentence, it would seem that they do not pose a particular security threat. It is difficult to understand why the prisoners are not allowed out of their cells for twelve hours a day (as is the situation in the Dóchas centre), a regime which allows prisoners to maintain a degree of normalcy.

The position in relation to education in Cloverhill is particularly dire. As was explained in the Prison Inspectors Report: 'It was thought that the prisoners here would not be detained long and therefore should have no need for a school within the prison. But it is now the practice that prisoners are detained for several months prior to final conclusions by the Courts.'[29] A Learning and Teaching Centre has now been built within the prison, although regrettably this is not yet in operation due to staffing issues.[30]

Overall, prison work and educational facilities in Cloverhill are inadequate and it is difficult to disagree with the conclusions of the CPT that 'the regime provided at Cloverhill Prison [is] particularly underdeveloped'.[31] In this regard at least, remand prisoners housed in Cloverhill are experiencing worse custodial conditions than convicted prisoners, despite their constitutionally protected right to the presumption of innocence. Facilities in Mountjoy and Cork Prison which hold convicted prisoners are superior and more varied and these prisons boast much higher rates of participation in work and educational programmes.[32] It is key to prisoners' psychological well being that they should be offered work or educational activities to occupy the day and this has led the CPT to recommend that 'the aim should be to ensure that *all prisoners, whether on remand or sentenced*, spend 8 hours or more outside their cells engaged in purposeful activities of a varied nature (work, preferably with vocational value; education; sport; recreation/association)'.[33]

(V) MENTAL HEALTH

It has long been established by international evidence that rates of mental illness are particularly high among unconvicted prisoners, higher even than those among the sentenced population.[34] Recent studies carried out specifically on the remand prison population have confirmed this trend in Ireland and, indeed, indicated that the problem may be significantly worse in this jurisdiction. Duffy[35] examined psychological distress, thoughts of suicide and self injury among male remand prisoners in Mountjoy and St Patrick's Institution while on placement with the Department of Justice Psychology Service as a Psychologist in Clinical Training. Some of the significant findings from the study were that 52 per cent of the prisoners involved had experienced suicidal thoughts in the past; 33 per cent had engaged in self injurious behaviour at some point in their lives, and, of this group, 70 per cent had self injured on two or more occasions with two thirds of attempters stating that their intent to die in the last attempt was high. Prisoners also experienced high levels of hopelessness with the study finding that 70 per cent of the sample scored in excess of the mean score for the Irish population using the Beck Hopelessness Scale. Over 60 per cent had feelings of personal inadequacy or inferiority. Furthermore, a comprehensive report on mental illness in prisons, by Dr Harry Kennedy, Director of the CMH *et. al.*, found that the rate of serious mental illness, such as schizophrenia or bipolar disorder, is at least twice the rate of similar studies conducted in prisons internationally.[36] The report found that the rate of severe mental illness among prisoners on remand is almost forty times higher than rates among the general community.

It is clear that, by its very nature, the prison environment is likely to exacerbate pre-existing mental illness and/or suicidal tendencies by placing individuals in an authoritarian environment removed from friends and family.[37] Remand prisoners also experience feelings of great uncertainty about the future together with a lack of apparent control over their fate. Liebling[38] has suggested that factors such as overcrowding, staff shortages, concern about being in prison and being a part of a large and constantly changing inmate population could explain the higher levels of mental instability among remand prisoners. The prevalence of mental illness and elevated suicide risk presented by remand prisoners makes effective screening upon entry to prison together with the provision of adequate psychiatric care crucial. However, the failure of the Irish Government to provide equivalence of care to prisoners in the psychiatric area is well documented.[39] Indeed, the appalling treatment meted out to two mentally ill remand prisoners while in Mountjoy Prison, including the use of strip cells, has led them to bring a legal action seeking damages for breach of their constitutional rights in tandem with the Irish Penal Reform Trust.[40]

Despite recommendations made as long ago as 1985 by the Whitaker Committee[41] and in successive years by the CPT, there are no in-house psychiatric facilities in Irish prisons aside from the Central Mental Hospital (CMH), and prisoners frequently experience delays in accessing beds in the CMH. Remand prisoners, like all prisoners, are therefore dependant upon intermittent visiting psychiatric care, and remand prisoners in Cloverhill have access to this type of service three times a week. The inadequacy of this type of service is highlighted by the fact that, in its most recent report, the CPT has recommended that a qualified psychiatric nurse should be present during the day in the medical unit at Cloverhill.[42]

(VI) OTHER RIGHTS

Currently, Irish prisoners who are remanded in custody cannot exercise their right to vote. Ireland occupies a strange no man's land in relation to prisoner voting in that, while prisoners are not barred in law from voting, they are not given the practical means to express their vote in that they are not given access to ballot boxes or entitled to have a postal vote. This regime applies to all prisoners, regardless of their legal status, unlike the position in Britain where the special status of both fine defaulters and remand prisoners affords them the right of suffrage.

Changes in the law, however, have been announced by the Government since the recent decision in *Hirst v. UK*.[43] In *Hirst* the European Court of Human Rights found the long established law preventing sentenced prisoners from voting in the United Kingdom to be in breach of Article 3, Protocol 1 of the ECHR. Under this Article, Convention Parties undertake to hold free elections at reasonable intervals 'under conditions which will ensure the free expression of the opinion of the people in the choice of the legislature'. Following a campaign led by the Irish Penal Reform Trust and pressure from opposition deputies in Fine Gael, the Government has now signalled its intention to provide all prisoners with a postal vote. Remand prisoners are also entitled to retain certain of their social welfare and housing entitlements while in custody. Subject to estate management, they can retain their local authority tenancies for the entire period as well as their rent supplement for up to thirteen weeks.

(VII) RIGHTS OF REMAND PRISONERS IN COURT

The case law on the rights of remand prisoners has shown, in O'Dalaigh CJ's words, more than a verbal commitment to the right to be presumed innocent and practical arrangements are now put in place to dispel any preconceived notions of guilt. Out of deference to the presumption of innocence, remand prisoners are no longer required to occupy the dock in most of the Dublin criminal courts and instead sit in a chair in the courtroom. Similarly, the courts have held that prisoners should not be seen by the jury in handcuffs, nor should photographs of prisoners in restraints be published by the media. The general undesirability of such images has been noted in strong terms by the Court of Criminal Appeal (CCA) in a series of cases. In *People (DPP) v. Davis*,[44] Hardiman J. held *obiter* that the publication of photographs of an accused person in restraints was capable of amounting to contempt of court and a trial judge would be permitted to forbid such publications in the interests of a fair trial. The learned Supreme Court judge based his ruling on the presumption of innocence attaching to defendants as well as the dignity of the individual. He approved the following statement from the Canadian case of *R v. McArthur*[45] as also representing the law in Ireland:

> The current state of our law and the administration of criminal justice in this country includes the presumption that the shackling of an accused during the course of his or her trial is *per se* prejudicial to the accused. The principle of our criminal justice [system] that any accused person is presumed innocent until proven guilty is tested severely by the use of any visible restraint during the conduct of a trial.

Indeed, the Court demonstrated a clear appreciation of the practical difficulties involved in preserving the presumption intact and it would appear that the judgment extends beyond the handcuffing of prisoners to any practice which would serve to taint the accused's character in the eyes of the jury:

> Every defendant suffers some degree of disadvantage simply by reason of the fact that he is accused. If he is incarcerated prior to and during the trial, the disadvantage is greater. The cardinal principle that a person is presumed innocent until proven guilty requires that a court should take all practical steps to ensure that such a person suffers no avoidable prejudice purely by reason of being accused or incarcerated.[46]

In *Davis* the CCA did not overturn the conviction due to the existence of 'overwhelming, uncontradicted and high quality evidence' which made another verdict unlikely. The Court did not shrink from doing so in the subsequent case of *People (DPP) v. McCowan*,[47] however, where it quashed the defendant's conviction for larceny on the grounds *inter alia* that the appellant had been held in handcuffs for a period of time sufficient for him to have been seen by potential jurors in the hall of the Circuit Court where he was to be tried. Hardiman J. stressed that the prejudice attaching to a defendant being seen in handcuffs had previously been noted by the Court and that the Court had resolved to quash the conviction for fear that, were it not overturned, 'none of these important matters will be taken seriously in the future'.[48]

Conclusion

The CCA's commitment to the presumption and its practical expression offers real protection to accused persons standing trial. Yet, it is a matter of some concern that the presumption does not appear to be similarly honoured in the less scrutinised corridors of the prison. It is true that significant concessions are currently made to reflect the remand prisoner's status, such as segregation from convicted prisoners (in the Dublin area) and the increased frequency of visits. However, serious concerns remain about conditions for remand prisoners in prisons outside Dublin (where separate accommodation is not provided) and about overcrowding and the lack of any structured activity involving work or education in Cloverhill. It is unacceptable that prisoners who in theory enjoy greater protection in reality are experiencing worse conditions than convicted prisoners in these important regards. The state's treatment of remand prisoners clearly tests its commitment to the presumption of innocence as a practical reality, not just as a philosophical principle. Discussing conditions for remand prisoners in England, Jones has argued that 'the same view of "no smoke without fire" which underlies the increasing legal restrictions placed on the right to bail also explains the indifference to the lot of the unconvicted prisoner'.[49] It can be argued that a similar level of apathy also exists in this jurisdiction, despite the increasing significance of this cohort within the prison population.

Notes

1 G. Williams *The Proof of Guilt* (3rd ed., Stevens 1963) p.184.
2 I. O'Donnell 'Prison Matters' (2000) *Irish Jurist* 153 p.172.
3 See further I. O'Donnell 'Putting Prison in its Place' (2005) 5(2) *Judicial Studies Institute Journal* 54 p.57.
4 J. Brosnan *A Quantitative Analysis of Pre-Trial Custody in Ireland*, submitted in fulfilment of the dissertation requirement for the award of Masters of Arts in Public Management, Institute of Public Administration, UCD (Criminal Justice Administration) (February 2005).
5 *Ibid.* p.64.
6 *Ibid.* p.71.
7 See further S. Jones 'Guilty until Proved Innocent? The Diminished

Status of Suspects at the Point of Remand and as Unconvicted Prisoners' (2003) 32 *Common Law World Review* 399.

8 In 1994, 2,387 of the 4,729 remand prisoners were 'brought up in court and not re-committed'. See further P. O'Mahony (ed) *Criminal Justice in Ireland* (IPA, 2002) p.597.

9 J. Brosnan *op. cit.* p.38.

10 Council of Europe, *Rec (2006)2E of the Committee of Ministers to Member States.*

11 Rule 96.

12 Irish Prison Rules 2005, Article 79.

13 See Irish Prisons Inspectorate *Report on Cloverhill Prison: Cloverhill Inspection: 4, 5, 6 November 2002 and 17 November 2002* (Dublin: Stationery Office, 2003) p.2.

14 *Ibid.* p.13.

15 *Report to Government of Ireland on the Visit to Ireland carried out by the European Committee for the Prevention of Torture and Inhuman and Degrading Treatment or Punishment* (Council of Europe: Strasbourg, 1999).

16 Irish Prisons Inspectorate *Report on Limerick Prison: Inspection 26th and 27th November 2002* (Dublin: Stationery Office, 2005); *Revisit Inspection of Limerick Prison 17th–18th February 2004* (Dublin: Stationery Office, 2005).

17 Irish Prisons Inspectorate *Report on Cork Prison 13th–14th September 2004* (Dublin: Stationery Office, 20053).

18 Irish Prisons Inspectorate *Revisit Inspection of Portlaoise Prison: 17th–18th May 2004* (Dublin: Stationery Office, 2004).

19 Irish Prisons Inspectorate *Third Annual Report of the Inspector for Prisons and Places of Detention for the Year 2004–5* (Dublin: Stationery Office, 2005) at Section 18.

20 Rule 37(1).

21 (1) A letter given by a prisoner for sending, other than a letter referred to in Rule 46 *(Letter to authorities)*, may be opened and examined by the Governor and he or she may confiscate the letter or any article enclosed therewith if he or she is of the opinion that:

(a) it is threatening in nature,

(b) were the letter or article sent to the person for whom it was intended, it could cause serious offence or distress to that person or other persons or there could be an interference with the course of justice,

(c) the prisoner has not adequately identified himself or herself as the sender of the letter,

(d) the person for whom it is intended has informed either the Minister or the Governor that he or she does not wish to receive letters from the prisoner,

(e) it would facilitate or encourage the commission of a criminal offence or hamper the prevention, detection, investigation or prosecution of a criminal offence,

(f) it could give rise to a legal action by a third party against the Governor or the Minister,

(g) it is contrary to the interests of national security,
(h) it is contrary to the interests of the security, good order and government of the prison or
(i) it infringes the rights and freedoms of another person (including the right to privacy of another prisoner).
(2) A letter sent to a prisoner under paragraph (1), (2) or (3) of Rule 45 *(Letters)* may be opened and examined by the Governor and he or she may confiscate the letter or any article enclosed therewith, if he or she, upon reasonable grounds, believes that were the letter or article to be given to the prisoner, that
(a) the maintenance of good order or safe or secure custody in the prison could be threatened, or
(b) it might facilitate a criminal offence or hamper the prevention, detection, investigation or prosecution of a criminal offence or
(c) it might, otherwise, cause an interference with the course of justice.
(3) A prisoner shall not, without the prior consent of the intended recipient, send a letter to the victim of his or her offence or the family of that person.

22 *Op. cit.* p.5.

23 Mark Kelly, Human Rights Consultants *Immigration-Related Detention in Ireland: a Research Report for the Irish Refugee Council, Irish Penal Reform Trust and Immigrant Council of Ireland*, November 2005 p.54.

24 *European Prison Rules 2006, op. cit.*, Rule 98.2.

25 *European Prison Rules 2006, op. cit.*, Rule 99.

26 Irish Prisons Inspectorate *Report on Cloverhill Prison op. cit.* p.6.

27 CPT *Report to Government of Ireland on the Visit to Ireland carried out by the European Committee for the Prevention of Torture and Inhuman and Degrading Treatment or Punishment* (Council of Europe: Strasbourg, 2003) at paragraph 49.

28 *Op. cit.* p.7.

29 *Ibid.*

30 I am grateful to Jim Mitchell, Press Officer, Irish Prison Service for this information.

31 CPT Report (2003) *op. cit.* paragraphs 46–48.

32 *Ibid.* paragraph 50.

33 CPT Report (2003) *op. cit.* at paragraph 50.

34 E. Dooley 'Prison Suicide in England and Wales 1972–87' (1990) *Brit. Jnl of Psychiatry* 40–45. See also S. Jones *op. cit.* 411–12 for the results of other English studies.

35 J. Duffy *Psychological Distress, Suicidal Ideation and Self-Injurious Behaviour Among Male Remand Prisoners* (Thesis completed in 1998 in Trinity College Dublin).

36 H.G. Kennedy, S. Monks, K. Curtin, B. Wright. S. Linehan, D. Duffy, C. Telijeur, A. Kelly Mental Illness in Irish Prisoners: Psychiiatric Morbidity in Sentenced, Remanded and Newly Committed Prisoners (January, 2006).

37 Dr Harry Kennedy *ibid.* has described prison as 'a toxic place for people with serious mental illness'.

38 A. Liebling *Suicides in Prison* (Routledge, 1992).

39 See, for example, *Reports of the Mountjoy Visiting Committee* (1996) and (1997) and CPT Report (1999) *op. cit.*

40 *Irish Penal Reform Trust, Lennon and Carroll v. Governor of Mountjoy Prison, the Minister for Justice, Equality Law Reform and Ireland* High Court, Gilligan J., 2 September 2005. This decision only dealt with the preliminary issue of *locus standi* and is currently under appeal to the Supreme Court.

41 *Report of Committee of Inquiry into the Penal System* (Dublin: Stationery Office, 1985).

42 CPT (2003) *op. cit* paragraph 62.

43 *Hirst v. UK (No 2)* Grand Chamber of the European Court of Human Rights, 6 October 2005.

44 [2001] 1 IR 146.

45 34 OTC 370.

46 [2001] 1IR 146 at 152.

47 [2003] 4 IR 349.

48 *Ibid.* at 354.

49 *Op. cit.* p.399

Chapter Eight

Guilty as Charged?

Most people think of the criminal justice system in terms of its adversarial features: legal arguments being thrashed out by opposing legal teams before a judge; bewigged counsel imprecating a jury as to a defendant's guilt or innocence; in short, there is an assumption that the culmination of a criminal investigation is the jury trial. The reality, however, is very different from this media-spun image. The vast majority of defendants (approximately 90 per cent) are tried summarily in the District Court. Further, and this is the point we are concerned with in this chapter, most of the public business of the criminal courts is taken up with the processing of defendants who have pleaded guilty. In 2004, for example, the Irish Circuit Court processed 1,648 offenders who pleaded guilty, which represented 78 per cent of its total caseload.[1] Although statistics are not currently available in relation to the rate of guilty pleas in the District Court in Ireland, it is likely, in common with the lower courts in other jurisdictions that the figure is probably much higher.[2]

The high rate of guilty pleas in Ireland, as in many other common law jurisdictions, is facilitated by various forms of plea bargaining. Plea bargaining has been defined by Guidorizzi[3] as 'the defendant's agreement to plead guilty to a criminal charge with the reasonable expectation of receiving some consideration from the state'. In other words, it is a benefit offered by the state in exchange for the tendering of a guilty plea. Despite official denial of the practice and Irish lawyers' general distaste for the subject, at least two forms of plea bargaining exist in this jurisdiction: prosecutorial plea bargaining (though subject to the DPP's consent) and also what has been termed 'implicit' bargaining (the discount in sentence which is traditionally given by a court in response to a plea of guilty). This latter type is sometimes not formally recognized as a means of plea bargaining. As Guidorizzi argues, however: 'Its use as a method of negotiating a guilty plea qualifies it as part of the process of plea bargaining.'[4] There has been some suggestion that a third type, 'judicial plea bargaining', may also exist – where the trial judge takes part in the discussions and indicates the probable sentence the accused may receive upon a plea of guilty – although this is probably without foundation.[5]

It is implicit bargaining or, in its more familiar guise, the guilty plea discount which will form the primary focus of the discussion in this chapter. Unlike the other forms, there is little by way of secrecy or distaste surrounding its role in the sentencing process. Indeed, many countries, including Ireland, have now given the principle statutory recognition.[6] The discount is central to the workings of the modern criminal justice process and it has even been argued in the UK and elsewhere that, were it to be abolished, the system would collapse under the pressure of more trials.[7] Despite its importance, in Ireland little research has been conducted into its operation and it is probable that any reevaluation of its merits with a view to reform would meet with considerable resistance within the legal profession. As de Londras[8] has noted in a rare treatment of the issue in an Irish context: 'The internalisation of concepts of how things should be, which takes place via formal education in such institutions as Blackhall Place and the Honorable Society of the King's Inns, has stymied the ability of components of the justice system to change the system from within.' It is submitted that the current state of research on the issue is highly unsatisfactory and that the following statement made by Baldwin and McConville[9] in relation to the English criminal justice system nearly thirty years ago accurately depicts the *status quo* in this jurisdiction:

> In this country (unlike the United States), no real debate has ever been generated by this principle and it would probably be regarded, in legal circles at least, as fanciful to

> question it or even to suggest a reassessment of the premises upon which it is based. Yet there is no other single consideration that so pervades the workings of the whole administration of criminal justice...

The concern of this chapter is therefore to attempt to ignite discussion on the merits of the principle, in particular, through questioning its compatibility with the presumption of innocence. The sentencing discount holds important implications for the presumption in that it appears to punish those who put the prosecution's case to proof and may even, in combination with a number of other factors, induce the innocent to plead guilty.

(I) The effect of the Discount

There is no fixed tariff for the discount and an understandable reluctance by appellate courts to state a figure. Received wisdom, however, places it at approximately a third of the sentence. This figure may also be adjusted to take into account the stage at which the plea of guilty was entered (with an early plea of guilty presumably attracting a discount in or around the standard 30 per cent and a late plea receiving less of a reduction) and this principle has now been given statutory recognition. Section 29 of the *Criminal Justice Act 1999* provides that the sentencing court, if it considers it appropriate to do so, shall take account of the stage at which the person indicated an intention to plead guilty and the circumstances in which this indication was given. In reality, it is also likely that the discount is applied to varying degrees by different judges in the different courts. In the absence of Irish studies, English surveys of sentences in the Crown Court have revealed significant disparities in the average discounts applied despite increased statutory regulation: the average reduction was 22 per cent in one study, 31 per cent in another and 40 per cent in another.[10] Further, a recent study on the practice relating to the guilty plea in magistrates courts has found that magistrates ranged from failing to allow for the plea at all to (a significant number) awarding over a third discount in sentence length.[11]

Viewed in the light of studies which indicate worrying inconsistencies in sentencing practice in Ireland and the substantial discretion afforded judges in determining sentence, it is probable that not all defendants can be certain of a discount at a fixed rate.[12] That said, however, the '30 per cent' principle remains an important rule of thumb for solicitors and counsel in advising clients. It is also in line with estimations of the amount of the discount in other common law jurisdictions.[13]

(II) RATIONALES FOR THE DISCOUNT

Three justifications are generally offered by advocates of the rule:

- it provides evidence of remorse;
- there are time and cost savings to be made by the state and the community; and
- there are the benefits which accrue to victims from a plea such as the avoidance of secondary victimisation.

In relation to the first point, the underlying premise appears to be that remorse may be indicative of some change having taken place in the offender, who will now be in need of less reform by the state or who will already have inflicted some degree of self punishment. The second argument takes a much more pragmatic approach in that the quick disposition of the case will conserve prosecutorial resources (through time spent by members of the Gardaí on organizing witnesses and giving evidence in court, etc) and also judicial resources by freeing up court facilities and thereby alleviating trial waiting lists. More recently, judicial attention has been focused on the trauma spared to the victim who will not be forced to relive their experiences in court or undergo the rigours of cross examination. The element of uncertainty as to whether the defendant will go unpunished is also removed and the victim may feel vindicated and perhaps be better able to put their experience behind them. It is questionable whether this is true of all cases, however, even those involving violence or sexual assault. Some victims want their 'day in court' and a guilty plea for a considerable discount in sentence may result in them feeling disempowered as actors within the criminal justice system.[14] Indeed, it is ironic that in the US one of the key criticisms of plea bargaining is that it allows 'criminals' to get away with light sentences, and in California attempts at abolishing plea bargaining were made in 1982 as part of a Victims' Bill of Rights.

Returning to the first and second justifications, it may be noted that they appear to be in conflict in that, if adhered to strictly, the rationale relating to a defendant's contrition would deny a defendant a reduction in sentence where the plea was purely tactical. The second rationale, on the other hand, focuses on the administrative benefits which flow from the expedited guilty plea on the basis that the amount of time and money expended on a guilty plea is much less than a trial. On this view, there remains a basis for reducing a sentence even where the guilty plea is tactical rather than a product of remorse.

It is also interesting to note that the Australian jurisdictions, following the American lead,[15] have recently developed a jurisprudence which decouples the sentencing discount from its traditional basis in the expression of remorse. In *R v. Morton*,[16] for example, the Victorian Court of Criminal Appeal baldly stated that 'a plea of guilty may be taken into account regardless of whether or not it is also indicative of some other quality or attribute such as remorse . . . A court may always take a plea of guilty into account in mitigation of sentence even though it is purely motivated by self interest.' Recent developments in England are also suggestive of a shift away from remorse-driven considerations.[17] In Ireland, the position is unclear. There is, however, case law to the effect that a person cannot benefit from the reduction where caught red handed or where there is a very strong prosecution case.[18] This is suggestive of the remorse rationale remaining to the fore of the discount's *raison d'être*, although it should be noted that in practice defendants are rarely questioned by judges as to their attitude towards the crime, with remorse being imputed to the defendant with the entry of a guilty plea. Moreover, in addressing the bench in mitigation, it is common for counsel to draw the judge's attention to resource implications and the time and effort which would have been required by the prosecution should the accused have chosen to put them to proof.

The underlying basis of the rule does hold some significance for an issue which will be discussed in more detail below: namely, the risks posed to innocent defendants by the sentencing discount. McConville[19] has argued that the shift to pragmatic considerations presents an ethical dilemma for advocates and increases the risk of an innocent person pleading guilty: 'Once the system is structured on administrative values and rejects repentance and factual guilt as conditionalities, the fear of an enhanced sentence on conviction after trial clearly runs the risk of inducing guilty pleas from those who are or may be innocent.'

(III) Arguments against the discount

A range of objections to the guilty plea discount has been voiced by American and English critics over the years. Perhaps the most comprehensive argument, however, has recently been made by Darbyshire[20] who, frustrated at the neglect of the issue by the Royal Commission on Criminal Justice, sought to underline its importance for Lord Justice Auld in his Criminal Courts Review.[21] Darbyshire provides a near exhaustive list of the negative implications of sentence discounts and other forms of plea bargaining. These include the difficulty in reconciling the principle with traditional justifications for sentencing; the alienation of victims from the outcome; the lack of transparency in the process; the way in which the guilty plea system facilitates lazy prosecutors and defence lawyers; inconsistencies in the application of the discount and the exacerbation of racial divisions. In relation to the final point, it is worth noting that research conducted by Hood[22] in the UK suggests that Afro-Caribbean offenders plead guilty less often than white offenders, leading to a situation where, by virtue of the sentencing discount, they may be experiencing indirect discrimination. Discriminatory effects have also been noted for ethnic minorities in other jurisdictions such as the United States.[23]

A point which merits further development is in relation to the incompatibility of the discount with sentencing rationales such as deterrence, incapacitation, rehabilitation and just desserts.

The courts and legislature in Ireland have failed to identify a coherent policy in relation to sentencing. However, a just desserts approach is favoured by the Law Reform Commission in their 1996 *Report on Sentencing*.[24] As noted by de Londras,[25] the fact that the accused has pleaded guilty does not impact in any way on either the severity of the offence or the circumstances of the offender and should not be a relevant consideration under a just deserts approach. O'Malley,[26] however, recognizes that a just desserts system may be tempered by ethically relevant considerations but warns against the clearly unethical prospect of innocent defendants being lured into a plea of guilty by the sentencing discount, particularly in a country where defendants enjoy a constitutionally protected presumption of innocence and right to trial. It is this vista which will now be examined in the following sections.

(a) Honouring the Presumption of Innocence

One of the main objections raised to the sentencing discount is its impact on the integrity of the criminal justice system and core values such as the presumption of innocence. It is difficult to reconcile the existence of the practice in Ireland with a legal system which professes adherence to the requirement of proof beyond all reasonable doubt. Indeed, it is very difficult to escape the conclusion that the defendant is being punished for exercising his or her right to put the prosecution to proof through the increased penalty imposed after an unsuccessful jury trial.

The response to this argument in legal circles is usually to the effect that the defendant who insists upon a trial is not being punished *more* than his counterpart but rather his counterpart is being punished *less* on account of his plea. The defendant who is sentenced after a contested trial receives the appropriate sentence; he or she is simply denied a reduction available to defendants who plead guilty. The argument is summarised in the English decision of *R v. Harper*:[27]

> The Court feels that it is very improper to use language which may convey that an accused is being sentenced because he has pleaded not guilty or because he has run his

> defence in a particular way. It is, however, proper to give an accused a lesser sentence if he has shown genuine remorse amongst other things by pleading guilty.

It is noteworthy that the European Commission in the case of *X v. UK*[28] has taken a similar view in rejecting a claim that the heavier penalty for contesting a charge amounted to a breach of the right to fair trial under Article 6 of the European Convention on Human Rights. This is also the position in Ireland. In *People (DPP) v. Gillane*,[29] Lynch J. noted:

> 'Now the first thing to be remembered about this case, as was the Applicant's right, he fought the matter tooth and nail. That is his perfect right. It doesn't add one day to the appropriate sentence, but it does mean that he is not entitled to the discount which is now given virtually as a matter of course... [when there is a guilty plea].'

With respect, such reasoning at best rests on a dubious distinction and, at worst, smacks of sophistry. The *effect* of the discount system operated in England, Ireland and other common law countries is that the defendant is punished for his or her decision to put the prosecution to proof and this presents a serious challenge to our ostensible commitment to the presumption of innocence and adversarial justice generally. Unsurprisingly, few defendants who are, unlike judges, confronted with the reality of the situation have difficulty in arriving at this conclusion. From their interviews with defendants who pleaded guilty, Baldwin and McConville[30] found that virtually all defendants viewed this type of reasoning as 'meaningless' and viewed the discount system, regardless of the legal window dressing, as a penalty imposed on those who unsuccessfully contest their case. As Bagaric and Brebner[31] observe: 'Arguments of this nature are logically flawed, and constitute no more than an appeal to confusion by invoking the perennial glass is half empty or half full subterfuge.' The force of this argument has been recognized in Scotland where traditionally no discount could be offered for a plea, given the incompatibility of the discount with the presumption of innocence.[32] In 1981, Sheriff-Principal Nicolson[33] wrote in his text on sentencing in Scotland: 'It would be quite unacceptable that, in a legal system which presumes innocence and which permits every person to go to trial, a person who was found guilty after trial should be punished more severely simply because he had not pleaded guilty.' Even now, with the introduction of the sentence discount into law,[34] the Scottish courts have displayed a marked lack of enthusiasm for it and in *Du Plooy v. HM Advocate*[35] noted: 'Any practice of making an allowance has to be kept within bounds, so as to avoid discouraging, or appearing to discourage, accused persons from exercising their right to put the prosecution to proof.'

(b) Inducing a Guilty Plea

The problem identified by the Scottish courts in *Du Plooy*, namely the likelihood of inducing defendants to plead guilty, represents another side to the argument that the practice is irreconcilable with the presumption of innocence. It is arguable that we are attenuating the presumption by buying out the right of defendants to insist upon trial. As Ashworth[36] argues: 'If waiver of the right to trial is permitted and if we are serious about the presumption of innocence, anything that represents a standing incentive to waive the right would seem to contradict or weaken the presumption of innocence.' The question must be posed therefore: *Are innocent Irish defendants being induced to plead guilty by the hefty discount offered upon tendering a guilty plea rather than run the risk of a trial?*

The possibility is not as fanciful as it sounds. In the absence of Irish research, international studies provide cogent evidence that innocent defendants do plead guilty. Indeed, as the English Royal Commission on Criminal Justice[37] observed, 'it would be naive to suppose' that it does not happen. The reasons for this are many and complex but as the research below indicates, the reduction in sentence for a guilty plea is a significant factor for defendants in making this decision.

English researchers have led the charge in respect of this type of research. Despite the existence of a large amount of critical literature on sentence discounts and plea bargaining in the US, there would appear to be a research gap in relation to the rate of inconsistent pleading. Only one American study, conducted by Blumberg,[38] has looked at the area and has indicated that a high proportion of those who pleaded guilty (51.6 per cent) protested innocence. Figures such as these must obviously be treated with caution given that maintaining their innocence might well be one way for convicted persons to salvage their reputations or even wrestle with their own conscience.[39] However, subsequent findings consistent with Blumberg's study make the claim that some innocent defendants plead guilty difficult to dismiss.

Dell[40] carried out a study on 527 women in Holloway Prison and found that 106 of the women denied having committed any offence. Of these 106 women, 56 pleaded guilty, or 12 per cent of the overall sample. Her study is also useful in highlighting the suggestibility of some offenders. For example, she was struck by the number of women among the inconsistent pleaders who had no previous convictions and the high proportion of women among this group (64 per cent) who said they had pleaded guilty in response to police persuasion. A study by Bottoms and McClean[41] a few years later found that it was at least possible that 18 per cent of their subjects had suffered wrongful conviction on at least one charge, despite eliminating from the study all cases where the defendant's statement ruled out any hope of a legal defence. Similarly, Baldwin and McConville[42] examined 121 defendants who at a late stage pleaded guilty in Birmingham Crown Court. They found that a high proportion of these defendants (over 50 per cent) had made some protestation of innocence 'with varying degrees of fervour and credibility' to some or all of the charges. Even more worrying was the significant cohort of defendants (36 per cent) who had made *strong* protestations as to their innocence. In the course of interviewing the defendants, the researchers were 'struck by the decisive influence that this reduction in sentence, whether real or assumed has upon them'.[43]

Finally, research carried out by the Royal Commission on Criminal Justice[44] in England suggested that approximately 11 per cent of defendants who plead guilty claim innocence but the Commission went on to state that 'there was little if any evidence' that this was because of the sentencing discount. Their dismissive attitude to the role of the guilty plea in encouraging inconsistent pleading, must be viewed in light of the Commission's approach to the issue which was dominated by the problem of cracked trials (where the defendant pleads guilty on the trial date). Further, their ultimate recommendation to balance this risk 'against the benefits to the system of encouraging those who are in fact guilty to plead guilty'[45] is a conclusion which seems to undervalue one of the most important rights in the whole criminal justice system – the right of a citizen not to suffer wrongful conviction.

It is important to look at the context in which the seemingly unthinkable happens and an innocent person pleads guilty. The defendant may feel it is futile to try to contest the case, despite their innocence. Innocent defendants do exist who have fallen victim to 'an unfortunate concatenation of events',[46] a tissue of lies or even a conspiracy of silence. Even absent these factors, the discount or a more lenient sentence may prove very attractive to a risk-averse innocent defendant who must consider lengthy remands, possibly in custody, and the gamble that a jury will vindicate his or her innocence. The dilemma is well described by Willis:[47]

> [For the defendant] the stakes will be generally high – acquittal or imprisonment; the outcome uncertain; a plea of not guilty likely to lead to further delays in the determination of the case; and the actual trial a lengthy ordeal to be endured . . . even for an innocent defendant, the guilty plea with an expectation of leniency can be an attractive soft option.

The potential for improper inducement is particularly marked in certain types of cases. The introduction in 1999 of a mandatory minimum sentence of ten years' imprisonment in this jurisdiction in respect of persons charged with possession of drugs valued at over €13,000 (s.15A, *Misuse of Drugs Act 1977*) has placed considerable pressure on such defendants to plead guilty.[48] This is on account of the fact that judges have interpreted the legislation in such a way as to disapply the mandatory minimum where a defendant enters an early plea of guilty or provides material assistance to the Gardaí. (In this situation, a typical sentence would probably be in the range of six to seven years.)[49] This is problematic as the greater the differential between the sentence which would be received after trial and the sentence received on a plea, the greater the coercive power of the discount. The encouragement of a greater number of guilty pleas was one of the primary motivations behind the enactment of the legislation. However, these risks act as a powerful disincentive to defendants with a reasonable chance of acquittal to contest their case. A recent report commissioned by the Department of Justice[50] on the criteria applied by the courts in sentencing under these provisions has noted that in all but one of the fifty-five cases studied the accused pleaded guilty, a statistic which suggests a much higher rate of guilty pleas than for indictable offences generally (78 per cent). The same author continues:

> In a criminal trial anything can go wrong; difficulties can arise with warrants, witnesses may be unavailable for a variety of reasons, there can be a flaw in the chain of evidence, technical errors may be made and so forth. However, the consequences of unsuccessfully testing the prosecution case in a s.15A charge are so severe, it would seem that one of the practical effects of the section has been to discourage the vast majority of accused persons from proceeding to trial unless the case against them appears to be obviously flawed.[51]

Although there is a clear implication in the report that the legislation has had a positive effect on busy court lists, the darker side of a system which produces a constant stream of guilty pleas is that the prosecution case is never tested and the Gardaí and prosecution are provided with little incentive to build a thorough, independent case. The function of the adversarial system of justice is, after all, to prove guilt in a public forum beyond all reasonable doubt. The borderline case where the accused forgoes trial to avail of the discount may be exactly the case where justice is best served through the public proof of guilt. Like plea bargaining generally, a system which provides a considerable incentive to plead guilty through sentence discounts 'turns the adversarial model on its head to one in which the individual is required to choose between a series of options which are more or less onerous rather than the assuring that the State is in possession of legally sufficient evidence in the first place; little if any check exists on the case for the prosecution.'[52]

Even for defendants charged with less serious offences, however, the benefits to be reaped by a plea are considerable and may influence the *form* of sentence eventually imposed,[53] rather than simply offering a reduction in the length of a custodial term or community sentence. This must exert a powerful influence over even the most resolute defendants and, as Ashworth argues, may well constitute 'constraint' in the decision-making process of the sort that has been found to be incompatible with the fair trial provisions of the European Convention on Human Rights.[54] Baldwin and McConville's[55] study of guilty pleaders in Birmingham Crown Court found that defendants who unsuccessfully contested their cases were much more likely than those who pleaded guilty to receive custodial sentences. Given that the study controlled for other factors such as sex, age, nature and number of offences charged, criminal record, etc, the researchers concluded: 'The fact that many more of those who contested their cases received custodial sentences than was the case with either of the other groups [guilty pleas and late changers to guilty pleas] cannot, if our analysis is correct, be explained other than in terms of the plea tendered.'[56] Considerable pressure may also be exerted by the practice discussed below of the prosecution accepting a plea of guilty to a significantly lesser charge.

A cynic might respond with an argument that the many protections afforded accused persons within the criminal justice system, most notably the advice provided by the defendant's legal team, can effectively counteract any risk of an innocent defendant pleading guilty. Yet, the advice furnished by defence counsel may well be a factor militating *in favour* of a guilty plea. In both Bottoms and McClean's[57] and Baldwin and McConville's[58] studies, legal advice given by a lawyer to plead guilty had featured strongly in the defendant's reasons for entering a plea. The sentence discount has the effect of putting defence counsel in the position of persuading a defendant who maintains their innocence in the face of a strong prosecution case to plead guilty in order to avoid a more severe sentence. Strong advice short of coercion may be given (putting pressure on a defendant to plead guilty is expressly forbidden by the Bar *Code of Conduct*) and may be assisted by what McConville *et al* have described in *Standing Accused*[59] as the procurement of a 'sweetener' from the prosecution, namely 'the dropping of a charge or an agreement between prosecution and defence as to the way a case will be presented in court so as to secure a light sentence'. Despite the reluctance to openly discuss prosecutorial plea bargaining in this jurisdiction, this practice is widespread in the Law Library, subject always to the final *imprimatur* of the DPP.[60] It is mostly well intentioned and is facilitated to a large degree by the non-confrontational relationships between prosecution and defence counsel.

More recently, McConville[61] has examined the guidance offered to practitioners by the ethical codes of conduct in a situation where an accused maintains their innocence yet wishes to plead guilty and argues that it should be understood within the broader political context. The guilty plea, through the political shift towards managerialism, has come to be celebrated in England as 'an ornament of the adversary system, as a jewel in its crown'.[62] It is argued that, by removing cases in which guilt is 'evident' from the system, it reserves the trial (and state resources) for only truly 'worthy' cases. The relevant sections of the *Code of Conduct for the Bar of England and Wales*[63] read as follows:

> Where a defendant tells his counsel that he did not commit the offence with which he is charged but nevertheless insists upon pleading guilty to it for reasons of his own, counsel must continue to represent him, but only after he has advised what the consequences will be and that what can be submitted in mitigation can only be on the basis that the client is guilty.

This guidance given above makes little mention of counsel's decision as to whether to accept instructions and can be contrasted with the barrister's duty when a guilty person enters a plea of not guilty. In that situation the rules state that the barrister cannot actively deceive the court by adducing evidence which he or she knows to be false. (It is important to remember that the entry of the not guilty plea itself does not amount to a deception as the defendant is entitled to put the prosecution to proof.) It would appear that no such restrictions are put in place where the converse situation obtains yet, unlike a plea of not guilty, the tendering of a guilty plea is a confession to having in fact committed the crime, not a recognition of the strength of the prosecution case or the likelihood of conviction. It is therefore difficult, as McConville argues, to avoid the conclusion that counsel is knowingly misleading the court.

While the pressures of managerialism are less acute in Irish criminal justice policy,[64] scrutiny of the *Code of Conduct of the Bar of Ireland*[65] reveals a degree of ambiguity around the problem of inconsistent pleading. As noted above, it is clear that a barrister cannot pressurize a defendant into pleading guilty and, in common with the English rules, counsel may not advance an ambiguous plea to the court or evidence which is inconsistent with the plea of guilty. However, the key instruction appears to be that 'a barrister should always consider very carefully whether it is proper, in the interests of justice, to accept instructions to enter a plea of guilty'. This is a stricter approach than that taken by the English Code in that counsel is seen to bear some responsibility for the effects of the plea, yet it is clear that the entering of a plea of guilty which conflicts with an assertion of innocence by the defendant is not prohibited.

By way of a closing remark, it should be noted that the criminal law may be accused of hypocrisy in excluding confession evidence induced by a threat or inducement yet refusing to acknowledge the real pressures which the legal system itself places upon an innocent defendant to confess. Findaly *et al.*[66] have remarked: 'It is a paradox [that] courts are diligent to prevent . . . pressure or inducement . . . to bring about an admission . . . and yet with . . . the plea of guilty such inducements have been institutionalised.' In this jurisdiction, the courts clearly recognize the powerful influence which may be exerted by a 'person in authority' in obtaining a confession.[67] Yet, the rights of the accused are not so jealously guarded where another authority figure in the form of the defendant's counsel provides an inducement to confess through a significant reduction in sentence or lesser charge.[68]

Conclusion

The discount is a stark reminder of the gap between rhetoric and reality in Anglo-American legal systems. These systems boast a jurisprudence replete with encomia to the jury trial, the presumption of innocence and proof beyond all reasonable doubt, yet most defendants plead guilty on the basis of a discount or reduced charge. In the words of one critic of the American plea bargaining system: 'The plea bargain convinces criminals that the majesty of the law is a fraud, that the law is like a Turkish bazaar.'[69]

There is no easy solution to the problem, given the entrenchment of the guilty plea in Irish legal culture and the pressure on resources. However, neither is there excuse for complacency in light of evidence that the sentencing discount principle seriously compromises the presumption of innocence. It is submitted that part of the long term solution, as for so many other problematic aspects of the Irish criminal justice system, lies in a detailed study of the operation and effects of the guilty plea discounts in both the lower and higher courts. In the interim, there is a strong case to be made for:

- reducing the sentence discount from its current rate of 30 per cent to 10 per cent so that vulnerable or undecided defendants are less likely to be affected by the discount;[70]
- requiring judges to state openly in court the amount of discount applied for a guilty plea;
- more stringent controls being exercised by the Office of the DPP on the practice of prosecutorial plea bargaining;
- clarification of the *Code of Conduct of the Bar of Ireland* in relation to inconsistent pleading;
- revisiting the system of mandatory minimum sentencing introduced by the *Criminal Justice Act 1999*.

The above proposals will at least ensure greater transparency in the operation of the plea as well as alleviating pressure on an innocent accused to plead guilty. It is important that the argument to reduce the level of the discount is not dismissed on bureaucratic grounds. As Ashworth[71] notes, the doomsday scenario painted by many advocates of the discount fails to consider how most countries on the European continent operate effectively without plea bargaining or discounts, and indeed, how the English and American systems did so prior to *circa* 1835.[72] Scotland's criminal justice system has also managed without it until the mid-1990s. If it is within the gift of the state and the legal profession to ensure the presumption of innocence is fully respected, and defendants are not punished for exercising their right to trial, then every effort should be made to do so.

As eloquently argued by Charleton and McDermott:[73]

> The presumption of innocence is something which is not to be regarded as a political shibboleth. It is the constitutional basis of the manner in which the system of law is to be administered in Ireland. Lawyers are supposed to believe in the ideology behind the law, as an expression of the desire to seek justice, apart from being also glibly required to state certain rules. They are there for the benefit of the community and not simply as an aid in legal argument.

Notes

1 Courts Service *Annual Report 2004*. (Dublin: 2004)These can be further divided into 1,465 guilty pleas (before trial) and 183 cases where defendants changed to a guilty plea. There were 355 jury trials (17%) and 115 *nolle prosequis* entered by the prosecution (5%).

2 The UK *Criminal Justice Business Quarterly Reports 1999–2000* state that the plea rate is 93% in the magistrates courts as opposed to 73% in the Crown Courts.

3 See further the author's extensive discussion of the issue: D. Guidorizzi 'Should we Really "Ban" Plea Bargaining: the Core Concerns of Plea Bargaining Critics' (1998) 47 *Emory Law Journal* 753 pp.755–7.

4 *Ibid.* p.757.

5 See comments of P. Charleton and P. A. McDermott 'Constitutional Implications of Plea Bargaining' (2000) *Bar Rev* 476 pp.476–7 who, having cited an article by C. Lysaght in the New Law Journal, 'A Tale of Two Judges' (1999) 149 *NLJ* 666, noted: 'If this comment refers to the Sheedy case, it is inaccurate. There is nothing to suggest that solicitors and counsel for the defence or prosecution acted in any way improperly in that case.'

6 Section 29, *Criminal Justice Act 1999* (Ireland); s.152 *Powers of Criminal*

Courts (Sentencing) Act 2000 (UK, replacing s.48 of the *Criminal Justice and Public Order Act 1994*); s.196 *Criminal Procedure (Scotland) Act 1995* (Scotland); s.16A(2)(g) *Crimes Act 1914* (Commonwealth, Australia); s.429(1)(u) Crimes Act 1900 (ACT, Australia); s.13 *Penalties and Sentences Act 1992* (Queensland, Australia); s.22 *Crimes (Sentencing Procedure) Act 1999* (New South Wales); s.5(2)(j) *Sentencing Act* (Northern Territory); s.10(g) *Criminal Law (Sentencing) Act 1988* (SA); s.5(2)(e) *Sentencing Act 1991* (Victoria); s.8(2) *Sentencing Act 1995* (Western Australia).

7 Professor Cross has claimed that 'the English system of criminal trials would break down if everyone charged with an offence in a superior court were to plead not guilty'. See R. Cross *The English Sentencing System* (London: Butterworths, 1971) pp.153–4. Burger C.J. in the US has also suggested that a small change in the guilty plea rate would have dramatic consequences in a speech to the American Bar Association cited in S. Schulhofer 'Is Plea Bargaining Inevitable?' (1984) 97 *Harv LR* 1037.

8 F. de Londras 'Kow Towing to the Twin Gods of Time and Money: The Guilty Plea Discount in Sentencing' (2004) 14(1) *ICLJ* 14 p.16.

9 J. Baldwin and M. McConville 'The Influence of the Sentencing Discount in Inducing Guilty Pleas' in J. Baldwin and A. Bottomley (eds) *Criminal Justice: Selected Readings* (Martin Robertson, 1978) at p.116.

10 For further details see A. Ashworth *Sentencing and Criminal Justice* (3rd ed, London: Butterworths, 2000) pp.144–6.

11 R. Henham 'Reconciling Process and Policy: Sentence Discounts in the Magistrates Courts' [2000] *Crim LR* 436.

12 In relation to inconsistency in sentencing see I. Bacik 'The Practice of Sentencing in the Irish Courts' in P. O'Mahony *Criminal Justice in Ireland* (IPA, 2002) p.348 and, in relation to the lower courts, C. Hamilton 'Sentencing in the District Court: Here Be Dragons' (2005) 15(3) *ICLJ* 9.

13 See K. Mack and S.R. Anleu 'Sentence Discount for a Guilty Plea: Time for a New Look' (1997) 1 *FJLR* 123 p.129.

14 Darbyshire 'The Mischief of Plea Bargaining and Sentence Rewards' [2000] *Crim LR* 895 p.905 draws attention to a study by E. Erez in 'Who's Afraid of the Big Bad Victim? Victim Impact Statements as Victim Empowerment and Enhancement of Justice' [1999] *Crim LR* 545, which argues that victims generally appreciate an opportunity to be heard.

15 The American courts have abandoned any adherence to remorse as a justification for plea bargaining with the acceptance of the 'Alford plea'. This allows a defendant to advance of plea of guilty while maintaining his or her innocence. The constitutionality of the plea was upheld in *North Carolina v. Alford* 400 US 25 (1970). See W.Pizzi 'Accepting guilty pleas from "innocent" defendants?' (1996) *NLJ* 997.

16 [1986] VR 863 at 867. See also *R v. Shannon* (1979) 21 SASR 442.

17 M. McConville 'Plea Bargaining: Ethics and Politics' (1998) 25(4) *Journal of Law and Society* 562 p.564 argues that this development

began with *R v. Cain* [1976] *Crim LR* 464 and was continued in a more nuanced way by the Court of Appeal. See also *R v. Fearon* [1996] 2 CrApp R (S) 25.

18 *People (DPP) v. M* [1994] 3 IR 306 at 319.

19 M. McConville *op. cit.* p.565.

20 P. Darbyshire *op. cit.*

21 In the event, Darbyshire's imprecations fell on deaf ears. The Auld Report simply noted that no system can prevent some innocent defendants from pleading guilty prior to expressing the view that a substantial discount was necessary to avoid guilty defendants simply 'playing the system'.

22 R. Hood *Race and Sentencing* (OUP, 1992).

23 Darbyshire *op. cit.* refers to a study by *San Jose Mercury News* in 1993 on 6,000 Californian defendants. Hispanics and blacks fared worse than whites in plea bargains.

24 Law Reform Commission *Report on Sentencing* (LRC 53-1996).

25 F. de Londras *op. cit.* p.17.

26 O'Malley *Sentencing Law and Practice* (Dublin: Round Hall, Sweet & Maxwell, 2000) pp.166–7.

27 [1967] 3 All ER.

28 (1972) 40 CD 64.

29 Unreported, CCA, 21 December 1998.

30 *Op. cit.* pp.118–9.

31 M. Bagaric and J. Brebner 'The solution to the dilemma of the guilty plea discount – I'm pleading guilty only because of the discount…' (2002) 30 *International Journal of the Sociology of the Law* 51 p.58.

32 *Strawhorn v. McLeod* 1987 SCCR 413.

33 C. Nicholson *The Law and Practice of Sentencing in Scotland* (1st ed., Edinburgh: W. Green Sweet & Maxwell, 1981) p.219 quoted in A. Ashworth *The Criminal Process* (1998) p.275.

34 Section 196, *Criminal Procedure (Scotland) Act 1995*.

35 2003 SCCR 640 at 644.

36 A. Ashworth *The Criminal Process* (2nd ed., OUP, 1998) p.276.

37 Royal Commission on Criminal Justice, 1993 *Report of the Royal Commission on Criminal Justice* (London, HMSO, 1993 (Cmnd, 2263)) at para. 7.42.

38 A.S. Blumberg *Criminal Justice* (Chicago: Quandrangle Books, 1967).

39 One is reminded of the quote from the film, *The Shawshank Redemption* (1994):

> Red: Everybody's innocent in here.
> Andy Dufresne: What about you?
> Red: Only guilty man in Shawshank.

40 S. Dell *Silent in Court* (Bell and Sons, 1971).

41 A. Bottoms and J. McClean *Defendants in the Criminal Process* (London: Routledge & Keagan Paul, 1976).

42 *Op cit.*

43 *Ibid.* p.117.
44 *Op. cit.*
45 *Ibid.* at para. 7.43.
46 This term is one which Charleton and McDermott (*op. cit.* p.480), note is used by a certain criminal practitioner in closing speeches to juries.
47 J. Willis 'Sentencing Discount for Guilty Pleas' (1985) 18 *Australian New Zealand Journal of Criminology* 18 p.141.
48 Section 15A of the *Misuse of Drugs Act 1977*, as amended by sections 4 and 5 of the *Criminal Justice Act 1999*.
49 P. McEvoy BL 'Research for the Department of Justice on the criteria applied by the Courts in sentencing under s.15A of the Misuse of Drugs Act 1977 (as amended)', 15 February 2005 available at www.justice.ie p.10.
50 *Ibid.*
51 *Ibid.* p.11.
52 M. McConville and C. Mirsky 'The skeleton of plea bargaining' (1992) 142 *NLJ* 1373.
53 See *R v. Howells* [1999] 1 Cr App R (S) 335.
54 See further A. Ashworth & M. Redmayne *The Criminal Process* (3rd ed., OUP, 2005) p.288 and also *Deweer v. Belgium* (1980) 2 EHRR 439.
55 *Op.cit.*
56 *Ibid.* p.120.
57 *Op. cit.*
58 *Op. cit.*
59 M. McConville, J. Hodgson, L. Bridge and A. Pavlovic *Standing Accused* (Clarendon Press, 1994).
60 Charleton and McDermott *op. cit.* p.476 cite Eamonn Barnes, former Director of Public Prosecutions, as stating: 'Prosecution counsel are not authorised to enter into any bargain or agreement about sentence and as far as I know they do not now ever do so.'
61 M. McConville 'Plea Bargaining: Ethics and Politics' (1998) 25(4) *Journal of Law and Society* 562.
62 *Ibid.* p.581.
63 5th ed, paragraph 12.5. For the current 8th edition see Code of Conduct, Section 3, 'Written Standards for the Conduct of Professional Work' at: http://www.barcouncil.org.uk/document.asp?languageid=1&documentid=2816#ParaLink10.
64 See S. Kilcommins, I. O'Donnell, E O'Sullivan and B. Vaughan *Crime, Punishment and the Search for Order in Ireland* (IPA, 2004) p.290.
65 Bar Council of Ireland *Code of Conduct*, 'Duty of a Barrister in the Code of Conduct of a Criminal Case' Paragraph 9.11.
66 M. Findaly, S. Odgers and S. Yeo *Australian Criminal Justice* (OUP, Melbourne) pp.114–15.
67 *People v. Murphy* [1947] IR 236.
68 Ashworth, *op.cit.* (1998) notes that the validity of this analogy was recognized by the Royal Commission on Criminal Justice, *op. cit.* who, despite their general complacency, seemed concerned that care be taken

during plea negotiations with vulnerable defendants who would be entitled to the support of an appropriate adult at a police station.

69 John Kaplan 'American Merchandising and the Guilty Plea: Replacing the Bazaar with the Department Store' (1977) 5 *Am. J. Crim. L.* 215 p.218.

70 This is also the figure recommended by Mack and Anleu *op. cit.* p.142.

71 *Op. cit.* p.282.

72 For an historical account of the development of plea bargaining see M. Feeley 'Legal complexity and the Transformation of the Criminal Process: the Origins of Plea Bargaining' (1997) 31 *Israel Law Review* 183.

73 *Op. cit.* p.480.

Chapter Nine

The Presumption Abroad

The indifference of the legislative and executive braches of government to the presumption of innocence is not particular to Ireland. Over the Irish Sea, New Labour have been producing criminal legislation at a frenetic pace with reforms that inevitably result in a diminution rather than strengthening of the rights of the accused. While an exhaustive analysis of the impact of recent legislative developments in England on the presumption is beyond the scope of this chapter, it is proposed to examine in some detail the *Criminal Justice Act 2003* as a major criminal statute which has been attended by much controversy. The legislative pace in England has also quickened since the September 11 attacks on the USA and the subsequent 'war on terror' and it is further proposed to examine recent counter-terrorism measures introduced in both the UK and the United States. While law relating to subversive activity is often viewed by some as *sui generis* or distinct from the 'ordinary' criminal law, to overlook these statutes would be to overlook some of the most serious abrogations of the presumption in countries to which Ireland has often looked in criminal justice matters.[1]

(I) The English Criminal Justice Act 2003

The 2003 Act has been described as the Labour Government's flagship piece of criminal justice legislation and was heralded, in terms now commonplace in New Labour rhetoric, as a means of 'rebalancing the system in favour of victims'.[2] It is a complex and wide ranging statute introducing extensive changes to police powers, bail, cautioning, and pre-trial disclosure, as well as trial by jury and sentencing. It has also overhauled mainstay principles of the criminal justice system such as the rule against hearsay evidence, the double jeopardy rule and the rules on the admissibility of bad character evidence. It is the provisions concerning the operation of the latter two rules which form the focus of the present discussion given their relevance to the presumption of innocence.

(a) Bad Character and the Presumption

The provisions concerning evidence of bad character are contained in Part 11 of the Act. Section 101 of the Act provides that evidence of the defendant's bad character is admissible if it can pass through one of the seven 'gateways' listed in subsection 1.[3] Many of these gateways will be familiar to English criminal lawyers, such as situations where the defendant has attacked the character of another (s.101(1)(g))[4] or where the evidence is necessary to understand other important evidence in the case (s.101(1)(c)) and in some respects the law has merely codified the existing common law position. However, scrutiny of the core gateway – (d) – which allows such evidence 'where it is relevant to an important matter in issue between the defendant and the prosecution', reveals that the law has been radically reformed. Whereas before bad character evidence was generally admitted where its probative value outweighed its prejudicial effect (*DPP v. P*),[5] s.101(d) (read together with s.103(1)) allows such evidence to be adduced on the basis that the accused has a general tendency to commit offences of this type.

Admittedly, the harsh effects of section 101(1)(d) – which amounts to no more than a general restatement of the primary rule of evidence as to relevance to the facts in issue – are somewhat ameliorated by the provisions of s.101(4) which sets down a general fairness criterion. Under this subsection, trial judges can exercise their discretion to exclude such evidence where it 'would have such an adverse effect on the fairness of the proceedings that the court ought not to admit it'. Indeed, the existence of this saver has prompted Roberts and Zuckerman[6] to argue: 'The net effect may well be to place *DPP v. P* on a statutory footing. When trial judges ask themselves whether bad character evidence "would have such an adverse effect on the fairness of the proceedings that the court ought not to admit it" they will naturally think back to how the PV > PE [probative value must be greater than prejudicial effect] test would have applied in these circumstances.' The difficulty with this argument is that the statutory rule as to bad character evidence in s.101(d) replaces the basic common law rule of inadmissibility of such evidence with a general rule that such evidence is *prima facie* admissible. Fairness is included very much as an exception to this general rule rather than a cardinal principle which admitted of exceptions in cases where the evidence had particular probative value and the importance of this shift in the legislation should not be underestimated. Analysis of the provisions has led Ashworth and Redmayne[7] to note that 'potentially at least, the new provisions are radical' and, despite the obscure wording of the legislation, it is difficult to disagree given the conceptual shift in favour of admissibility.

Further, even where a previous conviction is not admissible under this provision to show propensity, the Act allows that it may still be relevant to credibility or the 'question whether the defendant has a propensity to be untruthful'.[8] This runs contrary to both research conducted by the English Law Commission,[9] which found that jurors' assessments of an accused's honesty were in general not affected by the knowledge that they had committed criminal offences in the past, and psychological research to the same effect.[10] Juries may therefore not view the evidence as discrediting the accused but as highly probative of guilt.

Concern over the admission of such evidence is, moreover, compounded when one considers the Act in even greater detail. 'Bad character' under the Act is defined in s.98 as 'evidence of, or of a disposition towards, misconduct' on a person's part. This is further elaborated upon in s.112 which defines the key concept of 'misconduct' as 'the commission of an offence or other reprehensible behaviour'. Thus, 'misconduct' includes not just previous convictions to be used in evidence against a defendant, but previous allegations, acquittals and general behaviour as well. As noted by Munday,[11] the very concept of 'reprehensibility' 'is without a true fixed meaning; it tends to take on colour both from the context in which it is employed and from the qualifying adverbs that commonly accompany it'.

It is difficult to see how the presumption of innocence may be maintained if previous acquittals are allowed to play a role in determining guilt. Tapper[12] notes the very serious erosion of the presumption of innocence represented by a combination of sections 98 and 109 of the Act as the latter section mandates an assumption of the truth of bad character evidence. He observes that cumulatively 'these two provisions appear to be capable of creating a presumption, at least for the purpose of determining admissibility, that a person is guilty of an offence of which he has been acquitted'.[13] It will be interesting to see how the courts reconcile these provisions with the presumption of innocence in Article 6(2) of the ECHR should the provisions of the Act be challenged under the *Human Rights Act 1998*.

The traditional exclusionary rule on the admission of evidence of the bad character of the accused can be viewed as flowing inexorably from the presumption of innocence. Indeed, in Irish law this link has been made explicit. In *King v. AG*,[14] McWilliam J. held that: 'One of the concepts of justice which the courts have always accepted is that evidence of character or of previous convictions shall not be given at a criminal trial except at the instigation of the accused, as that could prejudice the fair trial of the issue of the guilt or innocence of the accused.' The presumption of innocence is obviously undermined by the adduction of evidence of previous bad character, as in reality the defendant is being asked to prove his or her innocence. As Murphy J. put it in *R v. Perry*,[15] the evidence 'conjures up a highly suspicious prejudicial atmosphere in which the presumption of innocence tends to be replaced with a presumption of guilt'. More specifically, the presumption is undermined through what is known as 'reasoning prejudice' or 'moral prejudice'.

The first type of prejudice results in juries concluding that the accused is the sort of person to commit a certain type of offence and convict them. This is reasoning of the 'give a dog a bad name and hang him' variety. As noted by the Law Commission,[16] this reasoning may not be illogical, as the evidence may well be probative of guilt, but the objection arises from jurors or other fact finders placing undue weight on evidence that the accused has engaged in previous wrongdoing and giving insufficient thought to the possibility that the accused has reformed. Further, jurors who consider it too much of a 'coincidence' that the accused has been arrested for the current charge may fail to allow for increased police scrutiny of known offenders and the continued tendency of police forces to 'round up the usual suspects'. In this regard, it is notable that a study by Hood *et al.*[17] in England found that a significant number of ethnic minority defendants complained about having their past held against them by the authorities when they claimed to have changed and have made a genuine effort to reform. This perception of unfairness is likely to be exacerbated with the entry into force of the new provisions.

The second type of 'moral' prejudice results in the jury abandoning its sworn oath and applying a standard of proof below that of beyond all reasonable doubt on account of the defendant's previous misconduct. In its most extreme manifestation, the jury will, irrespective of the strength of evidence on the present charge, seek to punish the defendant for earlier misconduct. This may occur on the basis that a person such as the accused has less to lose than someone without a criminal record or history of misdeeds and this in turn serves to minimize the regret that juries feel in convicting.

Both these reasoning processes offend the presumption of innocence by leading to a *de facto* reduction in the standard of proof. This is most obvious in relation to moral prejudice through which fact finders themselves employ a lower standard of proof for those with convictions. However, it is submitted that the standard of proof may also be indirectly affected by reasoning prejudice. If the prosecution uses bad character evidence to bolster a weak prosecution case this may also have implications for the criminal standard of proof. Evidence of the accused's bad character can be used to establish a *prima facie* case at trial or to bolster an existing *prima facie* case to the standard of beyond a reasonable doubt. In his critical appraisal of the Act, Munday[18] illustrates the practical problem here. He gives the example of a defendant who is prosecuted for burglary on the basis of some previous convictions; some circumstantial evidence such as a footprint from a trainer similar to one worn by the defendant and a lie told by the defendant as to his whereabouts on the date of the crime. The defendant in that situation, if convicted, will really be convicted on the basis of previous conduct rather than on the other evidence so that the *prima facie* case, the lowest threshold of proof, is in effect elevated to the highest form, that beyond a reasonable doubt.

It is noteworthy that some empirical support for the above theories has been garnered from a recent 'mock-jury' experiment carried out by Dr Sally Lloyd Bostock on behalf of the Law Commission.[19] Bostock found that 'evidence of previous convictions can have a prejudicial effect, especially were there is a recent previous conviction for a similar offence. Significant effects were found even though no information about the previous conviction other than the offence was provided, and where there was only one previous conviction'.[20] Further, certain types of conviction were found to be particularly prejudicial. Irrespective of the nature of the current charge, jurors were more likely to convict the defendant when told he or she had a previous conviction of indecent assault on a child, a finding which gives some support to common sense assumptions as to moral prejudice.[21] In the light of the findings, she has been critical of the reforms introduced by the 2003 Act: 'I think not enough account has been taken of the psychology of how people are going to use this information. A previous similar conviction, especially a recent one, is psychologically a very powerful piece of information.'[22] Added to this is the generally more punitive climate in which we live today. In Ireland this has been described by leading criminologist, O'Mahony,[23] as a 'hard-line consensus' or 'new militant penal tendency'. As Roberts and Zuckerman[24] note, modern jurors may be increasingly prone to moral prejudice: 'In an increasingly punitive penal climate, which is both cause and effect of historically unprecedented crime rates and widespread feelings of insecurity, the likelihood is even greater that jurors will project their fear and anger into scapegoating "criminals" for the ills of society.'

(b) Retrial for Serious Offences

Parts 9 and 10 of the 2003 Act introduce radical changes to the law relating to prosecution appeals and retrials for serious offences respectively. It is the latter, more controversial, topic with which we are concerned here. Part 10 provides for a possible retrial where a person has been acquitted of a 'qualifying offence' on indictment or on appeal against a conviction in proceedings on indictment. 'Qualifying offence' is defined in Part 1, Schedule 5 of the Act and includes twenty-nine offences, such as murder, manslaughter, rape, drugs trafficking and some of the more serious criminal damage offences. This list is much more extensive than that originally proposed by the Law Commission[25] or by the Home Office in *Justice for All.*[26] It is of further significance that the Act has retrospective effect in that it applies to acquittals secured *before* the 2003 Act came into operation. It is therefore likely that the impact of this legislative inroad into the double jeopardy rule will be considerable.

The criteria for the reopening of an acquittal are set down in ss.78 and 79 of the Act and are applied by the Court of Appeal upon application by the prosecution. The prosecution must be able to point to 'new and compelling evidence', defined as evidence which is reliable, substantial and 'highly probative of the case against the acquitted person'. It is noteworthy that evidence is 'new' if it was 'not adduced in the proceedings in which the person was acquitted'.[27] The broad definition given to new evidence means that the evidence in question could comprise evidence which could have been, but was not, adduced at the original trial therefore opening up the possibility that a second trial could be used to mend the prosecution's hand following a sloppy first outing. While the fact that the evidence would have been used in the first trial 'but for a failure by an officer or by a prosecutor to act with due diligence or expedition' is a factor going to the exercise of the judge's discretion to deem a retrial unfair in section 79, it is questionable whether this affords sufficient protection to the acquitted person. As noted by the Joint Committee on Human Rights,[28] a case could still be reopened in the following circumstances:

'(a) where evidence that was available was inadmissible at the time of the original trial, but the law has subsequently been amended to allow the evidence to be admissible (e.g. hearsay evidence);

(b) where the prosecution decided not to adduce admissible evidence at the original trial for sound tactical reasons, in circumstances that did not amount to a lack of diligence or expedition on their part;

(c) where the evidence was not adduced at the earlier trial, and this was because of a lack of diligence or expedition on the part of an officer or prosecutor, but the Court of Appeal decides in its discretion that the case should be reopened to allow the evidence to be used, because the seriousness of the crime and the likelihood of being able to give a fair hearing to the accused mean that it is in the interests of justice to do so.'

It is for this reason – the real possibility that the evidence in question may not in fact be new evidence – that the Committee considered that the provisions of the Act fell foul of Article 14.7 of the International Covenant on Civil and Political Rights (ICCPR) which prohibits the reopening of a case save in exceptional circumstances. Section 79 sets down an 'interests of justice' test and lists a number of considerations to which the court must have regard in determining whether a fair trial is possible, such as delay, media coverage and, as observed, prosecutorial laxity at the first trial. Only one application can be made for each acquittal.

While the provisions of the Act obviously offend principles of finality in criminal proceedings,[29] the concern here is with their impact on the presumption of innocence. In the particular context of the 2003 Act, it is a matter of no small moment that the retrial of the offence would be taking place against a background of a determination by the Court of Appeal that new, substantial, highly probative evidence had come to light. It is therefore at least arguable that the second trial would essentially be proceeding from a presumption of guilt rather than innocence. As Kennedy[30] writes:

> The campaigns for retrial will inevitably attract huge publicity. How can there be a fair retrial? A second jury might assume that, since our cleverest judges find the new evidence highly persuasive, their role is simply to endorse a conviction. The assumption at a retrial brought about

> because of new and compelling evidence will be that the defendant must be guilty. How does this square with the presumption of innocence?

It is submitted that the new provisions do not sit easily with the presumption and indeed, contradict it. As a response to some of the concerns voiced, the Government has given powers to the Court of Appeal to impose reporting restrictions to prevent a substantial risk of prejudice to a retrial. While this is a welcome safeguard, it is probable that the damage will have been done given the likelihood of intense media coverage of the trial up to that date. As noted by Ashworth and Redmayne,[31] the reforms raise the spectre of media campaigns to convict those who are regarded as having cheated justice, as well as encouraging victims to 'restructure their lives around the hope that "their" offender can be brought to justice, hiring private detectives or seeking to bug the suspect's home in the search for new evidence'. The implications of the new provisions for the criminal justice system call into question the wisdom behind the reform.

(II) Counter-Terrorism Legislation

It will come as no surprise to most readers to learn that the most egregious incursions on the presumption of innocence in the UK and USA have come about in response to the threat of terrorism. Terrorism has become an international bogeyman since the tragic events of 11 September 2001, even more so since the bombs in Bali, Istanbul, Madrid and most recently in London. There is a feeling, with which one can have great sympathy, that 'whatever it takes' to prevent the recurrence of such suffering and suppress the groups involved should be done. In relation to the rights of accused persons and suspects a similar sense of urgency prevails and the attitude is, generally, that these too must be sacrificed in pursuit of public safety. The emotional impact of the argument cannot be denied. While it is easy to empathize with the victims of terrorism, it is much harder to imagine oneself as someone wrongly accused in custody. The temptation for a fearful public to trade in rights to a paternalistic state is therefore great in the aftermath of such terrible events. Even normally staunch defenders of rights may baulk in the face of the terrorist threat. Indeed, in the wake of September 11 Professor Tribe, the famous constitutional lawyer quoted above in relation to the presumption of innocence, argued before the United States Committee on the Judiciary that while it may be right in more normal times to allow 100 guilty defendants to go free rather than convict one innocent one, the arithmetic should be reconsidered when one of the guilty might blow up the whole of Manhattan.[32]

Important questions should therefore be asked about what derogations from legal principle are permissible in times of emergency. There is a case for saying that terrorism and legislation for the prevention of terrorism should be regarded as a special case and that interference with a right may be more readily justified in the case of terrorism. Where, however, is the line to be drawn? At one extreme, Tony Blair has recently commented in the context of the debate on the *Prevention of Terrorism Act 2005* that 'the nation must recognize that no greater civil liberty exists than to live free from terrorist attack'.[33] This would be to write the executive a blank cheque, however, in the name of such freedom. Most commentators seek some middle way, through their recognition that there must exist lines beyond which rights should not be compromised. Brice Dickson,[34] Chairman of the Northern Ireland Human Rights Commission, for example, argues: 'Proscribing organizations that promote the use of violence for political ends is acceptable, but indefinitely detaining people without trial and using evidence likely to have been obtained by torture are clearly not.' Kennedy[35] expands on this approach by advocating a distinction be made between 'actions that involve incursions into our liberty to investigate or prevent acts of terrorism and the actions that are taken once persons are detained. No change should be countenanced which involves detaining people without charge and without the right to judicial review, or the lowering of standards when seeking to establish guilt.'

The courts, both on a domestic and European level, have also inclined towards this view. More recently, the House of Lords, in *Attorney General's Reference (No 4 of 2002)*[36] indicated that the pursuit of public security in the face of terrorism does not dispense with respect for the presumption of innocence guaranteed in Article 6(2) of the ECHR. As Lord Bingham noted: 'While security considerations must always carry weight, they do not absolve member states from their duty to ensure that basic standards of fairness are observed'.[37] It is particularly interesting to note his Lordship's explicit rejection of the Court of Appeal's approach in the same case, namely that it must be assumed that Parliament would not have made an exception to the presumption of innocence without good reason, on the basis that this gave too little weight to the presumption. This approach seems in line with the jurisprudence of the European Court of Human Rights. In *Heaney and McGuinness v. Ireland*[38] (discussed in Chapter 5), the European Court rejected arguments relating to state security in holding that s.52 of the *Offences Against the State Act 1939* violated the privilege against self-incrimination. The Court reiterated that Convention protections 'apply to criminal proceedings in respect of all types of criminal offences without distinction from the most simple to the most complex',[39] and ultimately found that 'the security and public order concerns relied on by the Government cannot justify a provision which extinguishes the very essence of the applicants' rights to silence and against self-incrimination guaranteed by Article 6(1) of the Convention'.[40] The 'essence' test is an instructive approach to the issue and has been described by Ashworth,[41] in his lectures on serious crime and human rights, as 'worth maintaining and refining' in striving to find the right balance between rights and public interest considerations.

There is good reason for insisting upon respect for fundamental rights, such as the presumption of innocence, even in the post September 11 legal and political landscape. First, it should be remembered that the presumption of innocence is a fundamental right of constitutional pedigree which seeks to protect the individual from wrongful conviction by the state. It is strongly to be argued that this core value, above all others, should not be yielded up in the current environment, as it constitutes the 'muscle' of the criminal law. This argument derives support from the House of Lords recent judgments in *R v DPP, ex parte Kebilene*[42] and *R v Lambert*[43] which seek to reinvigorate to some degree the spirit of *Woolmington*.

A second, significant argument is that the 'grave nature of the threat' cuts both ways. Just as the nature of the threat posed by terrorists to society is of an extremely serious nature, and the public interest in their conviction heightened, so the consequences of wrongful conviction for the defendant are correspondingly grave. As will be recalled from Chapter One, the dangers posed by wrongful censure by the state, the loss of liberty, opprobrium and psychological trauma, coupled with the 'moral harm' inflicted, require that a mistaken conviction should not be regarded in a similar light as a wrongful acquittal. A miscarriage of justice represents a much deeper wrong. The judgment of Sachs J. in the South African case of *State v. Coetzee*[44] eloquently highlights the double-edged nature of the argument that countering terrorism should trump rights:

> There is a paradox at the heart of all criminal procedure, in that the more serious the crime and the greater the public interest in securing convictions of the guilty, the more important do constitutional protections of the accused become. The starting point of any balancing inquiry where constitutional rights are concerned must be that the public interest in ensuring that innocent people are not convicted and subjected to ignominy and heavy sentences massively outweighs the public interest in ensuring that a particular criminal is brought to book... Hence the presumption of innocence, which serves not only to protect a particular individual on trial, but to maintain public confidence in the enduring integrity and security of the legal system. Reference to the prevalence and seriousness of a crime therefore does not add anything new or special to the balancing exercise. The perniciousness of the offence is one of the givens, against which the presumption of innocence is pitted from the beginning, not a new element to be put into the scales as part of a justificatory balancing exercise. If this were not so, the ubiquity and ugliness argument could be used in relation to murder, rape, car-jacking, house-breaking, drug-smuggling, corruption... the list is unfortunately almost endless, and nothing would be left of the presumption of innocence save, perhaps, for its relic status as a doughty defender of rights in the most trivial of cases.

Sachs J.'s argument serves to show that the choice presented by governments between liberty and security constitutes a false dichotomy. Murderers and rapists are not given lesser protection in the courts to those charged with lesser offences, although clearly their sentence will differ. Indeed, in his analysis of the above passage, Ashworth[45] makes the point that the rights of persons accused of more serious crimes are accorded an increased level of protection through the jury trial system.

It is of further note that, in the case of terrorism, harsh measures impinging on fundamental rights such as the right to be presumed innocent, are often counter-productive and indeed could serve as the best recruiting sergeant a terrorist organization could wish for. This has certainly been the experience of the British Government following the introduction of internment and other drastic measures in Northern Ireland. Indeed, the Government recently acknowledged internment as 'the terrorist's friend'.[46] While governments may argue for increased powers to prevent further atrocities, repressive legislation simply creates more victims, and the problems underlying terrorism thereby become more intractable. At a minimum, harsh measures may undermine support for the security forces and stem the flow of information from the relevant communities. This has recently been recognized by the Council of Europe which, in a set of guidelines on human rights and the fight against terrorism adopted by its Committee of Ministers on 11 July 2002, stated that 'it is not only possible, but also absolutely *necessary*, to fight terrorism while respecting human rights, the rule of law and, where applicable, international humanitarian law' while also reminding member states of the need to put in place 'long term measures with a view to preventing the causes of terrorism'.[47] Another lesson to be learned from Northern Ireland (and, indeed, the Republic of Ireland) is that the use of emergency powers can very quickly become normalized, resulting in 'seepage' into the framework of the ordinary criminal law. History shows us, then, that in the context of terrorism, it is particularly dangerous to be complacent about the rights of 'others'.

A final point relates to the ability to measure the terrorist threat. If rights are to be ceded, particularly fundamental rights, the state should be able to present empirical evidence to the effect that a curtailment of the presumption is both necessary and proportionate and will actually serve the purpose claimed in the fight against terrorism. The potential here for vague assertions about crime control and sweeping assumptions is great and as noted by Tadros and Tierney:[48] 'Certain [English] cases suggest a propensity for excessive deference on the part of the judiciary to the policy goals of Parliament.'

(a) United Kingdom

It is proposed in the section that follows to examine briefly three of the main pieces of legislation recently enacted in Britain in response to terrorism with a view to determining their impact on the presumption of innocence. It is common for such legislation to be permeated with a presumption of guilt: reverse onus clauses are usual, as are incursions on the right to silence. The logical conclusion of such a presumption of guilt, moreover, is to do away with the need for a criminal trial and proof to the requisite standard altogether and, as will be seen, this is what transpired in the UK in the months following September 11.

(I) Terrorism Act 2000

Not all counter-terrorism legislation was brought into effect following the attacks in New York. Indeed, some of the most wide-ranging and draconian legislation was already on the statute book prior to 9/11. New Labour introduced the Terrorism Bill in 1999 to replace existing legislation relating to Northern Ireland, namely the *Prevention of Terrorism (Temporary Provisions) Act 1989* and the *Northern Ireland (Emergency Provisions) Act 1996*. However, while many provisions are simply reenacted, there are a considerable number of innovations. These include the permanent nature of the Act; the expanded definition of terrorism to include international terrorism unconnected to Northern Ireland and the extension of jurisdiction to try terrorist offences which occur outside the United Kingdom.[49]

The definition of 'terrorism' under the Act merits scrutiny as all substantive offences created throughout the Act are linked to this definition in s.1 of the Act. It is defined as the use or threat of serious violence against a person or property or endangerment in order to influence the Government or intimidate the public, for the purpose of advancing a political, religious or ideological cause. The broad scope of the definition creates a risk that activity which would otherwise be lawful would fall within its terms, such as industrial action. The breadth of the 2000 Act can also be gauged from the large number of criminal offences it creates. For example, being a member of a proscribed organization (s.11(1)); supporting or 'furthering the activities' of a proscribed organization (s.12); directing the activities of a terrorist organization 'at any level' (s.56); 'possession of an item in circumstances which give rise to a reasonable suspicion that the possession is for a purpose connected with terrorism' (s.57); collecting 'information of a kind likely to be useful to a person committing or preparing an act of terrorism' (s.58); and 'inciting terrorist activity overseas' (section 59).

Some particularly controversial sections of the Act are sections 41 and 44 which allow for powers of stop and search without the traditional safeguard of reasonable suspicion. The potential for abuse was revealed in September 2003 when two entirely innocent persons, a peaceful protester and a journalist attending an arms trade fair at the Excel Centre in London, were stopped and searched. In line with the legislation, an order had previously been made by the Home Secretary under s.44 of the Act authorizing officers to stop and search any person without the need to prove any suspicion on the basis that it was 'expedient for the prevention of acts of terrorism'. In a subsequent challenge to the legislation taken by the individuals concerned, the Divisional Court held that the authorization was both lawful and proportionate to the gravity of the threat of terrorism. This decision has been criticized for the degree of latitude afforded the executive and is out of line with the less deferential approach taken in later decisions such as *AG's Reference No. 4 of 2002.*[50] As noted by Foster,[51] however, the account provides a useful illustration of 'the arbitrary potential of statutory provisions that fail to incorporate basic principles of the rule of law'.

Of equal concern is the number of provisions in the Act in

respect of which a burden of proof passes to the defendant. As discussed in Chapter Two a majority of the House of Lords in *ex parte Kebilene*[52] suggested that, once the *Human Rights Act 1998* was in force, legislative provisions which purport to reverse the burden of proof may have to be interpreted as imposing merely an evidential burden on the defendant, in order to be compatible with the presumption of innocence. The offence under consideration in *Kebliene* was s.16A of the *Prevention of Terrorism Act (Temporary Provisions) Act 1989* relating to the possession of articles for terrorist purposes. When the offence was reenacted in s.57 of the 2000 Act, therefore, the Government was careful to include s.118(1) and (2) which provide that the reverse onus of proof is satisfied if the person adduces evidence which is sufficient to raise an issue with respect to the matter unless the prosecution can prove the contrary beyond all reasonable doubt. This formula seems to ensure that a legal or persuasive burden will not be placed on the accused to establish a defence. Indeed, it has been observed that it may also slightly ease the evidential burden placed on the defendant by requiring simply the issue to be raised for it to negate the presumption in the statute of use of the articles for a terrorist purpose, unless of course the prosecution can prove otherwise.[53]

There remain, however, a considerable number of reverse onus provisions in the Act which are not listed in s.118 and which transfer the full burden of proof. These include defences under s.11(2) (membership of a proscribed organization) s.18(2) (money laundering); s.19(3) (disclosure of information); and s.21(5) (co-operation with the police in relation to other offences under the Act). Fortunately, their effect may be short-lived as the courts have once again mounted a staunch defence of the presumption of innocence. In the recent case, *Attorney General's Reference (No. 4 of 2002)*,[54] the House of Lords held that s.11(2) should be interpreted ('read down') under s.3 of the *Human Rights Act 1998* so as to impose an evidential burden. The decision is particularly significant given Parliament's clear intention to exclude the offence from the ambit of s.118 and to impose a legal burden on the defendant. The House, however, held that the imposition of such a legal burden on the defendant was not a proportionate and justifiable response to the problem of terrorism since a person who was innocent of any blameworthy or properly criminal conduct might fall to be convicted under s.11(1). There would be a clear breach of the presumption of innocence and a real risk of unfair conviction if such persons were compelled to exonerate themselves on the balance of probabilities. Indeed, the insistence of the Law Lords that security considerations did not provide an automatic licence for departure from such basic norms has been noted above.

(II) Anti Terrorism, Crime and Security Act 2001

The threat of international terrorism, however, has not been met solely by changes to the criminal law and laws of evidence. Notwithstanding the fact that 'with the full panoply of the Terrorism Act in force . . . the United Kingdom was the most legally fortified country in Europe',[55] the British Government has sought to sideline the criminal law through the development of alternatives to the criminal process, most notably detention without trial. The argument for this development is that preventative as well as punitive measures are needed to combat terrorism and that the authorities may have intelligence in relation to an individual but, due to the sensitive nature of the material, it cannot be placed in the public domain. Yet should intelligence, even 'good' intelligence, form the basis for detention of an individual in the absence of a criminal charge? Since the abolition of the death penalty, the deprivation of liberty is the most severe sanction available and it is for this reason that protections such as the presumption of innocence and the high standard of proof are afforded an accused. Regardless of the circumstances, it cannot be just to 'dispense with the system and the protections it provides and yet retain its most feared sanction'.[56] It should further be borne in mind that information received from foreign secret services may not have the same assurance of reliability as domestic sources and may be obtained by torture or include hearsay. Indeed, considerable scepticism now abounds as to the quality of intelligence assessments given the debacle on intelligence on Iraq.

Moreover, the argument that suspect terrorists who cannot be convicted by due process should not, in a post-September 11 environment, be considered immune is considerably weakened when 'extraordinary' measures are resorted to in response to much lesser social problems. The circumvention of the criminal trial and the requirement of proof beyond all reasonable doubt has been the subject of much discussion already in this book, and the development must be viewed in this broader context. As Walker[57] notes, while 'one consequence [of September 11] is that the ancient binary of guilt and innocence seems no longer to prevail' it must also be admitted that 'this melding has occurred elsewhere with sex-offender registers, anti-social behaviour orders, actions against the proceeds of crime and quasi-policing.' This is well illustrated by the British Government's most recent initiative on terror – the introduction of 'control orders' in the *Prevention of Terrorism Act 2005*. These orders have a close precedent in the form of anti-social behaviour orders and have even been dubbed 'anti-terrorist ASBOs'.[58] The very existence of ASBOs greatly diminishes the argument for control orders based on the prevailing emergency as they appear to be simply part of broader Government policy. As Beattie[59] argues, if we are to believe the argument that the gravity of the terrorist threat necessitates such drastic measures, 'it is alarming then that similar control orders – in the form of ASBOs – already exist in the UK and are issued in their thousands to contain a threat much less serious, namely, the perceived inconvenience of anti-social behaviour'.

Indefinite detention without trial was introduced by the British Government through Part IV of the *Anti Terrorism, Crime and Security Act 2001* (ATCSA) less than three months after the events of September 11. The Act differed from previous legislation providing for internment in Northern Ireland in that in applied only to individuals who were non-UK nationals. The reason for this lay, paradoxically, in the case law of the European Court of Human Rights which prohibited the deportation of individuals to countries where they may be subjected to torture or death even where these individuals presented a threat to national security.[60] As a result of such jurisprudence, such persons are essentially undeportable. Part IV therefore allowed for detention of an individual, even where deportation was impossible, where the Home Secretary (a) reasonably believed that his or her presence in Britain was a risk to national security, and (b) suspected that the person is an international terrorist.[61] In normal circumstances these provisions would constitute a clear breach of Article 5(1) of the ECHR (the right to liberty) and therefore on 11 November 2001 the Government issued a derogation from the European Convention on the basis of a public emergency threatening the life of the nation within the meaning of Article 15(1) of the Convention.[62]

If satisfied as to the above criteria, the Home Secretary can issue a certificate authorizing indefinite detention under existing immigration laws, subject to periodic reviews by the Special Immigration Appeals Commission (SIAC). Under s.26 of the Act a first review must be carried out after the expiry of six months since the issue of the certificate and thereafter every three months. The detained person also has the right to appeal the certification to SIAC who must cancel the certificate if it considers that there are no reasonable grounds for the Home Secretary's belief or suspicion or it considers that for some other reason it should not have been issued. At this appeal the detainees and their legal representatives are excluded from any part of the hearing which deals with the intelligence on which the detention order has been made. A special advocate, however, will be allocated to support the interests of the suspect in regard to material that neither he or she nor his or her legal representatives can see. This role is necessarily hampered by the provision that after the advocate has seen the confidential material, he or she is no longer allowed to speak to the suspect and their legal representative. Further appeals are restricted by s.35 of the 2001 Act which allows a decision of the Commission to be questioned in legal proceedings only where challenges to the derogation notice itself have been taken.

The Act represents an affront to basic concepts such as the rule of law and the presumption of innocence as there is no proven offence at all. In terms of the impact on the detainee, the procedure under the 2001 Act is very similar to finding that person guilty of a criminal offence or, in fact, worse given the absence of any release date. (In this regard, it is no coincidence that one of the detainees was released on bail in April 2004 due to his worsening mental state.) Writing in 2004 on counter-terrorism measures, David Blunkett, the then Home Secretary, commented: 'There are always certain rights which are nonnegotiable. There are some – for example the right to life, the prohibition on torture, the presumption of innocence, the right to a fair trial – where we cannot compromise on the principles.'[63] This apparent concern for the presumption of innocence *in the event of charge* is difficult to reconcile with the introduction of detention without trial for those persons in respect of whom there is insufficient evidence for trial.[64]

As outlined above, persons detained under the 2001 Act are deprived of their liberty on the basis of a reasonable belief or suspicion, not even on the civil standard of balance of probabilities. In *A & Ors v. Secretary of State*[65] it was argued that a high level of suspicion was required in the context of the Act. Disappointingly, however, the Court of Appeal upheld the orders on the basis that the right tests as to the standard of proof had been applied by SIAC. This was despite the Commission's description of the legislative test as 'not a demanding standard'. The Court held:

> I regard the expression 'not a demanding standard' in paragraph 71 as unfortunate but in using it, the Commission were in my view, making a comparison with standards by which facts are proved in judicial proceedings and were not departing from the statutory test. They wished to emphasise that the standard is a different one from that applied in ordinary litigation which is routinely concerned with finding facts. The context is different but, as Lord Hoffmann stated in *Rehman:* 'it is a question of evaluation and judgment' and 'the concept of a standard of proof is not particularly helpful'. All the circumstances must be considered and, while in some situations specific acts must be proved, what matters is the 'assessment made of the whole picture'.[66]

The dismissive approach taken by the Court of Appeal to the 'unhelpful' issue of the standard of proof stands in marked contrast to the rigorous parliamentary scrutiny of standards of proof under ATCSA's successor, the *Prevention of Terrorism Act 2005* which will be discussed presently.

To return to the decision in *A*, however, an even more worrying result of the decision was the concession that the

Commission could admit evidence which may have been obtained by torture or inhuman or degrading treatment from detainees at the hand of other state agencies throughout the world (such as Guantanamo Bay). In reaching this conclusion the Court laid emphasis on the fact that the process in question was not a criminal trial, thereby demonstrating its complete inability or indeed unwillingness to appreciate the reality of the situation for the detainees. Quite aside from the moral objections to this rather shocking decision and the obvious unreliability of such evidence, its adduction will serve to further undermine the low evidential standards required by the legislation.

In light of the above, the finding of the House of Lords in *A & Ors v. Secretary of State*[67] in December 2004 that s.23 of the 2001 Act (the detention section) was incompatible with the provisions of the ECHR is greatly to be welcomed. Although the Law Lords, sitting as an unprecedented bench of nine, could not order the immediate release of the twelve applicants, the effect of the judgment was to put paid to the policy of indefinite detention without trial. The House found s.23 to be incompatible with the Convention in two main ways. First, it was contrary to the derogation provision in Article 15 in that it was a disproportionate response to the emergency facing the country and secondly, detention under s.23 was unlawfully discriminatory on the basis of nationality or immigration status and was therefore a violation of Article 14. Lord Scott was particularly strong in his condemnation of the provisions:

> Indefinite imprisonment in consequence of a denunciation on grounds that are not disclosed and made by a person whose identity cannot be disclosed is the stuff of nightmares, associated whether accurately or inaccurately with France before and during the Revolution, with Soviet Russia in the Stalinist era and now associated, as a result of s.23 of the 2001 Act, with the United Kingdom…I am unable to accept that the Secretary of State has established that section 23 is 'strictly required' by the public emergency. He should, at the least, in my opinion, have to show that monitoring arrangements or movement restrictions less severe than incarceration in prison would not suffice.[68]

His Lordship's comments as to the necessity of the measures taken by the British Government were redolent of previous criticism of the Act expressed by the Committee of Privy Counsellors established to conduct a review of the Act under the auspices of Lord Newton.[69] The Committee expressed a strong preference for prosecuting terrorists under the existing criminal law and examined ways in which prosecution for terrorist-related offences could be facilitated. One measure which they advocated included the removal of the ban on the use of intercepted communications in court, also recommended by Lord Lloyd in his 1996 Report on terrorism legislation.[70] Other proposals put forward by the Committee included treating terrorism as an aggravating factor when sentencing; assigning a security-cleared judge to assume an investigatory role; the use of increased surveillance and, as a final resort, restrictions on liberty or deportation. In general terms, the Committee recommended that Part 4 of ATCSA should be repealed and replaced with a measure that 'does not require a derogation from the Convention on Human Rights'.[71] The same demand was made by the Joint Committee on Human Rights in their 2004 report,[72] and two UN Committees,[73] yet despite this mounting national and international pressure, the Government was only galvanised into action by the decision of the House of Lords in *A*.

(III) Prevention of Terrorism Act 2005

In the period following the delivery of the decision in *A* in December 2004, the Government indicated its intention to hold the men in custody until an alternative could be found. The order holding the men was due to expire on 14 March 2005 as the Act was subject to annual renewal by both houses each March. Yet the Government appeared to have been taken by surprise and waited until 22 February to rush out the *Prevention of Terrorism Bill*. Through a guillotined legislative process, the Act received royal assent on 11 March, a mere eighteen days after it was introduced. The *Prevention of Terrorism Act 2005* (PTA) provides for the use of 'control orders' to prevent terrorist-related activity, which will apply irrespective of nationality or immigration status. The ten suspects detained (as it transpired unnecessarily) in Belmarsh

Prison under ATSCA for over three years became the first subjects of these new control orders on 12 March, the day after royal assent was given.

Some comments deserve to be made not only as to the content of this new legislation but also as to the rushed manner in which the Bill was introduced by the Government, showing little regard for Parliament and the unprecedented nature of the powers proposed. This apparent desire to evade parliamentary scrutiny is extremely regrettable and must be regarded as a missed opportunity to have a serious debate on how far civil liberties can be surrendered in the present circumstances. As observed by Lord Lloyd in relation to the PTA: 'If ever there were an area on which it is desirable to achieve a consensus, it is in balancing the need for security against elementary human rights.'[74] In any event, the passage of the Bill, though expedited, proved controversial, and resulted in a game of parliamentary ping-pong between the House of Commons and the Lords on issues such as judicial oversight, the standard of proof and the inclusion in the legislation of a 'sunset clause' or date when the legislation ceases to have effect.

Despite the criticism levelled in *A* at the deployment of measures which are not strictly necessary (namely, the nuclear option of detention without trial), the Government opted for a measure which can only be described as the 'next best thing'. The Government scheme under the PTA creates two kinds of control orders, 'non-derogating' and 'derogating' orders, which can be approximated to orders releasing a person on bail subject to certain conditions and house arrest respectively. A derogating order is one which, as the name suggests, requires derogation from the ECHR because it deprives the suspect of his liberty by house arrest and is therefore in breach of Article 5 of the Convention. Under s.4(3)(c) a derogating order requires a prior resolution of both Houses of Parliament approving the derogation. As the Home Secretary indicated when introducing the Bill, the Government did not view it as necessary to derogate from the ECHR at that time. Derogating orders can be made by a court upon the application of the Secretary of State upon proof on the balance of probabilities that the defendant is 'or has been involved in terrorism-related activity'.[75] For a non-derogating order, on the other hand, the evidential standard is simply that the Secretary of State has 'reasonable grounds for suspecting' that the individual is, or has been involved in, terrorism-related activity. The Secretary will usually have to apply to the Court for permission, unless the urgency of the situation does not allow it and the Court may only refuse permission where it appears to it that the grounds relied upon by the Secretary of State are 'obviously flawed'.

Control orders are extremely broad in their scope in that the Secretary of State can impose 'any obligation' that he considers 'necessary for purposes connected with preventing or restricting involvement by that individual in terrorism-related activity'.[76] By way of illustration the Act lists a number of possible obligations, both negative and positive, such as prohibitions on the use of certain services and facilities; restrictions on work, association and communications; requirements to submit to electronic monitoring; and obligations to allow the authorities access to one's residence. Breach of any condition without reasonable excuse is a criminal offence, punishable by up to five years imprisonment.[77] Control order proceedings, like proceedings under Part IV of ATCSA, are closed and provision is made for the use of special advocates.

As already noted above, the idea for control orders came from the Newton Report[78] but it is important to place their recommendation in relation to 'restriction orders', as the Privy Counsellors called them, in the context of the overall report. The Report's preferred method of dealing with terrorists was prosecution where this was at all possible. In this regard, they made a number of suggestions such as the lifting of the ban on intercept evidence and only then proceeded to discuss their less favoured options. Their distaste for measures impacting severely upon liberty is evident from the wording of the report:

> It is possible that, even adopting some or all of the measures above, it may not be possible to prosecute in every case. The alternatives listed below would allow steps to be taken against both UK and foreign terrorist suspects which are less damaging to human rights than the current process (and so remove the need for derogation from the ECHR). These measures are less attractive than conventional prosecution and surveillance but in our view they are preferable to Part 4 as it stands.[79]

That the Committee was not contemplating the introduction of such extreme measures is clear from their overarching recommendation that, whatever form the new legislative measures take, the need to derogate from the Convention should thereby be obviated. While this approach has been clearly eschewed by the Government, through its decision to provide for derogating orders as a contingency power, questions must also be raised about the compatibility of non-derogating orders with Article 5 of the Convention. As argued by Metcalfe:[80] 'Although it may be possible to say with certainty that a particular requirement (*eg* reporting to a police station) does not breach Article 5, it is much less clear what the effect of multiple restrictions may be, particularly given the broad scope for serious interference with a person's enjoyment of several Convention rights'. This view has very recently been vindicated by the Court of Appeal[81] who upheld a finding by a High Court judge that a control order regime imposed on six Iraquis – which included 18-hour curfews – amounted to a 'deprivation of liberty' contrary to Article 5 of the ECHR. The court refused to accept that the regime constituted mere restrictions upon liberty of movement, having regard to the length of the curfew, the extent of the obligations and the intrusive impact on the respondents daily life.

The analogies between anti-social behaviour orders and control orders are obvious and have already been noted. Both are civil orders that are allegedly preventative in nature and which impose restrictions on an individual's movement, freedom of association or freedom of speech. They may do so for an indeterminate period of time and render breach of the order a criminal offence thereby attracting a swingeing penalty of up to five years imprisonment.[82] The hybrid civil-criminal mechanism used for control orders therefore attracts criticism similar to that levelled above at ASBOs in relation to the circumvention of the presumption of innocence. Control orders, even without contingency powers for house arrest of suspects, are objectionable in their reclassification of essentially criminal proceedings as civil in nature. That they are, in substance and reality, criminal in nature was recently recognized by Lord Lloyd, author of the 1996 report on anti-terrorism legislation: 'The Act imposes what are, in effect, criminal sanctions by a civil process; and it does so without the chance of a fair trial. The government argued that control orders are preventive, not punitive. But this is not how they will appear to the recipients.'[83]

Quite aside from this fundamental difficulty with the legislation, concern must be expressed at the condition listed in the Act that a person 'comply with a demand made in the specified manner to provide information to a specified person in accordance with demand'.[84] Given the absence of provisions relating to the use to which this forced information can be put and the fact that breach of such condition, if attached to an order, would render the suspect liable for up to five years imprisonment, it is at least arguable that the 'very essence' of the individual's privilege against self incrimination has been destroyed.[85] Other difficulties in the Act remain the low threshold for making control orders. The standard of proof for non-derogating orders remains exactly the same as the 'undemanding' standard required for certification under ATCSA. Further, the Act's silence in relation to the use of evidence obtained by torture casts further doubt over the safeguards provided by the Act.

On a more sanguine note, the raising of the standard of proof for a derogating control order to the balance of probabilities must be commended as, indeed, must s.8(2) which states that before making or applying for a control order, the Home Secretary must consult with the chief officer of the relevant police force as to whether evidence is available that could realistically be the basis of a criminal prosecution. According to s.8(4), the chief officer is responsible for keeping that question under continuing review. Further, hopes for a return to the normal channels of criminal prosecution may yet be revived as, although the legislation does not contain a 'sunset clause', the Government has promised that it would be bringing forward legislative proposals late in 2006 which will allow for a full reconsideration of the issues. Indeed, the government's belated introduction into law under s.5 of the *Terrorism Act 2006* of the offence of preparation of terrorist acts raises serious questions about the need for the use of executive detention. Had this offence been available earlier those detained under Part 4 of ATCSA could have been prosecuted for criminal offences. The likelihood of conviction would no doubt have been increased had the law been further amended to allow the use of intercept evidence. In light of the above, and the full panoply of powers available under the 2000 Act, a dim view must be taken of the British Government's readiness in 2001, and once again in 2005, to resort to alternatives to the criminal trial.

(b) United States of America

Across the Atlantic, the 'War on Terror' has been waged even more aggressively and parallel developments to those in Britain have occurred in terms of the indefinite detention of suspects and the use of the immigration law procedures to make assessments of grave criminality. In addition, in the United States there has been a clear paradigm shift away from the general criminal law and its concomitant protections such as the presumption of innocence, towards military law. This has occurred through the assignment of investigative tasks to military units, both inside and outside the territory of the United States, and the establishment of military tribunals for the trial of persons suspected of terrorism. It is proposed to examine below the main aspects of legislative and executive innovations since September 11 as they relate to the presumption of innocence. What follows is therefore not a detailed analysis of the USA PATRIOT Act, which is a massive, extremely complex piece of legislation and which holds serious implications for fundamental rights other than the presumption of innocence, such as rights to privacy and freedom of speech/association. A more in-depth analysis is available elsewhere.[86]

(I) USA Patriot Act

The symbolically named Act for the Uniting and Strengthening of America by Providing Appropriate Tools Required to Intercept and Obstruct Terrorism known by the acronym USA PATRIOT Act was the primary legislative response to the terrorist attacks on the Twin Towers and the Pentagon. As with the UK legislation, the legislative process was truncated and the Bill became law on October 26, having been introduced just over three weeks earlier. Given this narrow time frame, the public clamour for action, and the fact that many Congressional staff were locked out of their offices due to an anthrax scare, it is doubtful whether many members of Congress had time to read the Bill in any level of detail. There was a remarkable degree of consensus around the Act: only one member voted against it in the Senate and sixty-six in the House of Representatives. Members were urged to approve the legislation in bellicose terms by President Bush who declared: 'In order to win the war, we must make sure that the law enforcement men and women have got the tools necessary, within the Constitution, to defeat the enemy... We're at war, a war we're going to win.'[87]

As noted above, the Act is extremely wide-ranging, running to 342 pages and covering some 350 subject areas. A brief survey of its most significant provisions gives a clear indication that legal paradigms are being redrawn. The increased investigatory powers, for example, make serious inroads into rights such as the privacy protection of the Fourth Amendment. Section 213 of the Act provides for notification of the execution of a warrant to be delayed and therefore not communicated to the person to whom the warrant is addressed. In other words, this allows for a person's home to be searched and property seized as evidence without prior notice (notice may even be delayed for a reasonable period of time after the event). This represents a significant extension of the so-called 'sneak and peek' search powers which now apply not only to investigations of terrorism but to every federal criminal investigation. Further, the Act, by lowering the standard necessary to obtain warrants, also expands the ability of the Government to spy by wiretaps and computer surveillance and provides access to medical, financial, business and educational records.

The PARIOT Act amends existing substantive criminal law on terrorism. Of particular note is the sweepingly vague definition given to the new offence of 'domestic terrorism' under the Act as 'activities that (a) involve acts dangerous to human life that are a violation of the criminal laws of the United States or of any state; (b) appear to be intended (i) to intimidate or coerce a civilian population; (ii) to influence the policy of a government by intimidation or coercion or (iii) to affect the conduct of a government by mass destruction, assassination or kidnapping and (c) occur primarily within the territorial jurisdiction of the United States'.[88] In practice, these provisions have been applied to organizations such as street gangs and concerns have been expressed as to the impact of the legislation on freedom of association and speech rights.

This part of the Act also raises concerns about the related presumptions of *mens rea* and innocence. For example, assisting terrorism was an existing offence under American law, however, s.810 of the Act increases the maximum penalty from ten years to fifteen years and, in a situation where the death of a person results, to life imprisonment. What is significant about the provisions on assisting terrorism is that, due to the broad definitions of terrorism and support, any form of support is punishable and, despite the high penalties, there is no *mens rea* requirement. Under the legislation it suffices that the person concerned *should have been aware* that the support would be used for committing terrorist offences, which amounts to mere negligence. This represents a clear breach of the presumption of innocence in that a person could be convicted in the presence of evidence raising a reasonable doubt as to the offender's moral guilt. The failure to adhere to the presumption is very worrying in light of the fact that the offender may be sentenced to a term of life imprisonment. A similar criticism can be levelled against s.817 of the Act which now makes it possible to prosecute the simple possession of toxic or biological products without proof of intention to use these as weapons.

By far the biggest change to the legal landscape after September 11, however, must be the expansion of detention powers both under the Act and those assumed by the executive branch. Section 412 of the Act allows for the indefinite detention of immigrants and other non-citizens. Immigrants who are certified by the Attorney General as 'engaged in any…activity that endangers the national security of the United States'[89] may be detained under the amended legislation for an initial period of seven days after which they must be charged with a criminal offence or deportation proceedings instituted. The legislation allows for an important exception, however, where the detainee is ordered deported and this cannot be carried out within the requisite time period of ninety days. In this eventuality, where the Attorney General continues to suspect on reasonable grounds that 'the release of the alien will threaten the national security of the United States or the safety of the community or any person'[90] indefinite detention without charge is permitted. While there is a review of the certification every six months, the formal protection offered by a hearing in open court to test the state's case for detention is notably absent. Legal advice is available but solely funded by the detainee. As has traditionally been the case in immigration matters, the presumption of innocence does not apply.

Several cases of indefinite detention have been reported in the US due to difficulties in securing the co-operation of detainees' countries of origin. A good example is the case of *Clark v. Martinez*[91] where two Cuban nationals were detained beyond the ninety day period in a situation where deportation was not likely in the forseeable future. The Supreme Court affirmed decisions ordering their release as the Government had 'brought forward nothing to indicate that a substantial likelihood of removal exists'. It held that the legislation empowered the Government to detain non nationals beyond the ninety day removal period but only for so long as is reasonably necessary to achieve removal. In other words, the Government must be able to justify its continued detention of such persons.

It is unclear how many non-nationals are being detained under the PATRIOT Act due to the secrecy which surrounds such cases but the total number of detentions, including detentions in the framework of regular criminal investigations, could be as high as 1,200.[92] As discussed above in relation to the English anti-terrorism legislation, arbitrary detention violates due process and rides roughshod over the presumption of innocence. It is also likely to be counterproductive in alienating (and therefore stemming the flow of information from) Arab and Muslim communities within the United States.

(II) Executive Action

On 18 September 2001, Congress issued a Joint Declaration authorizing the use of 'all necessary and appropriate force against those nations, organizations, or persons [the President] determines planned, authorized, committed, or aided the terrorist attacks that occurred on September 11, 2001, or harbored such organizations or persons.'[93] In addition, Congress emphasized that the forces responsible for the September 11 attacks 'continue to pose an unusual and extraordinary threat to the national security' and that 'the President has authority under the Constitution to take action to deter and prevent acts of international terrorism against the United States.'[94] Although this Declaration represented a specific statutory authorization under the War Powers Resolution 1974, it was not a formal declaration of war. (Ironically, given the Administration's heavy use of war rhetoric, efforts by members of Congress to formally declare war were dismissed as unnecessary.) It is this document which has been relied on by the President, as Commander in Chief of the US Army, in adopting many questionable new powers such as the November 13 order authorizing the use of military trials and the indefinite detention of individuals as 'enemy combatants'. By declaring certain suspects 'enemy combatants', they can be held in military detention while awaiting trial by a military committee, thereby removing them from the reaches of the ordinary criminal law. The Bush administration has been careful, moreover, to restrict the application of international humanitarian law so that neither the Geneva Convention, nor the term 'prisoner of war' applies to the detainees.

Both citizens and non-citizens have been detained under this order. In mid-2002, two US citizens were arrested and detained as 'enemy combatants'. Both men, Hamdi and Padilla, were held incommunicado at military bases in the United States for the purposes of 'interrogation and intelligence gathering'. In June 2004 the Supreme Court delivered judgment in proceedings issued by Mr Hamdi.[95] They held that the Presidential prerogative which designated certain suspects of terrorist offences as 'enemy combatants' was authorized by the Congressional grant of authority for the use of force, although this did not provide for indefinite detention, was limited to detention in war zones and to 'necessary and appropriate force'. The Court went on to hold, however, that 'a state of war is not a blank cheque for the President when it comes to the rights of the Nation's citizens' and that 'due process demands that a citizen held in the US as an enemy combatant be given a meaningful opportunity to contest the factual basis for that detention before a neutral decision-maker'. Disappointingly, the Court appeared satisfied that a military tribunal constituted a 'neutral decision maker' and had no difficulty with the reversal of the burden of proof in such proceedings provided the person concerned was given an opportunity to mount a defence to the charges. Hamdi was subsequently released and returned to Saudi Arabia.

Judgment by the Supreme Court in the case of Mr Padilla was delivered on the same day but was dismissed on jurisdictional grounds and the Court did not rule on the substantive issues.[96] It should be noted, however, that in November 2003, the US 2nd Court of Appeals held that, after nineteen months of detention, the state had either to release him or show the basis for his detention beyond all reasonable doubt. The reference to the criminal standard of proof stands in sharp contrast to the reversals in the burden of proof tolerated by the Supreme Court in *Hamdi*. Following the *Hamdi* decision, the Bush administration has begun using Combatant Status Review Tribunals (CSRTs) to determine the status of detainees in a move which is designed to reflect the guidance provided by the Supreme Court. These tribunals are a variant on adminstrative tribunals already established to review the threat posed to the state by the detainees (Administrative Review Boards), with the important difference that the function of the CSRTs is to revisit the initial decision to classify an individual as an 'enemy combatant'. Most disconcertingly, there is a rebuttable presumption in favour of the Government's evidence, or in other words, a presumption of guilt.

The second category of detainees are non-citizens who inhabit the, now notorious, prisoner of war camps in Guantanamo Bay naval base in Cuba. The inhumane conditions in which these foreign nationals have been held have been well documented by the media, with press photographs depicting them as hooded and shackled in small wire cages which are exposed to the elements. In protest at these conditions, dozens of the detainees have gone on hunger strike and are being fed forcibly through nasal tubes. There are currently 558[97] suspected Taliban and Al-Qaeda members in Guantanamo Bay who have been detained for lengthy periods of time without having been charged, without the right to a lawyer and without trial. The legal wilderness in which these detainees found themselves was shored up by a line of authority[98] which suggested that enemy aliens outside the territorial sovereignty of the US could not rely on rights under the US Constitution and there can be little doubt that this formed part of the original usefulness of Guantanamo.

In a hugely significant decision, however, in *Rasul et al v. US*,[99] the Supreme Court held that the US, despite not having full sovereignty over the naval base, in effect still exercises full and exclusive jurisdiction over it. The Court held that '*habeas* [corpus] acts upon the person holding the prisoner, not the prisoner himself' so that US courts have jurisdiction where 'the custodian can be reached by service of process.' As Vervaele[100] has noted: 'With this important decision, the Supreme Court has put an end to the legal limbo of Guantanamo and reinstated the right to *habeas corpus* in the form of administrative military confinement and the incommunicado regime.' This basic legal safeguard would appear crucial in light of indications from the Administration that detainees will be kept in detention until the end of the 'war'. When asked in March 2002 to define this, Donald Rumsfeld replied: 'when we feel that there are no effective global terrorist networks functioning in the world that these people would be likely to go back to and begin again their terrorist activities.'[101]

The effect of *Rasul* was short-lived, however, as Congress voted on 14 November 2005 to effectively reverse the decision of the Supreme Court and to deny foreign detainees at Guantanamo Bay recourse to the US courts. The amendment, known as 'the Graham Amendment'[102] eliminated all federal court jurisdiction over *habeas* cases on behalf of the detainees, possibly including cases pending at the Bill's enactment. While the amendment introduces welcome Congressional oversight of the procedures the Department of Defence adopts for 'Combatant Status Review' panels (tribunals established post-*Hamdi* to allow detainees to contest their status as enemy combatants), including a ban on the use of evidence obtained by coercion, the equally important remedy of judicial oversight is dramatically curtailed. Technically other legal avenues such as claims for damages remain open to detainees although the removal of the powerful remedy of *habeas corpus* is likely to stem the flow of litigation from the detainees,[103] particularly as *habeas* is no longer available to those claiming they have been exposed to torture or other inhuman or degrading treatment.

The two exceptions to the prohibition on *habeas corpus* applications are that limited appeals can be made against (i) status determinations by Combatant Status Review Tribunals and (ii) final decisions of military commissions on the grounds that the Defence Department failed to apply its own rules, or that the application of those rules violated the Constitution or a federal statute. Even these applications, however, can only be brought *after* a determination has been made. Given that the Supreme Court had definitively ruled on the issue so recently, there remain questions as to whether the law offends the spirit of the separation of powers, if not its letter, or what one constitutional lawyer has termed the 'unwritten Constitution'.[104] Indeed, the actions of Congress evoke parallels with the decision of the Irish Government in the summer of 1996 to hold a referendum on preventative detention, despite the existence of a robust line of authority holding this to be a clear breach of the right to be presumed innocent.

For those Guantanamo detainees who are to undergo actual prosecution, their fate will ultimately be determined by military tribunal rather than the open civilian criminal courts. On 13 November 2001, without advance notice to Congress, President Bush signed an order allowing for the trial of non-US citizens suspected of involvement in terrorism before a special military commission. Such commissions were empowered to act in secret, to pass the death penalty by a two thirds majority and there was no right of appeal to the civil courts from convictions and sentencing. Under considerable pressure, the Department of Defense in March 2002 issued a 'Military Commission Order' outlining the procedures for trial in the tribunal. The order provides for the presumption of innocence and guilt to be established beyond a reasonable doubt. Further, defendants are to be given access to a military defence lawyer and a right to a unanimous verdict for any death sentences.

Serious concerns remain, however, about the fairness of such trials. Suspects who are acquitted by the military tribunals can have their verdicts reversed by the Defense Secretary which seriously undermines the integrity of any acquittal and the presumption of innocence which flows from it. Even leaving these issues aside, the order disregards a number of fundamental principles of evidence which may serve to undermine the formal application of the presumption of innocence. All evidence 'which would have probative value to a reasonable person' is admissible. This rule is sweepingly broad in its ambit and would include all evidence, however probative, without any regard to the traditional countervailing factor of prejudicial effect (see above in relation to the English *Criminal Justice Act 2003*). Presumably, evidence may be lead of previous bad character or previous criminal convictions which may have extremely limited probative value yet can have powerful effects on the tribunal of fact. The origins and manner of collection of the evidence will not be tested as the chain of custody no longer has to be shown and secret evidence may be adduced *in camera*. Finally, hearsay evidence is specifically included. Overall, it is difficult to see how the criminal standard of proof can be met with such unreliable evidence.

In this regard, the comments of Vice President Dick Cheney in relation to the trial of the alleged twentieth hijacker, Zacharias Moussaoui, are telling. When criticized for trying him in a civilian court rather than before a military tribunal, his explanation was that 'it can be handled through the normal criminal justice system without compromising sources or methods of intelligence...and there's a good strong case against him'.[105] His comments betray the lesser quality of evidence generally required under the military tribunal system and cast serious doubt over their *raison d'être*. The US Government contends that these tribunals will not jeopardize secret intelligence and will offer better protection to judges and witnesses. However, as the American Civil Liberties Union (ACLU) has noted: 'It is difficult to understand how the Administration can justify the use of a tribunal when the United States has successfully tried in our courts non-citizens accused of terrorist acts, organized crime, and others in situations where the safety of jurors and the disclosure of government intelligence methods were at issue.'[106] Indeed, members of Al Qaeda have in the past been tried and convicted before the general criminal courts in the US for their involvement in the

1998 bombings of the US embassies in Kenya and Tanzania.

The constitutionality of this shadow justice system has been challenged in the case of *Hamdam v. Rumsfeld*,[107] which concerns a Yemeni accused of driving a pick-up truck for Osama bin Laden in Afghanistan. In a further twist in the wrangle between the Supreme Court and the Administration, the Supreme Court has upheld this challenge. On 29 June 2006, the Court handed down a majority decision holding that (i) it had jurisdiction to hear the case despite the Graham Amendment (ii) the Federal Government did not have authority to set up these Military Commissions and (iii) that the Special Military Commissions were illegal under both the Uniform Code of Military Justice and the Geneva Convention.

The implications for Hamdam are that his trial must be in a court or commission with court-like protections. Further, the decision has prompted a public statement by the Bush Adminstration on 11 July 2006 that all detainees in US custody are entitled to humane treatment under the Geneva Convention.

The Bush Administration has consistently justified recourse to *incommunicado* detention without trial, trial by military tribunal and now the denial of the fundamental right of *habeas corpus* through claims that the individuals detained in Guantanamo Bay are among the most dangerous terrorists in the world or 'the worst of the worst' to use the Defense Secretary's phrase. However, the uncontested facts are that, as of August 2005, 245 detainees were transferred for release or to the control of other countries and 38 were found to be innocent.[108] A recent report by Amnesty International[109] indicates that nine of those conceded innocent remain at Guantanamo, among them five Chinese Muslims who may face persecution if returned to China but whose right to asylum is not recognized by the Administration. Further, studies of government transcripts of individual detainee cases conducted by bodies such as the National Journal[110] in Washington have argued persuasively that, although there are detainees against whom the evidence would appear to be substantial, there are others against whom the government has cited such common behaviour as wearing a Casio watch, carrying a gun, or staying in a guest house as evidence of a detainee's membership in Al

Qaeda or the Taliban. Most were not captured on a battlefield but were abducted in the mountains of Pakistan by warlords who handed them over to US forces for cash rewards. Hearsay evidence or evidence coerced from other detainees, using harsh interrogation techniques, is used to substantiate the cases against detainees in many instances.

CONCLUSION

The above brief survey of counter-terrorism measures in the United Kingdom and the US leaves little room for doubt that the most serious abrogations of the presumption of innocence occur in the context of measures to defeat terrorism. The indefinite detention of non-nationals in the US and Britain demonstrates that we are not so far away from the days of the Star Chamber. At the risk of self-contradiction, however, it is well to consider anti-terrorism measures in Britain against the backdrop of an increasingly fearful public and important inroads into due process. Significant incursions into the presumption in, for example, the *Criminal Justice Act 2003* detract from the argument that terrorism is a special case. As Lea has noted: 'In the context of such developments the reversal of the burden of proof and the lowering of the standard of proof in the area . . . of terrorism do[es] not stand out: rather they confirm the general trend.'[111] This argument has perhaps more application in Britain than the US, where the Administration has ignored fundamental rights through the application of a military regime and extra territorial detention. However, in the current political environment, there is certainly reason for questioning the traditional perception that special measures may 'contaminate' an otherwise healthy criminal justice system. While this still holds true to some degree, there is the issue, as Lea notes, of 'trickle-up' as well as 'trickle-down'. The increasing emphasis on crime control and the similarity of initiatives such as the ASBO and the control order serve to reinforce the impression that 'the sphere of anti-terrorist legislation is in tune with recent developments rather than distorting an otherwise due process oriented system'.[112]

NOTES

1 Little has been written about policy transfer in an Irish context, although the phenomenon has been recognized. S. Kilcommins *et al* note that during the debates on the *Criminal Justice (Community Service) Act 1983* that Deputy John Kelly noted: 'This is simply one more example in the ignominous parade of legislation masquerading under an Irish title... which is a British legislative idea taken over here and given a green outfit with silver buttons to make it look native.' See S. Kilcommins, I. O'Donnell, E O'Sullivan and B. Vaughan *Crime, Punishment and the Search for Order in Ireland* (IPA, 2004) p.182 fn.20. For a British perspective see T. Jones and T. Newburn 'Policy Convergence and Crime control in the USA and the UK: streams of influence and impact' (2002) 2(2) *Punishment and Society* 173. In Ireland, see, for example, Chapter 4 in relation to ASBOs which are a concept borrowed from Britain, and Chapter 5 in relation to the *Proceeds of Crime Act 1996* which draws heavily on the RICO legislation in the US. Other examples of policy transfer from both the US and the UK are mandatory sentencing and electronic tagging. Political rhetoric has also proved susceptible to globalization as demonstrated by Fianna Fáil's much vaunted adoption of the 'zero tolerance' approach to crime in the 1997 general election.

2 White Paper, *Justice for All*, Cmnd. 5563, (London: Home Office, 2002).

3 'In criminal proceedings evidence of the defendant's bad character is admissible if, but only if –

(a) all parties to the proceedings agree to the evidence being admissible;
(b) the evidence is adduced by the defendant himself or is given in answer to a question asked by him in cross examination and intended to elicit it;
(c) it is important explanatory evidence;
(d) it is relevant to an important matter in issue between the defendant and the prosecution;
(e) it has substantial probative value in relation to an important matter in issue between the defendant and a co-defendant;
(f) it is evidence to correct a false impression given by the defendant; or
(g) the defendant has made an attack on another person's character.'

4 It is important to note, however, that no distinction is drawn in the Act between evidence given in chief by the prosecution and questions which may be put to the accused during cross-examination. Accordingly, as P. Roberts and A. Zuckerman *Criminal Evidence* (Oxford University Press, 2004) note at p.514: 'Paragraphs (e) to (g) may be triggered *even if the accused chooses not to testify in his own defence*.' Emphasis in original text.

5 [1991] 2 AC 447.

6 *Op. cit.* p.517. See generally Chapter 11 'Evidence of Character'.

7 A. Ashworth and M. Redmayne *The Criminal Process* (3rd ed., Oxford University Press, 2005) pp.333–5.

8 Section 103(1)(b).
9 S. Lloyd-Bostock 'The Effects on Juries of Hearing About the Defendant's Previous Criminal Record' [2000] *Crim LR* 734.
10 See Law Commission Consultation Paper No. 141 *Previous Misconduct of A Defendant* (London: HMSO, 1996).
11 R. Munday 'What constitutes "Other Reprehensible Behaviour" under the Bad Character Provisions of the Criminal Justice Act 2003?' [2005] *Crim LR* 24 p.39.
12 C. Tapper 'The Criminal Justice Act 2003 (3) Evidence of Bad Character' [2004] Crim *LR* 533.
13 *Ibid* pp.547–8.
14 [1981] IR 233 at 241. See also DPP v Keogh [1998] 4 IR 416.
15 (1982) 150 CLR 580.
16 Law Commission *op.cit.*, paragraphs 7.7–7.9.
17 R. Hood, S. Shute and F. Seemungal *Ethnic Minorities in the Criminal Courts: Perceptions of Fairness and Equality of Treatment* (2003).
18 R. Munday '"Round up the Usual Suspects!" or What We Have to Fear from Part 11 of the Criminal Justice Act 2003' (2005) 169 *Justice of the Peace* 328 p.330.
19 S. Lloyd Bostock *op. cit.*
20 *Ibid.* p.753.
21 Law Commission *op. cit.* Appendix D.
22 Quoted in H. Kennedy *Just Law: The Changing Face of Justice and Why it Matters to Us All* (London: Chatto and Windus, 2004) pp.86–7.
23 P. O'Mahony *Criminal Chaos: Seven Crises in Irish Criminal Justice* (Round Hall Sweet and Maxwell, 1996).
24 *Op. cit.* p.507.
25 Law Commission Report No. 267 *Double Jeopardy and Prosecution Appeals* (London: HMSO, 2001).
26 *Op.cit.*
27 Section 78(2).
28 Joint Committee on Human Rights, Eleventh Report 2002–3, *Criminal Justice Bill: Further Report* p.17
29 For an in-depth discussion of this rationale for the double jeopardy rule see P. Roberts 'Double Jeopardy Law Reform: A Criminal Justice Controversy' (2002) 65 *MLR* 393 and I. Dennis 'Rethinking Double Jeopardy: Justice and Finality in Criminal Process' [2000] *Crim LR* 933.
30 H. Kennedy *op. cit.* p.81.
31 *Op. cit.* p.368.
32 Quoted in H. Kennedy *op. cit* p.50.
33 T. Blair: 'I'm not being "arrogant", I'm being responsible for our safety' *Daily Telegraph* 24 February 2005.
34 B. Dickson 'Law Versus Terrorism: Can Law Win?' [2005] 1 *EHRLR* 11.
35 H. Kennedy *op. cit* p.49.
36 [2004] UKHL 43; [2005] *Crim LR* 215.
37 *Ibid.* at para. 51.
38 [2001] 33 EHRR 264.

39 *Ibid.* at para. 57.
40 *Ibid.* at para 58.
41 A. Ashworth *Human Rights, Serious Crime and Criminal Procedure* (London: Sweet and Maxwell, 2002) p.132. It should be noted, however, that the author was not concerning himself with terrorism in these lectures: 'At an early stage of preparing these lectures it was decided not to focus on anti-terrorist measures but rather to focus on responses to other forms of serious crime, particularly drug trafficking, organized crime and serious fraud. Although the official reaction to the events of September 11 2001 has again raised deep questions about the commitment of governments to human rights, the focus of the lectures remains unchanged.'
42 [2000] 2 AC 326.
43 [2002] 2 AC 545.
44 1997 (3) SA 527, paragraph 220.
45 A. Ashworth *op. cit.* p.115.
46 Adam Ingram, Hansard, House of Commons Standing Committee A, Col. 73 (25 November 1997).
47 H (2002) 4 Strasbourg, July 2002.
48 V. Tadros and S. Tierney 'The Presumption of Innocence and the Human Rights Act' (2004) 67(3) *MLR* 402 p.429 citing by way of example Lord Woolf in *Lambert.*
49 [2004] UKHL 43; [2005] *Crim LR* 215.
50 For a fuller exploration of the Act see J.J. Rowe 'The Terrorism Act 2000' [2000] *Crim LR* 527.
51 S. Foster 'The Prevention of Terrorism and the Violation of Democratic Rights' *Justice of the Peace* 168 (2004) 9 p.11.
52 [2000] 2 AC 326.
53 C. Walker *The Anti Terrorism Legislation* (Oxford University Press, 2002) p.174.
54 [2004] UKHL 43; [2005] *Crim LR* 215.
55 C. Walker 'Prisoners of 'War All the Time" [2005] 1 *EHRLR* 50 at p.62.
56 B. Brandon 'Terrorism, Human Rights and the Rule of Law: 120 years of the UK's Legal Response to Terrorism' [2004] *Crim LR* 981 p.997.
57 C. Walker (2005) *op.cit.* p.50.
58 Hansard House of Commons Debates Com 311, 26 January 2005.
59 K. Beattie 'Control Order and ASBOs: taking liberties?' *Legal Action* April 2005 7, p.7.
60 *Chahal v. United Kingdom* (1997) 23 EHRR 413.
61 Section 21(2) of ATCSA defines a 'terrorist' as a person who '(a) is or has been concerned in the commission, preparation or instigation of acts of international terrorism; (b) is a member of or belongs to an international terrorist group; or (c) has links with an international terrorist group'. Section 21(3) further defines 'international terrorist group' as any group which is controlled by persons outside the United Kingdom and which the Home Secretary suspects is concerned in the commission, preparation or instigation of acts of international terrorism. Terrorism

under ATCSA has the same meaning as it does in the *Terrorism Act 2000*.

62 *Human Rights Act (Designated Derogation) Order 2001* (SI 3644 of 2001).

63 *Counter Terrorism Powers: Reconciling Security and Liberty in an Open Society: A Discussion Paper*, Cm. 6147 (February 2004) p.ii (introduction by D. Blunkett).

64 See further B. Brandon *op. cit.*

65 [2004] EWCA Civ 1123.

66 *Ibid.* para. 49.

67 [2004] UKHL 56. The House overturned the decision of the Court of Appeal ([2004] QB 335) in restoring that of SIAC ([2002] HRLR 1274).

68 *Ibid.* para.155.

69 Privy Counsellor Review Committee *Anti-Terrorism, Crime and Security Act 2001 Review: Report* (18 December 2003).

70 Lord Lloyd *Inquiry into Legislation Against Terrorism* (1996) Chapter 7.

71 *Op. cit.* BI: Conclusions at para. 4.

72 Joint Committee of Human Rights *Eighteenth Report: Review of Counter-Terrorism Powers*, Session 2003-4, HL 158/HC 713.

73 Committee against Torture *Conclusions and recommendations of the Committee against Torture on the United Kingdom of Great Britain and Northern Ireland, Crown Dependencies and Overseas Territories* (2004) and the Committee for the Elimination of Racial Discrimination *Concluding Observations of the Committee for the Elimination of Racial Discrimination, United Kingdom of Great Britain and Northern Ireland* (2003).

74 Lord Lloyd 'The Recruiting Sergeant' May 2005 *Counsel* 8 p.10.

75 Section 4(7)(a).

76 Section 1(3), PTA.

77 Section 9(4).

78 Privy Counsellor Review Committee *op. cit.*

79 *Ibid.* p.66.

80 E. Metcalfe 'Protecting a Free Society? Control Orders and the Prevention of Terrorism Act 2005' (2005) 2(1) *Justice Journal* 8 p.14.

81 *Secretary of State for the Home Department v JJ and Ors* [2006] EWCA Civ 1141 (1August 2006).

82 On this point see further K. Beattie *op. cit.*

83 L. Lloyd *op. cit.* p.10.

84 Section 1(4)(o).

85 See discussion of the case of *Heaney and McGuinness v. Ireland* [2000] ECHR 684 in Chapter Five.

86 A very thorough account is provided by J.A.E Vervaele 'Anti-Terrorist Legislation in the US: Inter Armes Silent Leges?' (2005) 13(2) *European Journal of Crime, Criminal Law and Criminal Justice* 201. See the following also for good synopses of the legislation: M.P. O'Connor and C.M. Rumann 'Into the Fire: How to Avoid Getting Burned by the Same Mistakes Made Fighting Terrorism in Northern Ireland' (2003) 24 *Cardozo Law Review* 1657; M. Jimeno Bulnes 'After September 11th:

the Fight Against Terrorism in National and European Law, Substantive and Procedural Rules: Some Examples' (2004) 10(2) *European Law Journal* 235 and P.A Thomas 'September 11th and Good Governance' [2002] 53(4) *NILQ* 366.

87 Remarks by the President to Employees at the Federal Bureau of Investigation (FBI) Headquarters, 25 September 2001.

88 Section 802.

89 Section 236A of the *Immigration and Nationality Act*.

90 Section 236A(a)(6) *Immigration and Nationality Act* (as amended).

91 United States Supreme Court, 12 January 2005, available at http://supct.law.cornell.edu/supct/html/03-878.ZS.html.

92 J.A.E. Vervaele *op.cit.* p.229, fn. 135.

93 Authorization for the Use of Military Force, Pub.L. no.107–40, 115 Stat. 224.

94 *Ibid.*

95 *Hamdi v. Rumsfeld*, US Supreme Court, 28 June 2004.

96 *Rumsfeld v. Padilla*, US Supreme Court, 28 June 2004.

97 The number and names of the detainees in Guantanamo were released by the Pentagon on 19 April 2006 in response to a freedom of information lawsuit taken by the Associated Press.

98 *Johnson v. Eisentrager* 339 US 763.

99 United States Supreme Court, 28 June 2004 available at http://supct.law.cornell.edu/supct/html/03-334.ZS.html.

100 *Op. cit.*p.249.

101 www.crimesofwar.org. An unfortunate side effect of the decision in *Rasul* may be that the US authorities may resort more frequently to the practice of 'rendition'. This is a process whereby detainees are removed to countries occupied by, or friendly to, the US under the supervision of US soldiers.

102 Senate Amendment 1042 151 CONG. REC. S12667 introduced by Senator Graham, passed by roll call vote, 49 – 42, 10 November 2005 and amended by S.Amdt. 2524, 151 CONG. REC. S12771 (14 November 2005).

103 It is estimated that at least 200 writs of *habeas corpus* had been lodged.

104 M.C Dorf 'The Senate Votes to Curb Habeas Corpus Petitions by Guantanamo Bay Detainees: How the Bill Threatens the "Unwritten Constitution"' 21 November 2005 available at http://writ.news.findlaw.com/dorf/20051121.html.

105 J. Seper & B. Gertz 'Bush made decision not to try Moussaoui in military court' *Washington Times*, 19 December 2001 at A1.

106 American Civil Liberties Union 'Press Release: Bush Order on Military Tribunals is Further Evidence that Government is Abandoning Democracy's Checks and Balances', 14 November 2001 available at http://www.aclu.org/news/2001/n111401b.html.

107 344 F.Supp.2d 152; 415 F.3d 33.

108 Department of Defense Fact Sheet *Guantanamo Detainees by the Numbers* 31 August 2005, available at www.defenselink.mil.

109 Amnesty International 'Guantanamo: Lives Torn Apart: the Impact of Indefinite Detention on detainees and their families' 6 February 2006, available at http://web.amnesty.org/library/Index/ENGAMR510072006.
110 C. Hegland 'Guantanamo's Grip' *National Journal* 3 February 2006.
111 J. Lea 'Terrorism, Crime and the Collapse of Civil Liberties' available at www.bunker8.pwp.blueyonder.co.uk/misc/terror.htm p.13.
112 J. Lea *ibid.* p.14.

Chapter Ten

Conclusions

It has been said of the due process rights of an accused person in Ireland that they have a 'look but do not touch, touch but do not taste' feel to them.[1] The brief survey undertaken above of the dramatically altered criminal justice landscape in the period following the enactment of the *Criminal Justice Act 1984* serves to confirm this impression. It is clear that the realization of the presumption falls far short of the rhetoric surrounding the principle. By way of gaining an overview of the impact of recent developments, it is useful at this juncture to view the criminal justice system through the eyes of the suspect-accused as he or she journeys through it. As noted in Chapter One, the significance of rights such as the presumption of innocence is only brought home by suspending momentarily one's view of the accused as an 'other' and imagining oneself or a relative confronted with the situation.

Let us take as our example a youth who has been charged with the theft of a large number of bicycles. In law he enjoys a constitutionally protected right to be presumed innocent. Under the new *Criminal Justice Act*, he may be detained in the Garda station for up to forty hours, inclusive of rest periods. He is questioned by the Gardaí, without his solicitor present, about some oil stains on his clothing and makes no reply as he is unsure of the law and does not wish to incriminate himself. As a result, the Guards warn him that adverse inferences may be drawn from his silence and used to corroborate the case against him which consists of largely circumstantial evidence. When he is brought before the District Court, the Gardaí object to bail on the basis that he will re-offend as soon as he is released and bail is refused by the judge. He finds himself in Cloverhill prison for a longer period of time than expected as the District Court judge refuses jurisdiction on account of the value of the property involved so his case will now be tried in the Circuit Court. He hates the prison as he is crammed into an 11m square cell with two other prisoners and there is very little to do except play pool and watch TV. When the case is listed in the Circuit Court, his barrister advises him that he has a reasonable prospect of an acquittal but this would depend on whether the jury believed his testimony and also there was a danger that the jury may draw an adverse inference from his refusal to co-operate with the Gardaí. If he pleads guilty, on the other hand, he will benefit from a discount in sentence and may even avoid custody. He decides to enter a plea of guilty, despite continuing to protest his innocence, as he feels a trial may be too risky and he doesn't think he can bear to spend much longer in custody.

This account serves to illustrate the reality of the Irish criminal justice system for an ordinary accused person who ostensibly is presumed innocent. The tangible benefits of the presumption as described by Tribe,[2] *viz.* a right to freedom and respect as an innocent member of the community, are little in evidence here. An accused may reasonably deride the presumption of innocence and prosecutorial burden of proof as a chimera or lawyer's sleight of hand. A similar conclusion may also be reached by a person accused of criminal anti-social behaviour under the new *Criminal Justice Act*, a person whose assets have been forfeited under the *Proceeds of Crime Act 1996* on the basis of previous criminal behaviour or, indeed, the innocent person who pays an on-the-spot fine to avoid court. Allegations as to substantive wrongdoing have been made against all of these persons, yet they will be denied a criminal trial or hearing and its concomitant protections. A further category of offenders who have been denied the benefits of the presumption are suspected child abusers due to a recent judicial exception carved out in the case law. Even restricting our view to the laws of evidence, it is clear that the burden of proof and reasonable doubt rules do not apply to cases where facts are within the 'peculiar knowledge' of the defendant, to persons who wish to raise the defence of insanity and to persons charged with offences of strict liability in Irish law.

Despite the growing insignificance of the presumption of innocence for accused persons, there is a consensus currently among politicians and journalists about the need to 'redress the balance' in a system which has supposedly swung too far in favour of the accused. The comments of the Minister for Justice, Equality and Law Reform in presenting the *Criminal Justice Bill* to the Dáil clearly reflect this view. Mention is rarely made of the powerful historical reasons why the system is structured in favour of the accused or numerous previous attempts at 'rebalancing'. It is tempting to adopt Ashworth's[3] suggestion that the term 'balance' should be banned from political discourse. The term conceals the real issues of the empirical evidence offered by way of justification for incursions into rights, to what extent rights must be compromised and recourse to any possible alternatives. Further, in a judicial context, the use of balancing tests to achieve fairness in criminal trials has proved particularly susceptible to the winds of public opinion on controversial issues. At a minimum, the following recommendation of the Irish Human Rights Commission[4] should prove a useful guide for legislators and members of the judiciary:

> A central pillar of human rights law is that any interference with individual rights must be justified by demonstrating that the interference is in pursuit of a legitimate aim, and that the interference is proportionate to the achievement of that aim. Furthermore, adequate and effective safeguards should be in place to ensure that the rights of the individual are not interfered with arbitrarily or unjustifiably.

It will be recalled that it was not my aim in this short account to attempt to explain the reasons why the presumption of innocence has, in recent years, formed the subject of attacks by the legislative and the judiciary, but rather to simply note in some detail the occurrence of the phenomenon. However, drawing on current trends and the experience in the UK and the US, where very serious dents have been made into the operation of the presumption of innocence, it is possible to make a number of suggestions about the future buoyancy of the principle in Irish criminal law:

- Further legislative and judicial inroads will routinely be made into the presumption on account of what Ashworth[5] has termed a 'creeping consequentialism' amongst the public and policymakers. This view holds that 'individual rights can be readily traded in exchange for anticipated consequentialist gains',[6] yet, as we have seen in the context of the *Criminal Justice Act 2006* for instance, 'the claims [of improved crime control] often run ahead of the evidence'. Attempts will be made in the near future to abolish the right to silence (through the drawing of adverse inferences) for all arrestable offences.
- The drift towards consequentialism identified above will coincide with further 'moral panics' following saturation media coverage of certain serious crimes. The Oireachtas will enact legislation which erodes safeguards such as the presumption in an attempt to be seen to be 'doing something' about the relevant problem.
- The current *ad hoc*, unprincipled approach to legislating will continue and will result in further serious oversights such as the failure to provide for a mental element in the offence of riot.
- Inroads into (or indeed the circumvention of) the presumption of innocence made by future legislation will be upheld by the superior courts, which have already endorsed significant dilutions of the principle. It is likely the constitutionality of ASBOs will be upheld domestically, save in the event of a successful appeal to the Strasbourg Court by the applicants in *McCann*.[7]
- Ireland will continue to fall prey to the vagaries of 'policy transfer' and future Ministers for Justice will continue to look to Anglo-American initiatives despite obvious differences in culture, population size and the size of our crime problem.
- Conditions for remand prisoners in Dublin will improve with the eventual opening of the Education Centre in Cloverhill. Conditions for remand prisoners nationwide (and all prisoners) may slowly improve with increased

scrutiny by the Committee on the Prevention of Torture (a visit is due this year) and increasing litigation in the area of prisoner's rights in the European Court of Human Rights.

A final suggestion concerns the concept of risk. It has been estimated elsewhere that in a few years time 'there will a greater focus on risk measurement as a guiding principle for offender management'[8] in the Irish criminal justice system. This preoccupation with risk and the reorientation of the criminal justice system towards the control of offenders and away from their punishment or reform has been famously expounded by Feeley and Simon.[9] To some degree, it can be argued that the state's preoccupation with certain risk groups is already evident through the proposals for anti-social behaviour orders and the introduction some years ago of sex offender orders.[10] Should this discourse of risk assert itself with even greater vigour, however, this will produce effects which are inimical to the presumption of innocence owing in large part to the fact that risk assessments have little need for the reasonable doubt rule. As cogently argued by Lea:[11]

> [In this situation] a rigorous criteria of legal proof such as beyond reasonable doubt loses its relevance. It does so because it is primarily aimed at specifying the requirement of firm evidence of individual criminal action. The notion of the balance of probabilities and even more that of reasonable suspicion, on the other hand, allow more space for probabilistic calculations of the likelihood of criminality. Such calculations are precisely the ingredients of actuarial and risk based knowledge.

The above prognosis offers few grounds for optimism in relation to the future of the principle and, indeed, that of other due process rights. Perhaps this is to ignore the successes of groups such as the Coalition Against ASBOs and the Irish Council for Civil Liberties in the recent past. It remains clear, however, that this is a topic which should be urgently addressed on both a micro and macro level, not just by civil liberties groups but by researchers, academics and politicians. In a micro sense, there are many other areas of the criminal law which are difficult to reconcile with the presumption and which should be highlighted. Examples include the law on self-induced intoxication,[12] which holds that recklessness in relation to a criminal act is to be inferred from the prior act of consuming alcohol; the assumption under the *Criminal Justice Act 1994*, once a criminal conviction is secured for a drugs trafficking offence, that all assets acquired in the previous six years are the proceeds of drug trafficking and the subsequent confiscation of those assets on the balance of probabilities; and institutional practices whereby the DPP directs trial on indictment in a given case or, in the alternative, summary trial conditional on a plea of guilty. From a macro perspective, crime control is becoming more central to Western societies, yet surprisingly little has been written on this in comparison with other criminological issues.

Our complacency as a society to the steady erosion of the due process rights such as the presumption of innocence has clear implications in that, in extremis, we risk drifting incrementally into a police state. In this connection, Chakrabati[13] wrote recently on the presumption:

> The presumption of innocence, like innocence itself, is more easily compromised than reclaimed. It seems to me that we would not be living with the chilling spectre of the anti-terror 'control order' (indefinite punishment based on secret intelligence) if we had been more critical of his older cousin, the Asbo.

As Chakrabati makes clear, public apathy in relation to assaults on the presumption of innocence creates a fertile breeding ground for future and further divergence culminating in very serious attacks on our liberty. Given the discussion above, which casts doubt on the claim of our criminal justice system to be oriented towards the accused, the lessons to be learned on this side of the Irish Sea are clear. The apotheosis of this drift away from due process protections, as we saw in Chapter Nine, is a land without law and detention without the right of *habeas corpus*. We ignore this trend, its causes, effects and dangers at our peril lest in the more egregious attacks on the presumption in the UK and the US we catch a glimpse of our future.

NOTES

1 S. Kilcommins, I. O'Donnell, E O'Sullivan and B. Vaughan *Crime, Punishment and the Search for Order in Ireland* (IPA, 2004) p.174.
2 L. Tribe 'Trial by Mathematics: Precision and Ritual in the Legal Process (1971) 84 *Harvard Law Review* 1329.
3 A. Ashworth 'Crime, Community and Creeping Consequentialism' [1996] *Crim LR* 220 p.229.
4 Irish Human Rights Commission, *Observations on Additional Proposals for Amendments to the Criminal Justice Bill 2004* (8 March 2006) p.1.
5 A. Ashworth *op. cit.*
6 *Ibid.* p.225.
7 *R* (*on application of McCann*) *v Manchester Crown Court* [2003] 1 AC 787.
8 I. O'Donnell 'Crime and Justice in the Republic of Ireland' (2005) *European Journal of Criminology* 99, p.128.
9 M. Feeley and J. Simon 'Actuarial Justice: the Emerging New Criminal Law' in D. Nelken (ed.) *The Futures of Criminology* (London, Sage, 1994).
10 *Sex Offenders Act 2001.*
11 J.Lea 'Terrorism, Crime and the Collapse of Civil Liberties' available at www.bunker8.pwp.blueyonder.co.uk/misc/terror.htm at pp.12–13.
12 See further N. Lacey, C. Wells and D. Meure *Reconstructing Criminal Law* (Weidenfield and Nicolson, 1990) pp.189–209. The argument runs that the case law (*DPP v. Majewski* [1977] AC 433) establishing that *mens rea* for crimes of recklessness is supplied by the voluntary prior consumption of alcohol offends the presumption of innocence and the requirement that the prosecution prove all aspects of guilt beyond all reasonable doubt.
13 S. Chakrabati and L. Casey 'Mob justice or yob control?' *The Guardian*, 19 March 2005.

Index